HOW TO BE SEVENTY

BOOKS BY GEORGE MIKES

ABOUT US
How to be an Alien
How to be Affluent
How to be Decadent
How to be Inimitable
English Humour for Beginners

ABOUT OTHER PEOPLE
How to Scrape Skies
How to Unite Nations
Italy for Beginners
Switzerland for Beginners
Little Cabbages
Uber Alles
Eureka: Rummaging in Greece
Any Souvenirs?: Central Europe Revisited
East is East
Tango: a Solo across South America
Not by Sun Alone: a Jamaican Journey
Boomerang: Australia Rediscovered
The Prophet Motive: Israel Today and Tomorrow
The Land of the Rising Yen: Japan

ABOUT LIFE
Down with Everybody
Shakespeare and Myself
Wisdom for Others

ABOUT HISTORY
The Hungarian Revolution
The AVO: a Study in Infamy

ABOUT A CAT
Tsi-Tsa: the Biography of a Cat

NOVELS
Mortal Passion
The Spy Who Died of Boredom
Charlie

How to be Seventy
An Autobiography

GEORGE MIKES

ANDRE DEUTSCH

First published in 1982 by
André Deutsch Limited
105 Great Russell Street London WC1

Copyright © Georges Mikes
All rights reserved

Printed in Great Britain by
The Thetford Press Limited
Thetford, Norfolk

ISBN 0 233 97453 9

LIFE ONE: SIKLÓS
Early Memories: Count Metternich *1*
Preface *4*
Archdukes and Whores *9*

LIFE TWO: BUDAPEST
Maturity? *45*
Malice in Wonderland *66*

LIFE THREE: LONDON
Lala *101*
Murder *132*
My Political Career *144*
How to be an Alien *157*
Two Kings *169*
The Mogul *180*
Our Cricketing Career *182*
Daylight at Midnight *189*
Revolution *196*
The Decline of Invective *203*
Abstract Paintings *207*
Snobs *213*
A Gentleman at Last *220*
Mania *226*
The Last Anecdote *230*

LIFE ONE
Siklós

Early Memories:
Count Metternich

Reliable documents have convinced me – I would never have suspected it otherwise – that I am quite an old man.

I was born in Siklós, in those days a village in the south of Hungary. It is still in the south of Hungary but by now it has become a town. As far as I know I am the only English writer to have been born in Siklós. But one can never be sure. It is a different world, of course; but the point is that it was also a different era.

When I talk to my daughter Judy (born in 1949 in London) about the War she listens to me in the same way that I listen to someone telling me about the Crimean or the Peloponnesian wars. Interesting episodes of history, no doubt. The fact that I remember World War Two so clearly is bad enough; but to have been alive during World War One is surely going a bit too far.

I was born in 1912, on February 15, a subject of Francis Joseph who acceded to the throne in 1848. This makes me, at a stretch, a contemporary of Metternich and Talleyrand. The Kaiser ruled Germany, Bulgaria had a Czar, the last Sultan of Turkey had recently been dethroned and radio – let alone television – was not yet invented. I am older than the BBC but younger than the Magna Carta. The alphabet and the wheel were already known and used. The wheel was more used on horse-drawn carriages than on motorcars, at least in Siklós. When we children heard the noise of an automobile, we rushed out to the street to have a look at it. I am older than such states as Czechoslovakia and Yugoslavia, and I gained my independence before Poland and Finland gained theirs.

(I do not know why I am spending so much time and effort on

proving that I am really quite old. Nobody seems to doubt it.)

In 1912 Austria-Hungary was one of the five great powers of the world, or at least that's what most people believed. A man called Khuen-Héderváry was Prime Minister of Hungary when I was born. By now he has been almost completely forgotten, even in Hungary, while I am still remembered. In the midst of great and permanent political excitement people failed to realise how happy they were. One issue of the day was electoral reform, usually referred to as 'manhood suffrage'; a serious enough political question, to be sure. It caused – according to contemporary newspapers – 'unprecedented tension' and the country was deeply shocked when after a demonstration 'thousands of street lamps were smashed'. Another grave problem was whether reservists should be called up and kept in the army in peace-time. The year of my birth became the year of the Great Obstruction, when Members of Parliament made immensely long and pointless speeches followed by awesome noises with trumpets, whistles, rattles and motor-car horns, to prevent the proper procedure of Parliament. The din was, I am sure, much more entertaining than an average Parliamentary oration. Few people in Hungary remember any speech delivered that year; everybody knows of the Great Obstruction and the rattles, whistles and horns. The Austrians struggled with Polish, Czech and Ruthenian nationalists. The Hungarians bravely and nobly asserted their own independence vis-à-vis Austria while they oppressed their own minorities as fiercely as they could. In the year of my birth they were especially devoted to extinguishing Croatian nationalism forever, but by the time I was a small schoolboy Yugoslav troops were occupying Siklós for a while. Russia and Turkey were being 'liberalised', not for the first or the last time in history. The Russian people remained as oppressed under the new constitution and the Third Duma as they were before; Christians suffered as much under the Young Turks as they had suffered under the mad Sultan Abdul Hamid, while Armenians suffered much more. The one hopeful thing was that the international horizon was cloudless; the outlook was rosy. The Czar met the Emperor of Germany in a ship on the Baltic Sea and the meeting testified 'the firm and lasting friendship between Germany and

Early Memories: Count Metternich

Russia'. To be sure, there would be difficulties and disputes, but one thing was absolutely certain: there would be no European war. I was lucky to have been born in 1912.

What was the news the British public read in *The Times* on 15 February 1912? In the Commons there was a debate on the Address. The Prime Minister, Mr Asquith, made a statement about Lord Haldane's planned private visit to Germany and Mr Bonar Law in his speech from the opposition front bench 'hit hard'. Lloyd George was Chancellor, Winston Churchill was First Lord of the Admiralty. The King and Queen opened the new session and in spite of the cloudy weather 'along the route their Majesties were heartily cheered by the crowd'. It was planned to build a new road to the West – it is still not quite finished. A meeting between the creditors of Horatio Bottomley, MP, was adjourned; the Foreign Minister of the 'Nanking Government' (Sun Yat-sen's Southern Republic) was clamouring for recognition once again but 'the request was ignored'. M. Mathieu Moreau, a well-known sculptor and former Mayor of the 19th Arrondissement, died in Paris; the Princess Royal, accompanied by her two children, left Cairo for Alexandria; Lord Sandhurst became Lord Chamberlain (in place of Lord Spencer) and at Warwick the County Hurdle Race Handicap was won by Mr Barr's Mink, while the Chandler Handicap Steeplechase was won by Mr Faber's Black Witch. The wind was mainly from the east and south-east (light to moderate).

Not a word in *The Times* about my birth. But there was a piece about it in *Siklós és Vidéke* (Siklós and Neighbourhood). My father was its editor.

Preface

I put the Preface here because I did not want to begin this book with an apologia and explanation but I must say a few such words on certain subjects and I feel that a Preface should be, at least, *near* the beginning.

I am writing this book burdened with two initial and perhaps insuperable disadvantages. The first is that I am a happy man and I cannot help it. I am perfectly content with my lot and enjoy every minute – well, shall we say almost every minute? – of my life. A friend asked me recently – and I discerned some irritation in her voice – if I was ever depressed. If 'depressed' means *sad*, then of course I am occasionally sad. The illness or death of someone near to me, a major or even minor blow befalling me or those I love, injustice witnessed or frustration endured does not cheer me up. If someone kicks me hard it hurts me just as much as it hurts the next man. But if 'depressed' is used in the now generally accepted sense of the word: waking up in the morning in a terrible mood, a prey to melancholy, splenetic, lachrymose or suicidal feelings that life is not worth living, then – I informed my friend – I could truthfully claim or reluctantly admit that I had never been depressed in my life. Every morning when I wake up I am full of beans, happy to be alive and looking forward to the day. Several girlfriends have left me in disgust because of this. Few people can bear cheerfulness and exhilaration before 11.30 a.m. Graham Greene wrote in his autobiography, *Ways of Escape*: 'Writing is a form of therapy; sometimes I wonder how all those who do not write, compose or paint can manage to escape the madness, the melancholia, the panic fear which is inherent in the human situation.'

Madness and melancholia? Panic fear of what? I really have no idea what he is talking about.

Preface

This is a frightful admission of superficiality and a great drawback for a writer. I have touched on this subject in a recent article in *Encounter*. In an autobiography one is bound to quote oneself sooner or later, so I might as well start committing this sin right now. I was dealing with a piece written by an American professor on the future of humanity. According to him humanity had no future at all, it was doomed to go through a few more disasters before complete annihilation. This view, this *weltanschauung*, made me pale with envy. Dark and unmitigated gloom always makes me envious. I am fully aware of the sad fact that I am just not gloomy, despondent and atrabilious enough.

The fact that I am not one of the great writers of this age – perhaps of all ages – is not due to lack of talent, power of observation and expression. It is due to my damned pleasant and equable nature and to my (I must apologise for the phrase) sunny temperament. All I can plead in extenuation is that I am not happy because I have achieved much, but because I have learnt to be content with little.

Great writers from Sophocles through Dostoevsky to Kafka, Koestler and Solzhenitsyn are all preoccupied with gloom, disaster, ruin and evil. George Orwell predicted utter catastrophe for the West by 1984, and Spengler expected it much sooner. The West has survived pretty well. Nevertheless, what chance has a man got who expects everything to turn out well? Who accepts almost everything as it comes, with a shrug of the shoulders? What insight can I gain to the depths of the human soul when I myself have no depths – indeed practically no soul to speak of? What can I possibly understand about human suffering when I am always satisfied or, at least, ready to put up with my lot? I am the man who is thrown out of the window at the fortieth floor and falling past the twentieth, says to himself: 'Nothing has happened up to now – I'm sure it will be all right.'

The other drawback is that, comparatively speaking, nothing has ever happened to me. Most of my friends have been in prison. I have done no more than see the inside of two prisons: one during the Hungarian revolution when I visited the town of Sopron as a television reporter, the other when I was shown round an experimental institution in Sweden. Many of my friends died in Auschwitz or were executed or tortured by the ÁVÓ, Rákosi's political police. My own most dramatic clash with tyranny was to be 'asked' – together with a BBC television crew – by the Hungarian police to accompany them to Kecskemét police station, only to be released an hour later. Many of my friends died on various battlefields and fought in various armies. All I achieved on the military field was to be rejected by *two* armies, the Hungarian and the British. Other people have stories about exhilarating and adventurous journeys. All my travel stories I have already told, and they were far from being stories of adventure. Again, others had harrowing illnesses. As a child I had all the illnesses in the book but as an adult I have been unromantically healthy, spending only one week in bed with a virus infection during the last forty years (it was in 1957) and otherwise never having even the 'flu. I am almost embarrassed when I hear people discussing whether they had a good or bad night. I go to bed and sleep till the morning.

It is true that I lived throught the *blitz* in London; was in houses and a restaurant hit by bombs; was nearly – but only nearly – parachuted into Hungary. I witnessed occupations of countries, saw revolutions, crash-landed in Argentina, was expelled from my own native land, met a few famous – even great – people and found some of them quite interesting; but such events are trivial compared with the stories thousands of my contemporaries could tell.

'But if nothing ever happened to you,' the reader may ask, 'why write an autobiography? After all, it is not compulsory.'

I could answer: 'Not compulsory, just compulsive.' Perhaps. But this is not the main reason. Nothing much has happened to me in the generally accepted sense of the word 'adventure'. I did not kill anyone with the single exception of a Norwegian sailor called Ejnar Dybwad; I have committed no grave crime worth recording; was never knocked down in a brawl – indeed was never even beaten either by my parents or by any teacher; I have no idea how to handle a gun; I was never bankrupt; I never grew rich; I have never been chased across the moors or across anything else. No, nothing like that. But I did experience *real* adventure: the big stuff. I was born in a village and at the age of

Preface

thirteen I moved to Budapest. This was a greater adventure than James Bond could ever dream of. And coming to London in order to live among those strange English people – that was an even greater adventure. These two migrations made a tremendous impression on me. They filled me with awe and wonder, with horror and delight; and – for better or worse – they formed me and made me what I am. Then I have met a large number of people – some famous, most of them not – and I have found them a bottomless source of fascination. I have come to the firm conclusion that the world would be considerably duller without people. Perhaps a better place to live in, but duller.

The big events in life are not the murders, motor-car chases and gun fights, which are few and far between and pretty boring, on the whole. 'The fundamental changes,' wrote Golo Mann, 'are the slow and undramatic ones, which happen every day and finally add up to something big.' Sudden revolutions in the life of nations, and murders, elopements, divorces and other disasters in the lives of individuals are not the *causes* of great changes but the *results* of slow, almost unnoticed, formative week-day events. What was more important in the life of Europe, the undramatic building of thousands of miles of railway lines which by altering distances brought great changes to communities, industry, outlooks, national consciousness and the class-structure, or the July Revolution of 1830 which chased away the Bourbons (who in any case had died out, without realising it, about four decades earlier) and put a well-meaning but ineffectual ditherer in their place? And which was the more important event in my life: being nearly blown to smithereens by a flying bomb at a railway station in Berkshire, or saying good-bye to my girlfriend in Budapest and acquiring a new girlfriend in London? She – the London one – was a tall, amusing but unemotional and very upper-class county woman with the stiffest of upper lips. She came to me every weekday afternoon for three years. She told her husband that she was going out shopping. I asked her once whether her husband did not find it peculiar that she spent so much time shopping but never bought anything. She looked at me sadly, almost pityingly. 'You will always remain a bloody foreigner,' she said. 'What has shopping to do with buying things?'

How to be Seventy

* * *

Some years ago my new Japanese translator, Nao'omi Kuratani, came to see me in London. We met for the first time. He had just translated my book on Japan, called *The Land of the Rising Yen*, and brought me a copy.

'I have transliterated your name Mick-ash, as you yourself pronounce it,' he informed me. 'I hope you don't mind.'

'Well, of course not. That's my name.'

'Oh yes, but it's not quite so simple as that. On your previous books published in Japan your name appeared as Mikes (to rhyme with likes) and now you have lost all the advantages gained by your former works. Most people won't realise that the writer Mick-ash is identical with that chap Mikes. They think it's somebody else, another fellow. I hope you will forgive me.'

'Not only forgive: I am grateful to you. You see, for a boy coming from Siklós, Hungary, it is an achievement to become a reasonably well-known writer in Japan, but not – let's face it – a tremendously big achievement. But to become *two* well-known writers in Japan . . . that's quite something!'

The three lives of these two people are described on the following pages.

And now back to Siklós.

Please read on. But you have been warned.

Archdukes and Whores

The first person I met in Siklós was my mother. You utter the word 'mother' – particularly in Central Europe and in America – and people are moved to tears. Everybody's mother is the most magnificent person in the world. Everybody's mother is beautiful; everybody's mother is the best cook – just nobody can cook so well as everybody's mother. And, of course, everybody's mother is the best mother who ever existed. My mother was no exception – except in one respect. She was a lovable person and I loved her dearly. She was a pretty woman. But she was the lousiest cook. No, that's not quite correct. She was no cook at all, she could not make scrambled eggs if she tried, and nothing was further from her mind. Cooking was the job of Auntie Anna, the maid who had been with us for donkeys' years, in fact that 'maid' was a venerable old woman when I was born (she died a few years later). Many years afterwards, my mother – when she lived in America with her second husband – had to learn how to cook and it was then that she developed – slowly – into the lousiest cook in the world. She was really quite remarkable: she could make a simple soft-boiled egg uneatable.

She was almost unique in another way too: in my whole life I only met one other person so completely lacking in guile and malice. She always believed the best of everyone, trusted everybody and was constitutionally unable to hate anyone. The one exception mentioned – who was even more trusting and less malicious – was her father, Miska Papa (to be pronounced: Mishka Papa) who when, say, Hitler raised him to a paroxysm of rage, would exclaim: 'He's not a nice man at all.'

I doubt if the second person I met in Siklós was my father but eventually we did meet. When my maternal grandmother – i.e. Mishka Papa's wife, whom we called Róza Mama – came down to see me – I was about three days old – she, the mother of two daughters, wanted to be sure that I was really a boy. So my swaddle, or whatever they called those old-fashioned things, was opened and I peed into her face. She often told me this story, somewhat reproachfully. I never liked her much and no doubt I was expressing my views about her in the only way I then could.

My father was a lawyer, a man with deep blue eyes and a small moustache. He was of middle build and always very neatly dressed – a predilection he failed to bequeath to his elder son. Like all little boys, I adored my father but it was Ómama, his mother, who presided over the family and overshadowed everyone else. She was extremely fat, moved with great difficulty, her hair was snow-white and she looked to me as old as the hills although she must have been just under sixty when we were introduced to each other. Her mother tongue was German as her family moved to Hungary from Austria. She spoke Hungarian fluently and without any foreign accent but she made many very funny mistakes, some of which still survive in our family. In this funny language she scolded her maids loudly and angrily and I always thought that they hated her. In fact they adored her and, indeed, the last of them – as we shall see – demonstrated a touching, almost obsessive, degree of loyalty and love. Ómama had a remarkably vivid brain. She was very much interested in public affairs and, after the invention of the radio, was always listening to the news, trying to get varied views on events. She had a delightful, self-mocking sense of humour and loved to be teased.

She was the eldest of eleven children and her brothers and sisters had innumerable offspring, some of whom I never met and some of whom I kept confusing with one another. But not Ómama. She knew everybody and followed everybody's career with the utmost interest. She was informed of everybody's fortunes, good or ill luck, illness, advancement in his job, setbacks and disasters, marriages and births – but no divorces as those were quite unimaginable in a middle-class family – until one happened very close to her. If a third cousin's granddaughter living in a distant part of Hungary (and Hungary was a big country in those days) fell ill with German measles, gloom and

Archdukes and Whores

anxiety descended upon us all until she got better. If she died, scenes of Greek tragedy were enacted. No, worse than that: scenes of Biblical disaster, with loud wailing, tears, sobs, rantings against Heaven. These went on for weeks, even if Ómama had not set eyes on the poor deceased girl for twenty-five years. There was only one other family which she knew as well as she knew ours: the Habsburgs. She was perfectly informed about even the most obscure Archdukes and Archduchesses and if an Archducal couple's fifth son was mentioned in the newspaper, Ómama would be able to tell us his full life-story, with his parents' and grandparents' life-stories thrown in for good measure. I am sure she knew that complicated family considerably better than did the Emperor Francis Joseph (no Emperor to the Hungarians, just King).

There was only one contact between the two families: I mean between the Habsburgs and us. It was Uncle Pepi.

Uncle Pepi was Ómama's cousin and, as far as she was concerned, the pride of the family. He was, indeed, a man of double distinction. He was – or rather had been – the physician of Crown Prince Rudolf and he had also translated the great Hungarian poet Sándor Petöfi into German. I have no idea what sort of doctor Uncle Pepi was. Many doctors kill their patients but Uncle Pepi cannot be suspected of having killed Rudolf, since the Crown Prince killed himself at Mayerling without any medical assistance. The Petöfi translations, however, are here for everybody to judge. I find them pretty feeble, but as my knowledge of German is quite inadequate I may be unfair to Uncle Pepi's memory. In any case, none of this mattered at all – not to Ómama. Whether he was a good doctor or a bad one, whether he translated Petöfi well or abominably, it was all the same to her. The main thing was that we had a royal physician and a translator of Petöfi's in the family.

I do not remember Ómama's husband, who was a lawyer practising in Siklós, because he died when I was two. They had three children. Aunt Berta died before I was born. My father was Ómama's younger son; his elder brother Uncle Marcel was a timber merchant who lived in the Bánát, next door to Transylvania, a part of Hungary which became Romania after World War One.

Uncle Marcel's visits were always red letter days for several reasons. First of all, he was something of a romantic hero. (He did not look like a romantic hero: he resembled my father very closely but had a somewhat bent back which, to a lesser extent, I managed to inherit from him – a mistake on my part because my father had a neat little figure.) Uncle Marcel lived in a somewhat unhappy marriage with a Viennese lady. In the town of Lugos there was a most coveted and admired young lady called Alice Fraenkel, the daughter of a leading lawyer. She was a Doctor of Chemistry, a witty and highly cultivated woman who spoke a number of languages fluently and was as well versed in old and recent literature as the best literary critics in Paris or London. On top of all that she was very rich, so the golden youth of Lugos was all after her. But the only man she wanted was Uncle Marcel, a middle-aged, married man with a bent back, almost twenty-five years her senior. Uncle Marcel decided to divorce his wife and a scandalous divorce suit greatly entertained the gossip-lovers of Lugos while causing Uncle Marcel much distress. When he came to Siklós in those days he would discuss his affairs with my parents in angry and excited tones. He always started in a whisper – to conceal matters from me – but ended by shouting wildly and cursing his wife. (They had a small daughter, my cousin Erzsi, who became a doctor and whose whole life was subsequently overshadowed by this divorce.) When the case was over at last, Uncle Marcel went to Dr Fraenkel and formally asked for the hand of his daughter. He was thrown out. Upon which Marcel and Alice eloped together. This caused a tempestuous scandal, the talk of the town for a long time to come. After the elopement Alice's parents had no choice: they had to agree to the marriage. The whole of Lugos foresaw that the marriage could not possibly last, and that for its short duration it would be unhappy. It was, in fact, one of the happiest and most movingly beautiful unions I have ever observed in my life. Uncle Marcel and Aunt Alice were devoted to each other. I simply adored her and still do – she is happily still with us. She became as well-versed in the affairs of our family as she was in French, English, German and Hungarian literature, and as Ómama was in the Habsburgs. Even today I often learn from her letters what is happening to my own brother, with whom I am in constant correspondence. And I get all the news about distant and half-forgotten relations.

In addition to loving my new Aunt Alice from the first moment, I had other reasons for looking forward to Uncle Marcel's visits. He was delightfully vulgar and used all those shocking words which were taboo. Ladies shrieked and pretended to faint left and right when Uncle Marcel made his scatological jokes, yet they loved the jokes and egged him on all the time. Whenever he said 'shit' or 'arse', the whole gathering collapsed in helpless laughter and feigned shock. Later I suspected that this studied vulgarity was a clever device. My father was a witty man – even today I meet people who tell me that they never met anyone wittier and quicker on the uptake – and Uncle Marcel lacked his wit. He had to compete with his younger brother somehow, so he stole some of the limelight this way.

The two brothers adored Ómama and they loved teasing her. We had a house in the main square of Siklós and Ómama lived with her widowed son-in-law (Aunt Berta's husband, the official village doctor who never opened his mouth) more or less opposite. Marcel and Alice stayed in our house – and family gatherings in the evenings were also held there. The eminence of our family was Ómama's favourite subject, and she would often extol the virtues of its members, particularly of that honoured physician and eminent poet, Uncle Pepi.

'But why do you keep talking of Uncle Pepi, Mother,' Uncle Marcel would ask, 'Why don't you ever mention Dóra, who is a whore in Eszék?'

My grandmother would be rendered speechless. Did Marcel mean that Dóra was a naughty girl? No, Marcel did not mean a naughty girl; he meant a whore. That was a wicked slander, Ómama protested, Dóra was a girl of impeccable virtue. Under pressure she would then concede that Dóra might be a little flirtatious.

'Flirtatious?' asked Uncle Marcel or my father. 'If jumping into bed with Tom, Dick and Harry for moderate fees means being flirtatious, then she is flirtatious. But if she is just flirtatious, how did she contract syphilis?'

Ómama would change the subject and start talking of her brother Imre, another pride of the family, although not quite so eminent as the royal physician. Uncle Imre was director of engineering, or something like that, of the state railways at Lugos (the town where Uncle Marcel lived) and he had reached the Fifth Remuneration Grade. That was a tremendously important thing. Any civil servant who reached the Fifth Grade was entitled to be called 'Your Dignity'. The title sounds ridiculous in English and although it sounded only slightly less ridiculous in Hungarian, it was an eagerly coveted distinction.

'Why do we keep talking of Uncle Pepi and Uncle Imre?' my father would ask. 'What about Lord Zsiga who is a waiter and a criminal?'

Zsiga was my paternal grandfather's brother who got his title – from my father – because of his lordly manners. Ómama declared coolly that Zsiga was no ordinary waiter but a headwaiter and the most honest person in the world.

'He may be a headwaiter,' my father replied, 'but his two sons never rose to such heights of eminence. The other day I was travelling through Zagreb and meant to have lunch at the station restaurant. Hardly had I started studying the menu when the waiter threw himself upon me, embraced and kissed me. It was Lord Zsiga's younger son. Other guests thought the scene unusual.'

And so it went on endlessly. According to Ómama the family consisted of His Excellencies, 'His Dignities', poets and other great men – practically Archdukes and Archduchesses all of them – while according to her two sons it consisted of whores, criminals and – in the best case – headwaiters.

There was one occasion when my father himself acted as a waiter.

He finished his legal studies at Kolozsvár (now Cluj, in Romania) University. He was already engaged to my mother and very keen on getting his degree and getting married, but he failed in Private Law at the finals and that meant delaying his marriage for about six painful and much resented months. At last the six months were up and my father passed his exam. He had to take part in a final ceremony in Kolozsvár wearing tails. As soon as the ceremony was over he – still in tails – rushed to the railway station to catch a train to Budapest where his fiancée lived. He had no time to change.

The train stopped somewhere *en route* for twenty minutes. Passengers dashed out to get refreshments. A young lady spotted my father rushing around in tails, and waved to him: 'Waiter, a coffee please.'

As the girl was sufficiently pretty, my father went to the counter, bought a coffee and served her. Then a middle-aged, portly gentleman shouted at him, curtly: 'Coffee for me too.'

My father examined him and replied: 'No. Not for you.'

'What do you mean?' the man asked astonished. 'You serve her but not me?'

'Precisely. I serve her but not you.'

The man still did not want to believe his ears: 'But why?'

'Because she is a pretty young girl and you are an ugly old man.'

The man gasped for air. He demanded to see the manager but my father told him to go and find him himself. A flaming row ensued, abuse was exchanged and the train started moving. My father ran after it and in spite of his somewhat inhibiting garment succeeded in jumping on, a feat which his irate and flabbergasted opponent failed to achieve.

My father Alfred, usually called Freda, and Uncle Marcel were extremely able musically but lacked musical education almost completely. For this they blamed Ómama.

'Why did you not see to it, Mother,' they would ask, 'that we should attend to our piano lessons properly?'

'Because I couldn't climb on the roof.'

This conversation – or varieties of it – which I heard more than once, puzzled me until I learnt what it was all about. There was a piano teacher, a middle-aged lady, engaged to teach the two boys, but while they loved sitting down to the piano and playing tunes they knew by ear, they hated scales and five-finger exercises, so they used the simple device of climbing on the roof whenever the piano teacher showed up. She reported to Ómama that her pupils were on the roof again, daring her to climb up and bring the piano with her. Ómama rushed out, scolded the boys, made dire threats but the boys just laughed and invited their very fat mother to climb up.

'You will come down, all right, when you are hungry,' she told them.

'True. But by then *she* won't be here and you won't be cross.'

They did climb down when the coast was clear and occasionally even taking risks when they had to go to fulfil another musical engagement they loved: they were regular bell-ringers of the neighbouring Catholic Church.

In the circumstances it was perhaps not quite fair to blame Ómama for the flaws in their musical education. And they lived to regret their truancy bitterly. Both loved music, it played an important part in their lives and they wanted to play better than they could. My father could play the piano all right in his own fashion and had an amazing musical memory. He went to the opera when in Budapest, or occasionally in Pécs, the nearby large town, and went – much more often – to the local cinema (where a pianist supplied the music in the pre-talkie days), then came home, sat down to the piano and played the whole opera or the whole repertoire of the cinema pianist with amazing accuracy. Occasionally – to amuse us – he would fill a dozen or more glasses with various amounts of water. When hit with a fork, these glasses gave out different sounds, depending on the amount of water they contained. He could tune the glasses to perfection and played lovely – though simple – tunes on them with a fork or a knife as if they were a xylophone.

Uncle Marcel did even better. He played the piano for many hours every day and started composing songs. He set famous poems to music or composed pseudo-folk songs. He sent some of his musical compositions to the local radio and as the Romanians were keen to show that they were doing something for the minority culture of the Hungarians, these songs were sometimes performed on the radio. After World War Two, when

Archdukes and Whores

Romania became a Communist satellite, Uncle Marcel's timber yard was confiscated and Uncle Marcel expected to be treated as an enemy of the proletariat, a former capitalist. But not at all. The Communist Party was also keen on showing that it was a friend and supporter of Hungarian culture and Uncle Marcel received a pension – a reasonable one by Romanian standards – as a retired composer. From that time on, he devoted all his time to music, became very prolific and his songs were quite well known. He was ninety when he died. I have received two books from Auntie Alice, published in Lugos, and analysing the achievements of Marcel Mikes, composer. It is no use running away from your destiny and climbing on roof-tops: your fate, indeed your talent if genuine, will catch up with you.

I myself was punished for the sins of my father. My father and later the rest of the family were determined not to commit the same mistake about me as Ómama had committed about her sons. There were differences: after we had moved to Budapest there was no roof-top within my range, so I had to sit through those boring and hopeless piano lessons. And – an even greater difference – I had no musical talent at all, having inherited my mother's musical abilities, which were nil. Yet I was tortured with piano lessons for eleven years. I could not learn how to play the piano – I cannot play even badly – but I did learn to hate music. This feeling has been slowly changing in recent years, but it is too late. I cannot enjoy serious music to the extent I should be able to if only the roof-tops in Budapest had been a little lower.

My father did not compose music: he was interested in writing. He wrote many a sketch and song for local performances, full of local references and making fun of local dignitaries and celebrities. There were many amateur performances and my father's pieces were extremely popular. He also wrote an operetta, its music composed by the Director of a local school, Sándor Szóhner, and the two authors went to Pécs and sought an interview with the director of the theatre.

The director saw them, only to tell them abruptly that he was not interested in the work of provincial amateurs. But somehow he was prevailed upon to listen to my father's reading and Szhóner's music, whereupon he accepted the operetta then and there and it became one of the greatest successes of those years. My mother and I were in Budapest and could not attend the first night. Indeed, we reached Pécs only for the last night, the very last performance. It was a magnificent feeling to be the author's son and I was determined to become a playwright myself – a dream I nearly realised but, after two great disappointments, was unable quite to fulfil.

People have often talked to me about my father with great – yet critical – admiration. They all agree that he was one of the wittiest men they ever met. They also agree that he was pretty ruthless. When in company he would select a victim, a stupid or shy man, and would pull his leg, pursue him relentlessly, torment and embarrass him and – whether the poor man fought back or surrendered meekly – would destroy him amid the loud and malicious laughter of the gathering. For many years I thought this was a brilliant and amusing thing to do, and I tried to emulate my father. One day – I was about sixteen – a friend of mine (later the consultant of a large Budapest hospital) came to see me, sat down opposite me and told me off in a reasonable and friendly manner but in no uncertain terms. He explained to me that perhaps I could think a little faster than most of the others but that I was abusing this gift, I was becoming a bully and the cheap victories I gained were no credit to me. To pull someone down and then kick him when he *was* down was a nauseating performance. And so on. This was one of the rare occasions when a few well-spoken and well-meant words had their full effect. Never again did I make fun of anyone just because he was an easy victim. I tried to become the protector of the weak and the scourge of the strong. Alas, I never achieved quite this degree of nobility, I am just not noble enough by nature, but sometimes, when some fool sticks his neck out, and some devastating remark is on my lips, I still see my friend Tibor's disapproving look and swallow my remark.

All respectable families have a skeleton in the cupboard and I longed to find one in ours – if only to prove our respectability. I searched and searched and my labour has been rewarded. But

Archdukes and Whores

the skeleton I found is, I confess, a thin one; it hardly rattles.

My maternal grandfather, Mishka Papa, came from the same region of southern Hungary as my father. *His* father was a gendarme in the middle of the last century. When he retired, he – as a reliable former public servant – got a job as a rent- and debt-collector. He had to go around the villages (in the cold, in the snow, in the mud or – in the very best case – in the white, lung-destroying dust) to collect small sums from peasants and shopkeepers and hand the money in at the end of the week. While away, he slept in village inns. One evening he met a bunch of crooks and confidence tricksters, who induced him to play cards with them. He was an honest man, a babe in the wood and an easy prey for them. In a short time he lost all his own money and some of the company's. Panicking, he staked more and more in a wild attempt to save the day, and he lost it all. When left without a penny, he said good night to the crooks, went up to his room and hanged himself.

The result of this was that Mishka Papa became the most scrupulously, ridiculously and even insanely honest man in the world. Just to mention a tiny but typical example: in those days (and in these days too) it was a popular pastime in Budapest to travel on the trams without buying a ticket. It was quite easy to cheat: the trams were nearly always overcrowded. The conductor was busy at one end, so one got in at the other. Then one simply got off before the conductor could reach one; or if the conductor worked fast, and was approaching with unexpected speed, one jumped off the moving tram, it was easy enough. But Mishka Papa was always searching for the conductor. If he was at the other end he would fight his way through angry crowds in order to reach him. Once or twice – when he just could not reach him in time – he travelled one or two stops farther in order to be able to pay – then walked home in the heat or in the rain.

As I have always appreciated exciting cleverness more than dull honesty (one of my many failings) I'm inclined to feel that Mishka Papa's self-sacrificing honesty is the *real* skeleton in my family's cupboard.

* * *

How to be Seventy

I never understand – but often admire – people who remember every detail of their childhood. They can recall anxieties, pangs of loneliness, jealousy and fear; they remember nightmares and joys as if they were children even today. Perhaps they are.

My childhood was happy. I cannot remember harrowing events, perhaps because there weren't any. Or perhaps there were but I remember only the pleasant things. Happiness is, after all, in the beholder's eye. I had more or less the same childhood as my sister, but mine was delightful while hers was miserable. I had kind and understanding parents, she had strict and ill-disposed ones but we both had (again more or less – more about this later) the same parents. She had clear and enduring memories of dreary and galling episodes which in my memory were quite pleasant ones – or else I did not remember them at all. I recall only two events which shook me deeply and must have been formative influences.

When I went out on a walk with my father he was greeted by everybody with courtesy and obvious pleasure. His friends shouted '*Szervusz Frédikám!*' and the peasants (many of them my father's clients) raised their hats respectfully. He stopped to chat with people, as was the general habit in Siklós streets, and nearly everybody had a kind and flattering word for me, too. I was a spoilt little brat. As I have already said: nobody – parents, teachers or any other adult – ever beat me or even slapped me. Of course, I got – very occasionally – into fights with other boys but there is a world of a difference between fighting, even losing a fight, with an equal and being beaten by some superior authority when you cannot hit back. One evening my mother and Auntie Anna, the maid, were pickling cucumbers for the winter. They were filling huge jars. I had a toy spade in my hand and made a mock gesture as if I wanted to smash one of the jars. I hit it harder than I meant to and I did smash it, the cucumber splattered all over the kitchen floor and the water from the huge jar caused a minor flood. My mother, who had the temperament of a saint, either flared up for once or else decided that I ought to be punished for such a heinous crime and told me that I was to go out into the world. This 'going out into the world' was a phrase I had frequently heard in fairy tales. The poor heroes were chased away from the house; they had to go out into the strange and menacing world and fend for themselves. They were cut off from all family ties, thrown out. I always felt very sorry for the children to whom this happened but they were nothing to do with me, they were heroes of stories from books who communicated with fairies, witches and kings, while I had never met a fairy, a witch or a king. And now, incredibly, it was happening to me! The door was opened and I – wearing my night-shirt and still carrying the offending spade – stepped out into the darkness of our garden. I was 'out in the world'.

I did not panic. I never do in moments of utter disaster. I remain cool as a cucumber (an apt simile in this case) and contemplate my position with amazing sang-froid, on a purely practical level. (But as I am not totally insensitive, reaction comes later, a kind of delayed-action bomb, usually in the shape of desperate, deadly tiredness.) In this case I pondered over the immediate problem: where to go, to whom to turn. Ómama – living across the square – was an obvious choice. But I was not sure. As I had been sent out into the world, perhaps I was not supposed to turn to a member of the family. That must be against the rules, I felt. I looked at the spade in my hand. Before the idea of becoming an agricultural day-labourer could occur to me, the door was opened again and I was readmitted to the family hearth. I had to promise never to smash large cucumber jars with my spade again. I kept my promise honourably: I never smashed even small ones.

Any budding psychologist can see that this episode had a tremendous influence on me. I have no doubt about that, but I wish I knew in what way this influence manifests itself. I am not afraid of being left alone; I am not terrified of being expelled from any circle, and when I did have to leave the circle I belonged to – my family, my friends and my country – I rather enjoyed the experience. Yet I know that this event was extremely important in my life. It is imprinted on my mind. I can see it with amazing clarity and vividness, the film running in front of my eyes, although I have forgotten many other seemingly more important events. Perhaps it was the only time in my childhood when I felt abandoned and rejected; when I felt completely let down; when

How to be Seventy

my mother's love was denied me for a minute and a half.

The effect of the other episode is clearer.
Siklós had a football team and was slightly football mad. The star of the local team, a clever left-winger and dribbler, was Tsinna, a barber's assistant who frequently came to our house to shave my father, so I could admire him from quite near and even talk to him. One Sunday afternoon – I was about eight years old – I received three crowns from my father to go and watch a Siklós-Dárda match. (Dárda was a neighbouring village, even smaller than Siklós.) I went with my friend Márton Vida and his Fräulein – a Fräulein being an Austrian governess. Arriving at the pitch, we learnt that the match, for one reason or another, was off. I ought to have returned the three crowns to my father, but I didn't. I went to the local stationer's and bought a few sheets of paper. It seems I had already acquired the mad fascination every writer feels for his deadly enemy: clean sheets of paper. This purchase, while psychologically understandable, was quite stupid as I could use as much paper in my father's office as I pleased. And here lay the root of the trouble.

My father passed my cupboard in the corridor and noticed the clean sheets of paper. (Apparently he had never heard of the cancellation of the football match, or had failed to connect it with the three crowns handed to me.) He asked me whether I had taken those sheets from his office. I replied, quite truthfully, that I had not. My father told me that it did not matter in the least if I had taken the paper – I was permitted to do so – but it mattered a great deal that I should always speak the truth, so perhaps I would like to think again and refresh my memory. Did I or didn't I take the paper? No, I did not. I was given my third, fourth and fifth chance but I stuck to the truth: I had not taken the paper. Very well, if that was so, where did I get it from? Here lay the danger. I could not – or I absurdly felt I could not – tell my father about the three crowns. So I said I had received the paper from Tibor Kaufmann, a schoolmate and the son of the stationer. Why should he give me paper? Because I did him a small favour. What was the favour? I helped him with his homework. I thought this was very clever and all dangers had passed. But not at all. My father took his hat and walking stick and told me that he would go over to the stationer's and ask Tibor Kaufmann about it. This happened after dinner and I went to bed quickly. When my father came back, my mother told him that I was asleep. I heard my father reply: 'Tibor Kaufmann was also asleep, but he was wakened. Wake *him* up too.'

I faced my father who was sad, grave and disapproving. Tibor Kaufmann had told him that he had not given me any paper and I had done no favour for him. So did I or did I not take the paper from his office? No, I did not.

The punishment that followed was dire. I was sent into exile. I was banished from civilisation. I was a liar and did not deserve any better. My father would not speak to me and I was to have my meals at a little table, next to the family table, all by myself.

Next morning my mother had a heart to heart talk with me. She, too, was frightened and upset. At lunchtime, when my father came home I went up to him – following my mother's advice – and falsely confessed that I *had* taken the paper from his office. He kissed me, forgave me and told me most seriously once again that the paper did not matter but he wanted his son always to speak the truth.

I had acted wrongly and I knew it. I had embezzled three crowns. But I also knew that I had got into the worst trouble of my life by speaking the truth and had succeeded in clearing myself and regaining my father's affection by telling a lie.

I saw this story as I wanted to see it. I thought a great deal about these traumatic events but it took me about twenty-five years to remember that, in fact, I was lying in the first place too, inventing the gift from Tibor Kaufmann and that 'small favour'. But that would have spoilt the picture I was determined to paint for myself, so I failed to see it. I only saw the victory of Lie over Truth.

I am sure that this paradox helped me to develop my appreciation of the grotesque. I came to the conclusion, at the age of eight, that virtue did not pay; that the truth may get you into trouble and a lie may get you out of it. I cannot say – luckily – that these ideas became my guiding principles in life, but they did help to turn me rather cynical and sceptical as far as terrestrial justice is concerned.

God and the two Pistas. Pista is a diminutive of the Hungarian version of Steven. One Pista was my cousin (my father's sister's son) and the other my grandmother's sister's son. The first Pista was a little old man even at the age of five and was called Papus, 'little Father', by the whole family; the second Pista was of dark complexion and nicknamed Csóri, i.e. little Gipsy-boy. They were twelve years older than I (born in 1900), inseparable friends and great heroes in my eyes. They were university students at that time. Papus became an eye surgeon, Csóri an architect. Papus lived in Siklós, he came over to us every day at lunch-time and was very strict with me: he forced me to eat all the food I detested (my mother was too weak to force me to do anything) and he always saw to it that I learnt my lesson and prepared my homework properly. Consequently I did not like Papus all that much in my young days. But Csóri was always kind and funny and treated me as an equal. So I just loved it whenever he came over from neighbouring Pécs to visit his dearest friend at Siklós.

The other participant of this story, God, played a less important part in my life. I fully accepted what I had been told and taught about him. I do not have much of an analytical mind, neither am I of rebellious disposition. So I was nine years old before I ever questioned what I had been told about God. There he was, I nodded, omnipotent and omniscient, a forbidding and vengeful creature – terrible in his wrath – altogether not very likeable but one must love him. As it was my duty to love him, I loved him.

The two Pistas were walking in our orchard and during the conversation I mentioned God.

'Who?' asked Csóri with mock surprise.

'God,' I repeated.

'Oh, that old bearded idiot?' asked Csóri.

And then something remarkable and unforgettable happened. Namely nothing. The dog did not bark. The heavens did not open up; there was no thunder, fire and deluge; Csóri was not struck down by lightning. There he stood, facing me, smiling as if he had not uttered the most terrifying blasphemy I had ever heard. I waited a minute or two but God failed to react, failed to stand up for himself. Csóri is still with us, a delightful man, healthy, robust for his age, quite happy as far as I know and very rich. God, on the other hand, is no longer with us, at least no longer with me. He disappointed me terribly in that orchard. Then and there he lost his chance with me. He has never recovered – except for a very brief period.

One day large blue placards were stuck on the walls all over Siklós and I went to read one in Kossuth Lajos Square. It seemed to announce some sort of an open meeting but I could not make head or tail of it. Then a man came up to me and said menacingly: 'If you dare to tear this down, I'll give you a hiding you'll never forget.'

The man was a hunchback, called Finta. I was terrified of him because of his deformity and sinister appearance. I had never talked to him before. I was not only terrified but even more surprised. Never in my life had I torn down a placard; the idea had never crossed my mind.

Later I heard that the placard called on people to gather in Kossuth Lajos Square for a meeting against the Jews.

Oh yes, the Jews . . . I knew. I had seen people in long kaftans, little round hats, side whiskers, always in a great hurry. They looked poor, like the peasants, yet they were very different from the slow-moving, slow-thinking, dignified peasants who made up the bulk of the population of Siklós. It was explained to me that the Jews were dirty, dishonest, not nice at all and one must beware of them.

One day I was coming home from school and one of my school-mates – a poor boy, son of a washerwoman, whom I was quite fond of – shouted to someone in the street: 'Jew! Dirty Jew!'

And he ran away.

I looked around to see whom he was talking to. There was no man in a kaftan there; indeed there was no one else there except myself. He must have been talking to me. What a silly joke, I thought.

I told my mother about this incident and she said yes, we were Jews. I did not understand. We never wore those ridiculous kaftans or those little round hats, we had no side-whiskers, we were not dirty and I had always thought we were 'nice' people, while they were not. What did we – we! – have to do with those comic yet sinister characters dressed in black? All the same, my mother insisted, we *were* Jews.

This happened in the early twenties when an angry wave of anti-Semitism was sweeping over Hungary. The White Terror was not less cruel and bloody than the preceding Red Terror of Tibor Szamuelly, indeed it was more vicious, more vindictive, more systematic and lasted longer. Admiral Horthy, the new Regent of Hungary, was a vain man of very limited intelligence but he had been an aide-de-camp to King Francis Joseph and he had impressed a British fellow-admiral, sent to investigate conditions in Hungary, as 'a Christian gentleman in a Christian country'. So all was in perfect order as far as England and Western Europe were concerned, occasional massacres of the Jews were disbelieved (or 'wildly exaggerated') and, in any case, Horthy was a bulwark against 'barbarous, Asiatic Communism'. But for these two bulwarks, Hitler and Horthy, barbarous, Asiatic Communism would still exist only east of Poland – if at all.

During the Premiership of Kálmán Tisza, Hungary was the most philosemitic country of Europe. She not only tolerated Jews but positively invited them from the great reservoirs of Russia from where they fled the pogroms. Greater Hungary (prior to the end of World War One) had twenty million inhabitants of whom less than half were of Magyar stock. The Hungarians proudly claimed their full national rights vis-à-vis Austria, yet at the same time oppressed their own numerous national minorities: Slovaks, Croats and Romanians. 'A Slovak is not a human being' was one of the popular slogans, and practical politics lived up to this ideology. Kálmán Tisza (father of the war-time Premier, Count István Tisza) was keen on improving statistics and strengthening the Hungarian 'majority' (in fact, a minority – people who *declared themselves* to be Magyars). The Jews seemed to be excellent material for his purpose. A persecuted minority welcomed here, would be grateful to Hungary. They would be only too keen on calling themselves Magyars when the census came. And while these first generation 'Magyars' might look a bit peculiar, Tisza had no doubt that the second and third generation would be totally assimilated.

His calculation seemed to be correct. Hungarian Jews became great Magyar patriots, more Catholic than the Pope, imitating the silly habits of the gentry, fighting duels and serenading women with gipsy music accompaniment and – almost without noticing it – forming a Hungarian middle class. This started before the time of Kálmán Tisza. Hungary, like other backward countries, used to have a rich and haughty aristocracy and an oppressed peasant class, with nothing in the middle. This vacuum was filled by Germans and Jews who became the factory owners, industrialists, bankers and professional people. Later Magyar civil servants and small landowners also helped to swell the ranks of the middle class and all these elements got mixed up with each other: the Jews got gentrified, the gentry got Judaised while the Germans became gentrified *and* Judaised *and* Magyarised – and yet, as we were to see later, remained Germans.

Anti-Semitism was never quite dead in Hungary but it manifested itself in snobbish contempt and ridicule rather than in anything more wicked. All went well – indeed very well – until the end of the First War. The Jews – over-patriotic Hungarians to the last man – went to the front, fought and died in a pointless war with which Hungary should never have become involved – and were proud of their sacrifice. After the lost war – in which Hungary had also lost about two thirds of her territory and her population – scapegoats were badly needed. The Jews and Count Tisza were made responsible for everything. Tisza was murdered; so were many Jews. Many others were beaten up or tortured and all were humiliated, although they were as innocent of causing or losing the war as István Tisza himself.

The Jews of Hungary reacted to this new wave of persecution in two ways. A small minority was defiant: very well then, we *are* Jews and we have nothing to do with these Asiatic hordes of

Magyars. Palestine is our home, we shall try to get there but as long as we have to stay in this backward country we insist on being treated like human beings. But Zionism was a not too significant movement in Hungary, it was regarded as unpatriotic by the majority of the Jews and damaging to themselves. The Zionists insisted that the Jews were not Hungarians, but the majority maintained that they *were* Hungarians, Hungarians of the Jewish faith. This was not a policy, carefully thought out: it was a sincere and desperate cry in the wilderness. They were assimilated (as were the German Jews), their mother tongue was Hungarian, their background and culture was Hungarian and they were almost without exception great chauvinists. During the war they felt they had proven their devotion to Hungary. They were outraged by the anti-Semitic attacks and massacres, and they were also deeply hurt and puzzled. But then they found an explanation which they were only too eager to accept: anti-Semitism was a temporary wave, instigated by a small, misguided and resentful minority, a natural reaction after a lost war. The noble and chivalrous spirit of the Magyars would soon prevail and people would realise once again what splendid fellows the Jews really were. In the meantime one must stand up for oneself, fight slanders and calumnies and prove that even under unjust attack the Jews remained faithful patriots.

My father and all his friends belonged to this majority group. My father was asked to become President of the Jewish Community. He had a problem. The problem was the pig. Every winter a pig appeared in our house and occupied the otherwise empty pig-sty. The pig was well treated, indeed, too well treated and fattened up as much as possible. I visited the pig several times a day and grew fond of it. Then one day at about five in the morning I would wake up to the heart-breaking shrieks, roars and squeals of my friend the pig. It lasted a very, very long time and I would tremble and cry. The noise slowly became less violent, a few more howls, then faint groans and then silence. My friend was dead. He had been murdered. I learnt later that the butcher – who came to our house to kill the pig and then do all the work on it – sat on its back and killed it with a knife, cutting – first trying to cut, then, at last, cutting – its jugular vein. By ten in the morning fresh sausages were ready and I loved them. They were the highlight of the winter, those fresh sausages, although the day of the year when the pig was killed was dark and dreaded. Thinking back, I do not understand my enjoyment of those sausages. Or perhaps I do. Somehow I succeeded in dissociating the two things: the killing of the pig was very sad; the sausages were very good and the two had no connection. I was a precocious brat. As irresponsible and as good in fooling myself for my own benefit as most adults.

When my father was asked to become President of the Jewish Community (a large and prosperous one) he said he would accept the job, he would carry on the fight and do his best but he was not a religious man, and would not pretend to be one. In fact, he was having a pig killed every year – he said – and proposed to go on doing so. If the Jews of Siklós were ready to have a President who had his own pig killed annually, very well; if not, they must choose someone more suitable. The Jews of Siklós wanted my father, and the pig, while not forgiven, was – so to say – swallowed.

My own Jewishness started with my mother's explanation that yes, we were Jews. Not to this day have I quite overcome the shock. I did not understand the situation. I did not want to be a Jew. I found it intolerable to be a Jew. After that dark lie about the origins of those few sheets of typing paper, I took my father's admonition to heart and I have remained a reasonably truthful person all my life. For a few years – later on – absolute veracity became a mania, an obsession with me, so that I would not wish 'good day' to a man if I felt I could not wish it sincerely. Even when I had relaxed a good deal I still remained, on the whole, a truthful man, partly because I think it's the right thing to be, partly because no one with my rotten memory can afford to be a liar. But for a long time I lied about my origins. I left the Jewish faith as soon as I could legally do so (doing it without the knowledge of my parents) and became a Roman Catholic. In Budapest I always lied about my family background, denying my Jewishness – a hopelessly stupid thing to do in a town where everybody knew everything about everybody else. I got so involved with this lie that in the late thirties – when anti-Jewish

How to be Seventy

laws started coming into force and it became obvious that I could not hide my origins (about which no one had any doubts in any case) any longer – I decided to leave the country. I was much less afraid of Hitler than of the possibility – nay, certainty – that my 'Jewish origin' would become public knowledge.

Here in England I kept up my lie. Why I did so I cannot tell. I lied about it to my first wife, Isobel, who learnt it after our marriage, and not from me. She shrugged her shoulders and laughed. A much-loved girl-friend found out the truth after a year of intimate friendship. She (a Catholic) told me that she loved Jews and that I was the first non-Jew in her life. She was delighted to find out that the first non-Jew was yet to come. (She hated to be a Christian and wanted to be a Jew. She denied her Catholicism almost – but not quite – as determinedly as I denied my Jewishness.)

We are all products of our age and environment; we are all creatures of circumstance. I am no exception – only very few and very outstanding people are. Today I know that I acted as a few hundred thousand other Hungarian Jews of my age acted or tried to act as long as it seemed possible. Today I look at my attitude with head-shaking disapproval; I am even mildly ashamed of it. Yet I cannot quite overcome it.

I was two years old when World War One broke out, so my memories of it are somewhat hazy.

Father was a very thin man, very fragile and not in robust health. He was called up, nevertheless, and we all moved to Pécs – the county town of Baranya – where we rented rooms in the flat of Mr and Mrs Miklós Sugár, who became and remained friends of my parents. They lived above the coffee-house called 'Otthon' and I often visited that coffee-house with my parents and admired the gipsy band leader, the 'Primás'. While the rest of the band was seated, he could stand – a doubtful advantage – and walk about from table to table. I was so fascinated by him that Father bought me a tiny violin. I walked about in the Sugárs' flat, producing the most frightful, ear-piercing sounds from my violin, imagining that I was the great man, the gipsy Primás. This is my most vivid memory from the War.

Archdukes and Whores

But I have others. My father worked in a military court as a clerk and never rose above the rank of private, which perfectly satisfied his military ambitions. Eventually he was invalided out of the army and early in 1917 we moved back to Siklós. The place was full of soldiers, coming from or going to the Serbian front. There were a number of Czechs among them who spoke no Hungarian at all and many of them courted my cousin, Ilonka (the elder sister of Papus and Micike). There was one among the soldiers with whom she was constantly fighting, not metaphorically but literally: wrestling. They tortured each other, got hold of each other's necks and would not let each other go for minutes on end. I was told later that they were not wrestling but kissing. Strange. I was a bit worried the next time Mother wanted to kiss me, but her kisses were gentler. Ilonka later married that officer from northern Hungary. His name was Dezsö Einzig, he had a very deep and beautiful voice – he could sing magnificently – was the son of the rabbi at Brezno (now Slovakia) and was a dentist. I visited them later on and in their house there was a loo with two seats next to each other. That's what I call a closely knit family.

I was six when the war ended. Hungary – according to her ancient traditions – was on the losing side. New states were born: Yugoslavia (then called SHS) and Czechoslovakia; Romania swallowed Transylvania and became a large country. We were taught that the treaty of Trianon – our Versailles – was the greatest injustice in history (and like Versailles, it was not only an injustice but a very stupid treaty). We were also taught to hate the Czechs, the Serbs, the Croats and the Romanians who had all stolen parts of our country. We were commended never to forget – not even for one single moment – the injustice of Trianon and to dedicate our lives to one single purpose: regaining the lost territories.

Before I could dedicate my life to rectifying the injustices of Trianon, Siklós itself was occupied by the Serbians who stayed there for about three years. In those days the injustice of Trianon was never mentioned. (To be accurate: the Treaty of Trianon was signed only in 1920; immediately after the war we talked about lost territories and injustice, not about 'Trianon'.) During the Serbian occupation we could dedicate our lives to football and marbles. The disturbing thing about the Serbs was that they behaved extremely well, were very popular and many people said that they were much nicer than the Hungarians with their White Terror, which was raging on the other side of the frontiers or, rather, the 'lines of demarcation'. But Siklós was, in due course, given back to Hungary and the Serbs had to withdraw. Everyone dreaded this withdrawal, supposing that the Serbs would loot houses, rape women and burn the village to the ground. But they behaved impeccably, no one was harmed, no property was damaged. The kind and civilised Serbs moved out; the Hungarian White Terrorists moved in.

On the return of the Hungarian Army, led by a general called Károly Soós, various organisations made welcoming speeches. My father welcomed them in the name of the Jewish Community, my mother in the name of Jewish Women. The General shook hands with all the other speakers, but not with my mother and father.

At school we were taught once again that the Serbs were beasts and the Magyars the cream of creation. I believed it unhesitatingly. We were taught once again to dedicate our lives to regaining Greater Hungary. I was enthusiastic and decided to reconquer as much territory as I could.

One day I saw my mother sorting out some tiny socks and headgear and asked her what those things were.

'For a baby,' she said. 'Just in case another baby is born. One never knows.'

My mother's foresight proved remarkably prophetic. A few months later she travelled to Budapest (as she often did to visit her parents) but this time I was informed that a little brother, called Tibor, was born during that visit. Thus ended my five and a half years' reign as an only child. Bad luck, I felt, but there was nothing I could do about it. (A sister, too, was born later but she came *between* Tibor and me.)

I was taken to Budapest to see my little brother in whom I was not at all interested. It has been noted before that no child rejoices in the appearance of a rival. In our case the age difference between us was rather wide, so my jealousy, I believe, was disguised as indifference. I did not dislike Tibor; I was not consciously jealous of him; I just regarded him as a superfluous nuisance. Perhaps my dislike of babies was generated by that experience. I think babies are terrible bores and children should begin at the age of two. Even my own children failed really to interest and fascinate me until they started walking and talking.

In later years Tibor's significance as a nuisance grew. I had to see about his homework and I had to teach him Latin – a subject which I adored and in which I excelled while he was as indifferent to Latin as I was to him. My pedagogical methods were simple. I explained to him, say, the mysteries of the *accusativus cum infinitivo* and expected him to take them in after one hearing. Then I asked him questions. If he gave me the right answers, all was well. If not, I beat him up. It was a plain and effective method while it worked. I failed to notice, however, that Tibor had grown a lot, becoming very strong and much more athletic than I was. After a few somewhat ferocious beatings he asked me – mildly and courteously – to rely more on explanations than on brute force. But I believed in brute force. The next time I attacked him he counter-attacked and – more in sorrow than in anger – gave me a thorough thrashing. I was terribly surprised but I had to face realities. I changed my educational methods and ceased to believe in brute force.

When he was about four Tibor uttered an immortal saying.

We had a well in our courtyard – the courtyard itself was situated between a large front-garden and the orchard. The well was an old-fashioned contraption: the bucket, tied to a long rope, had to be lowered by turning a large wheel. Once down it filled itself with water and had to be brought up by turning the wheel in the opposite direction. This system was hard, so eventually it was decided to replace it with an electric pump. While this work was being done – while the old well-head was gone but the new pump was not yet installed – there was a dangerous hole in the courtyard. The well was deep: one could fall about 150 feet before reaching the water and the water itself was very deep and dark.

How to be Seventy

The hole was covered up by planks but it was still far from safe, so stiff warnings were issued about not going near it. To Tibor especially it was made clear that approaching the hole was a heinous crime. Upon which he nodded, went to the hole and nearly fell in. He was caught by the scruff of his neck in the nick of time. When the first great excitement was over and Mother had regained her breath and voice, she realised that something had to be done in order to avoid repetition. As she was no strict disciplinarian, she told Tibor that he would be dealt with by Father in a fearful manner. (Father was no great disciplinarian either but he could be strict when he made an effort.)

About two hours were to pass before Father came home from the Court. They were tense. Tibor did not say much but he was obviously preoccupied. At last Father arrived and was informed by Mother about the events of the morning. We boys were then called in from the garden and sat down to lunch. Father, quite shaken himself, looked grim and glum. However, before he could utter a word, Tibor spoke.

'Let's not talk of wells.'

After a moment's silence, laughter broke out. Tibor was surprised. He failed to see the joke; he had simply made what seemed to him an appropriate and helpful remark. But we all appreciated the brightness of his proposition. The phrase: 'Let's not talk of wells' became and has remained a favourite saying of the family and has been handed down to new generations. It is more than just a comic remark. It has universal validity. Almost every day, for example, we hear politicians interviewed on television. They are asked a difficult or inconvenient question and – without blinking an eyelid – they start fluently talking about something which has absolutely nothing to do with that question. They are not honest enough to say with Tibor 'Let's not talk of wells', but, clearly, it is his policy they are following.

Tibor was about fifteen or sixteen when he visited Ómama, travelling down from Budapest to see her. Ómama – as always – was living with her widowed son-in-law, Mishka Márkus. Uncle Mishka, who had the comfortable job of official village doctor, was a small man with a beard and spectacles, one of the most taciturn of human beings. It was quite impossible to have a conversation with him. In later years when we went down from Budapest to stay with Ómama and him, he would look at us on arrival and declare: 'You look well, child' or 'You don't look too well, child'. At our departure he would look at us again and declare: 'You look better, child,' or 'You don't look better, child'. That was all. Not a word in between. And he was no more reckless with money than he was with words. Every evening Ómama had to ask for money for next day – to give her a weekly sum was absolutely out of the question. When Ómama mentioned money, Uncle Mishka's interest in the newspaper he was reading became increasingly intense, and he did not hear her. She would try again five or six times, louder and louder, and finally he would look at her – but only to make it clear that he hadn't heard a word. She had to repeat her request many times before he grasped what Ómama was talking about. When he got the idea, at last, he took out his purse and put a few silver pengoes on the table and went back to reading. An outburst from Ómama followed: did Mishka have any idea what the price of beans or chickens or soap was? They would all starve on that miserable pittance. Uncle Mishka took out his purse again and gave Ómama another pengo. And later another. Then a third. After that he would dish the money out in fillers, i.e. pennies.

Once when Tibor was there a letter arrived, informing Uncle Mishka that Ómama's sister Auntie Paula would arrive from Eszék (now called Osiek in Yugoslavia) at 9.30 p.m. Uncle Mishka told Ómama that he would go to bed at nine, as usual and would see Paula the next morning. Ómama remonstrated with him. *She could not stay up, but wasn't it a little unfriendly of him* not to greet someone whom he had not seen for eighteen years.

'That's the point,' replied Uncle Mishka. 'As I haven't seen her for eighteen years I can wait another day.' And he went to bed at nine.

Ómama, before retiring herself, remarked how lucky it was that the house had just been redecorated (on her insistence) and looked quite decent.

It was this redecoration which caused all the subsequent trouble. Ómama and Uncla Mishka had retired and Tibor had gone out. When he returned at ten o'clock he heard painful moaning coming from the loo. He went to examine the situation. The light was on in the loo – an old-fashioned one with a wooden throne – so obviously it was occupied. But no one emerged from it and the moaning became louder and more agonising. So Tibor went to the door and opened it. There was an elderly lady – obviously Auntie Paula whom Tibor had never met – sitting on the throne – which had been repainted that day. As no one was about when she arrived, no one had warned her about the fresh paint. She had sat on it and she was stuck. Hard as she tried, she could not get up. Tibor, a stickler for etiquette in all circumstances, said: '*Kezét csókolom.*' (The appropriate greeting: 'I kiss your hands.')

'Good evening,' replied the lady with as much dignity as one can muster when stuck to a freshly painted lavatory seat.

'My name is Tibor Mikes.'

'I am Auntie Paula.'

The formalities over, Tibor took his aunt by both hands, put his right foot next to her on the loo seat, shouted '*ho-ruck!*' – the traditional cry of furniture removers – pulled hard and lifted her from the seat. The fresh paint was ruined and so was Auntie Paula's behind. Then Tibor – like the little gentleman he was – bowed formally and retired.

Aunt Paula never spoke of this incident again; Tibor has not stopped talking about it till this day.

There was a lot of excited talk, whispering and obvious worrying at home. My father had to have an abdominal operation. It was not very serious and all went well. But the wound refused to heal and doctors became worried. I remember my mother and later a nurse helping him to dress the wound. He carried on with his work but became rather weak and instead of going to his office – a few steps further away in the same house – he received his clients and dictated to Gizi, his secretary, in the drawing room. But faces became more and more serious, everybody was worried and then, suddenly, Father departed for Budapest, accompanied by Mother.

Archdukes and Whores

I became very worried when I noticed that Ómama was in a terrible state, crying more and more. She tried to control herself in my presence but was not very successful. One afternoon I went over to her and found a number of old ladies – all with white hair and thin black velvet ribbons around their necks – all of whom were sobbing desperately. When I arrived they tried to pull themselves together and hide their tears. A telegram was lying on the table. I wanted to read it but it was snatched from me. I ran home, ran out to the orchard, climbed up a pear tree and cried there for a long, long time. This scene – crying in that tree – remains one of my most vivid childhood memories. When years later I got back to Siklós, one of the first things I did was to return to our old house and the orchard. But the house had been divided into small units, the orchard was built over and the pear tree had disappeared.

Next morning my cousin Micike came to see me. She tried to be firm and to suppress her tears.

'I have some sad news to tell you. Your father . . .'

She broke down and began to sob.

But she did not have to finish the sentence.

I was ten years and one month old and quite on my own. Mother was in Budapest and I do not remember where my little brother was at the time. Auntie Anna, the old maid, was dead by that time and I missed her very much.

Ómama's grief cast a biblical gloom over those days. She was in the habit of crying bitterly and for weeks whenever a tenth cousin she hardly knew died, and now she had lost her favourite son, at the age of forty-four. She did not simply cry all day and all night; she shrieked, howled and wailed all the time, crying out to Heaven and terrifying me out of my wits. When I think back to those days, they are filled with Ómama's overpowering grief much more than with the death of my father. Ómama was in Siklós; my father was dead in Budapest.

The coffin arrived and was put up in my parents' bedroom. There was a little window cut in the coffin and my father's face could be seen through the glass.

How to be Seventy

'Don't look,' my mother told me. 'I want you to remember him alive.'

I did not look and have seen very few dead people since. People very close to me have died, and I have failed to turn up at their deathbeds. I have been strongly condemned for this by some members of my family and they may be right. Perhaps I have complex reasons for staying away, but it seems to me that I have decided to keep them in my memory not as corpses but as happy and smiling people, as I remember my father to this day.

The funeral started from our house and half Siklós was there. The Jews came, of course, to say farewell to the President of the Community. Many of them were close friends. The business and financial community came because my father used to be the lawyer for the local bank and many other smaller institutions; the professionals came to mourn a colleague; and the solemn, grave and dignified peasants – many of them clients of my father – were also there. Pale and shaken relations came from all over the country, most of them complete strangers to me. They kissed my face, stroked my head and whispered remarks about the poor little orphan. But even in that huge crowd it is Ómama's broken-hearted, forlorn sobbing that remains most clearly in my mind. When the coffin was lowered into the grave – a horrifying moment – she collapsed and I felt that the world had come to an end.

But I realised soon enough that the world would go on. I adored my father and could not imagine life without him, his jokes, his gentle leg-pulls, his stories, our chess-games – but I also loved my mother, trusted her and was not afraid of the future. Yes, confidence in my mother was the main factor. Whether courage played a part in it too . . . I doubt it. I think it was mostly indifference. I care for very, very few people and not all that much for myself. I am *interested* in my fate; but I am not all that much involved.

I heard rumours that we might leave Siklós. I dismissed them. Who could leave Siklós?

There is one episode in connection with my father's death which

Archdukes and Whores

I learnt many years later from Tibor who now lives in America. He heard it from Mother – who also lived there during her last years. Mother had a great deal of girlish charm even at the age of seventy. Her skin was like a peach, rosy and smooth and she could blush like a girl of fifteen. She often did. She blushed before telling this story, but to tell it was obviously a deliberate decision. She wanted her sons to know. She had never told it to anyone before and now she tried to seem casual – just an old lady remembering something of her past. Not being aware of her face turning crimson, she thought she succeeded in being casual.

She recalled various details of Father's illness. Something went wrong with that operation and the wound became infected. After the Second World War he would probably have been cured by two penicillin injections but this was after the First World War, before the penicillin age. Whatever medicine existed at that time, Hungary was desperately short of everything. Father arrived in Budapest in a very grave condition. He was taken to the nursing home 'Liget' where the consultant (called Chief Physician) was Dr Dezsö Halmos, his brother-in-law. (He was the widower of Mother's sister, and he is to play a great part in this narrative.) He did everything he could to save Father, and so did all the other doctors, but the infection caused meningitis and it was soon apparent that his condition was hopeless.

'He was not told, of course,' Mother continued the tale to Tibor, 'but he knew it perfectly well. I wasn't told either and I didn't know. He had nurses with him day and night. One day – it turned out to be his last – he was lying in bed, looking at me. According to medical science he ought to have been dead, but he could still speak without difficulty and he turned to the nurse and asked her to leave the room.

'The nurse was surprised.

' "Leave the room?"

' "Yes. I want to be alone with my wife."

'The nurse left. He turned to me and said: "Undress, Margitkám, and come to my bed."

'I got frightfully worried. What was I to do? I did not want a hopeless effort to kill him; on the other hand I did not want to refuse perhaps his last wish. I could hardly control myself. I told him that I had to go out for a moment. I rushed to the doctor on duty and told him what had happened.

' "Nothing can harm him any more," he said. "He has not long to live. Besides he cannot make love. That is absolutely impossible." '

There was a brief silence. Mother blushed again, even more than earlier and added: 'But he didn't know your father.'

Siklós remains a pleasant and joyful place in my memory, full of kind and smiling people. Everybody had a kind word for me when I, still a child, walked its streets. Even the policeman – who often came to our house delivering various official documents – never passed me without uttering a few friendly words and stroking my head.

There were, of course, a few odd people such as Laci Weisz, a tobacconist, whose wife was very ill. He detested her and hoped that she would die, the sooner the better. When people asked him: 'How's your wife, Lazi?' his eyes would light up and he would reply 'Very poorly, thank God'; or sadly 'Unfortunately, she's much better'. Once a customer of his asked him: 'And tell me, Laci, do you plan to marry again?' Laci grew thoughtful, then replied gravely: 'I should not deserve that this one should die if I even thought of marrying another.' (I do not admire Laci Weisz's compassion; but I still do his sincerity.)

Another irascible man was Feri Heisler, the vinegar manufacturer. He was tiny and excessively fat, resembling a giant football more than any human being I have ever seen. One day he burst into my father's office in a frenzy of rage. He wanted to sue a man for slander. They had met in the street and the other fellow had asked him: 'And where are you *rolling along to*, Mr Heisler?' I am sure Father saw the hilarious possibilities of a trial in which the central issue was Mr Heisler's rotundity, but he had to think of his client's interests first, so he tried to calm him down but to no avail. Heisler was outraged, he simply could not swallow such an insult.

'How would you feel if someone asked *you* . . .' He stopped. My father was the thinnest and most fragile of men, so it was

Archdukes and Whores

extremely unlikely that anyone should ask him where he was rolling to. But he took the point.

'I would not object to a *similar* question. In fact, the other day I met someone in a neighbouring village and he asked me: "What ill wind blew you here, Dr Mikes?" It's the same thing.'

'But is it the same thing?' asked Mr Heisler suspiciously.

'Entirely.'

'And you didn't mind?'

'Not in the least.'

Whereupon Mr Heisler departed, satisfied.

But by far the greater part of the people of Siklós appeared to be as calm and cheerful as they were friendly, and I have often wondered what drove them mad. I have wondered the same thing about people of other places too, but ultimately the whole world is a big Siklós. What changed those kind and dignified peasants? What got into those friendly, almost humble policemen who used to stroke my head? Was it the Nazi madness which infected the air and took away their senses? Or is it true that you cannot get nastiness out of a man unless it is already latent inside him?

In 1944, during the days of Nazi rule in Hungary, two of those kindly, smiling, head-stroking policemen came to fetch Ómama. She was ready to go but she could no longer walk. She was too fat and too heavy, the policemen could not carry her. So they threw her into a wheelbarrow and pushed her to a disused granary, serving now as a temporary concentration camp. The kind and friendly souls of Siklós, fully appreciating the policemen's sense of fun, laughed and jeered at the old woman in the wheelbarrow, rolling along the cobblestones. Some of them shouted at the policemen: 'Well done! Kill the fat old Jewish swine.' Ómama was nearly ninety.

There was only one person who cared for her, Margit the maid. (No member of the family was left in Siklós, they all had died or moved away; and even if they had been there, they would have been rounded up themselves, in no position to help.) Margit was the one honest person thrown among thieves. She spent hours in front of the granary calling the jailers murderers and beasts and refusing to go away. She appeared with food twice a day but the guards refused to take it from her. Then they got fed up with her and told her that unless she shut up she, too, would be taken away. Yes, that's what she wanted – she replied. She wanted to be near the Old Lady and to help her.

But the Old Lady was taken away and Margit – bless her memory – had to stay behind. What happened to Margit? No one knows. But we know what happened to Omama. She survived the journey to Auschwitz. She survived three days in the murderously overcrowded wagons, lying – well, there was no space to lie down – in her own and other people's excrement and urine. On arrival she was selected to die. There are witnesses who saw her carried to the gas chamber and thrown in.

I visited Siklós once again, many years later, in 1970, when I was filming for the BBC doing a piece for them on Hungary called 'One Pair of Eyes'. The village was now a bustling, busy and dull place. Of its several hundred Jewish population, three people survived and had returned from Auschwitz – three brothers, strangely enough, called Breuer. Under the new Communist regime the people looked, perhaps, a little tired but they were kind and courteous once again. I almost expected the policemen to stroke my head.

An elderly woman, when she found out that I was the son of the lawyer Mikes, told me: 'I served as a maid with many families. They were all nice people although . . . well, forgive me for saying this . . . although they were Jews.'

Then, feeling unsure of my reaction, she repeated: 'You will forgive me?'

I looked at her. Was she one of those who had laughed and jeered at my grandmother in the wheelbarrow? Had *she* shouted: 'Kill the fat old Jewish swine!' How could I know? Why did I *want* to know? What could I do a quarter of a century later? I forgave her.

LIFE TWO
Budapest

Maturity?

I was thirteen years old when I acquired a sister. She came *between* Tibor and me which was rather clever of her.

We – Tibor and I – were sent to holiday to Petrozsén, Transylvania, to some distant relations whom we did not know at all. They were not, in fact, true relations of ours: the three boys of the family were cousins of our cousin Hédy. Considering that we hardly knew Hédy, either, the tie seemed far from close.

Hédy was a sweet, plump girl. I had met her once at my maternal grandmother's, Róza Mama's, place in Budapest and later she came to spend two or three days with us at Siklós. She had a tragic story.

My mother had a sister, Ibolyka (Violet), who was – according to unanimous family reports – a great beauty. Ibolyka married a doctor called Dezsö Halmos. Hédy was born in April 1914 (so she was two years younger than I) and her mother never recovered from the birth. She lingered on for a few months and died at the age of twenty in August, 1914 – a memorable date in history which, in fact, plays a part in this story.

Hédy's father, my Uncle Dezsö, was heartbroken. He decided to commit suicide. But as war had just broken out he had second thoughts. He still wanted to die but he would do it not uselessly but in a patriotic and public-spirited way. He volunteered for the army and was among the first people to be sent to the Serbian front, where he committed one act of reckless folly after another. He was captured twice. On both occasions he jumped on a horse and rode away. On the first occasion they shot his horse under him. Although a doctor and not a fighting soldier, he continued to take wild risks throughout the war (later on the Russian, and finally on the Italian front). He won many decorations for bravery and emerged unscathed.

How to be Seventy

Róza Mama, Ibolyka's mother, took her daughter's death tragically. Her terrible grief was genuine, but it had – like everything about her – an histrionic element in it. She decided to dedicate her life to the memory of her daughter, and she hated Hédy. It was an unadmitted and unconscious hatred but she hated her all the same. Indeed, she told Hédy once that she had killed her beloved and beautiful daughter, a cruel remark which left a life-long scar on Hédy. It poisoned her childhood, very unhappy in any case. Her mother she never knew; her father was fighting a glorious but somewhat senseless war on faraway battlefields to start with, and later showed no interest in his daughter. Róza Mama would not take her in, in fact she refused to look at her. So Hédy was pushed around to aunts and other relations, kind and understanding people in most cases but she had neither parents nor a home. In the end she landed with her father's sister, Auntie Elza, Mrs Bauer. The Bauers were nice, if somewhat primitive, people and rather poor. In spite of Auntie Elza's kindness and love, Hédy felt like an orphan and an outsider. Elza had three boys of her own. She treated Hédy with care and affection: but Hédy wanted to be the little orphan so she felt like the little orphan.

It was this Bauer family with whom we were to spend our summer holiday for reasons which were a little mysterious to me. Hédy was there, too, of course. I went to a boy-scout camp for a few weeks and as the eldest of the Bauer boys, Bandi, was the local Chief Scout, I had the time of my life. We had a grand time altogether in Petrozsén and I grew very fond of the three Bauer boys, older than I but always kind to me, treating me as an equal and laughing at my jokes. A few days before our return was due, we were informed that my mother and my Uncle Dezső would come to fetch us. I found nothing peculiar in this arrangement and was astonished, indeed bewildered, when Uncle Dezső informed me that he was going to marry my mother. My very first reaction was to start crying bitterly and to go on sobbing for a long time. It was partly the shock, partly the effect of the tales of the Brothers Grimm. I had learnt from those tales that people with step-fathers and step-mothers were the most miserable and pitiable creatures on earth, so I felt very sorry for myself and

Maturity?

Tibor. My second thought was the peculiarity of my situation. I had never heard the expression: 'deceased wife's sister'. I only realised that Hédy my cousin was now to become my sister: Dezsö my uncle was now my father; and, in a sense, my own mother, by marrying my uncle, was to become my aunt. In Tibor alone could I find reassurance: he seemed to be a rock in this sea of confusion – he was to remain my brother.

I need not have worried. Everything worked out well. Hédy and I fully accepted each other as brother and sister from the first moment to the last. Tibor was much younger than us and in those days this mattered a lot. He was our little brother, too young to be our friend.

I accepted my step-father, too. Overcoming some strong inner resistance, I called him Father, which pleased him. I never felt that he might have treated me differently had he been my real father. Hédy, too, was happy in her new, permanent and affectionate home, although her deprived childhood had made her a little suspicious and she watched people's relationship to her and to her brothers with eagle eyes. She observed that she was not her own father's favourite and was quite pleased with this fact: the one thing she dreaded was a 'my child – your child' division. (Frederick Karinthy, the brilliant humorist, had a second wife. Karinthy had a boy from his previous marriage, so did his new wife and a third son was later born to them. One day a frightful din emanated from the nursery and Mrs Karinthy asked her husband to investigate. He came back after a short while and reported: 'Oh, it's nothing much. Your son and my son are beating up our son.') According to Hédy's acute observation Tibor was Father's favourite, I was Mother's favourite and she herself was adored and protected by Mishka Papa. After his wife's death he came to live with us, so he was permanently present to protect Hédy, who needed no protection. Hédy would come and talk to me while I was trying to read a book. I ignored her. Mishka Papa watched the scene most disapprovingly. Hédy went on talking. Then she came and started pulling the book away but as I held on to it firmly and went on reading, she changed her tactics

How to be Seventy

and started twisting my nose and pulling my ears. I acted as if I had noticed nothing and so did Mishka Papa. Then, at last, I told her: 'Hédy... please...'

Upon which Mishka Papa came to Hédy's defence with a severe reprimand to me: 'How can you be so rude to that poor child?'

We all found this extremely funny and Hédy often made Mishka Papa perform as St George, slaying us, the dragons.

It was my step-father (we called him Apu, Father now) who became the prominent – and most eccentric – personality on the scene. He was an eminent doctor, devoted to his patients, had a vast practice and worked extremely hard. At the end of days when he had seen a hundred patients – and such days were far from infrequent – he was happy, buoyant and ready to go on playing bridge till three in the morning. However, if there had been the occasional half hour between patients – a rare event – he was not only upset and depressed, feeling that his practice was going to the dogs, but also deadly tired. Similarly, when he was called out three times during one night, he was full of beans next day and happy as a lark; but when an epidemic abated and he had no night-call for a week he was sleepy all day, very quiet and went to bed early.

He was a highly cultured man, interested in every subject under the sun. When he qualified as a physician, he decided that he wanted to see the world before he settled down. He applied to the Cunard Line in London for a job, and got it. As he was an alien, he had to serve under a British doctor. This was lucky for him. Only very large ships carried two doctors, so those were the ones he had to serve on. He spent his three years with Cunard on the largest ocean liners. There was no part of the world, from China to the Solomon Islands, from Montevideo to Sydney which he failed to visit and explore. Once, on his way to New York, some passengers invited him to play whist with them. He accepted, as he had often done before, with others. When it came to settling the score, he found to his horror, that they had been playing for enormous stakes. But he had won. Indeed, he had won 3,000 dollars – a veritable fortune in those days. They were to spend four days in New York and he decided to blow it. It was not easy to blow 3,000 dollars in four days before World War

Maturity?

One, but he managed it.

As a result of his service on English boats, he learnt to speak fluent English. He got also used to drinking tea with milk, a custom unheard of in Hungary. I feel almost certain that – apart from English residents in Budapest – my father and mother were the only people who drank that – to me – horrible liquid for breakfast.

He adored my mother. He overwhelmed her with gifts and was very generous to her. He also made her life hell. He had a strong sadistic streak and took great pleasure in tormenting the woman he loved. Mother with her sweet and meek nature was an eminently suitable victim. As she was also a bit of a masochist, on the whole she enjoyed it.

Food was a permanent *casus belli* or rather *casus explosionis* because these wars were brief, eruptive and one-sided.

One recurring reason for discord was my mother being late for lunch. She never cooked those lunches herself, she could not cook at all. We had two maids, sometimes a staff of three. We always had lunch very late, at 2.30 or 3, but in spite of this – or perhaps because of this, thinking that she had plenty of time – Mother was often late. She went out shopping and forgot about the time. When she realised how late it was, she rushed home but she never took a taxi. Father begged her to take taxis but she – never exactly parsimonious in other matters – refused that single extravagance. She came home by tram and ran all the way from the tram stop. When she was late, Father was angry; when he saw her running he was livid. Yet, Mother was late for lunch about once a week, however late we ate. She always gambled on the possibility that her husband would be later still. Sometimes he was; sometimes he wasn't.

The other, even more frequent, reason for rows was food, or the way the table was laid. I do not believe that Buckingham Palace could be more fastidious in gastronomic formalities than Father was; and I know for certain that the last Habsburg Emperor who really counted, Francis Joseph, was considerably less fastidious. All sorts of mishaps occurred. Perhaps the soup was cold. Perhaps the wrong type of forks were laid on the table. Perhaps vegetables were not served from the right dish. Perhaps a napkin was not properly ironed.

How to be Seventy

The rows always took the same course. Father had a strong, deep, indeed beautiful voice. He started with a polite question:

'Margitkám [my dear little Margit], don't you think this soup could be a little warmer?'

Mother – knowing full well what was coming – tried to be diplomatic: neither to contradict him, still less to encourage him.

'Perhaps it could be a tiny bit warmer but I don't think it is freezing.'

Father would say – his voice rising in strength but his courtesy unimpaired – that he had asked most humbly, many times, that the soup should be not only not freezing but piping hot and he should like to know why such a modest request of his could not be fulfilled. And so it went on: his voice getting louder and louder until he was shouting and roaring and the chandeliers started shaking. But he never used a rude word; indeed he always remained exceedingly courteous. (It happened only once that he threw a whole roast goose out of the – unopened – window.) He always 'begged to enquire', he 'humbly requested to be informed', he would be 'extremely grateful to be told' why that soup could not be warmer. The Battle of Waterloo could not have produced more deafening noises than Father's humble enquiries. Finally Mother, having promised twenty-five times that she would take the utmost care in the future and never again, under any circumstances, would soup be served below boiling point, would lose her nerve, break down under these courteous but ear-splitting enquiries and start sobbing. We children would go on eating in deadly silence. Mishka Papa would sit in pained silence but would never interfere. Father would then go down to his surgery where, as a rule, a dozen patients were already waiting. An hour later a gigantic bouquet would arrive from a nearby florist, with a letter containing Father's humble and sincere apologies. He was sorry – nay, inconsolable – that he had been carried away. He assured my mother that it would never but never happen again; he also told her that he adored her and his life would be meaningless without her. The row was over. At least until the next time that Mother was late for lunch or the soup was cold. Or both.

* * *

Maturity?

He was strict with us children, too. That we had to have good marks at school, that went without saying. We usually did. Our table manners had to be impeccable and – unless we forgot – we took the utmost care lest he should 'beg to enquire' why one or the other of us held his or her fork less elegantly than was ordained by books on etiquette. And – this was a most troublesome rule – we had to eat up everything put on our plate. If we disliked a dish we were permitted to have a small portion of it, but never to refuse it entirely. So when we had something on our plate we particularly detested, we very slowly ate all its accompaniments – potatoes, salads and such – without touching the unwanted food itself, and we waited for the telephone to ring. It invariably did ring, as many patients knew when Father had lunch and also knew that he answered all calls personally. Sometimes he had ten calls during one lunch. As soon as he left the room, we shoved the unwanted food onto Mishka Papa's plate. When Father came back he noticed, of course, that our plates had suddenly become empty and that Mishka Papa was struggling – always successfully – with a huge heap of food. Mishka Papa looked guilty and avoided Father's gaze. Mother, who had witnessed everything, remained neutral and never gave us away – she found the whole system rather funny. Father never said a word.

Except on one occasion. A man, a native of Siklós, who became a successful painter in Budapest, came to have lunch with us in order to discuss a portrait which he was to paint of Mother.

The telephone rang, as usual. Father stood up but before going out – for the first and last time, perhaps to show that he *knew* what was going on all the time – said to us: 'And do eat up everything while I'm out.'

The painter, who used to be a poor boy at Siklós, was astonished and remarked: 'When *my* father had to leave the table, he always told us: "And *don't* eat up everything while I'm out."'

Many years later Mother and Father lived in New York state, in Long Island. He still worked there as a doctor, at a blood bank – and needless to say they had no cook at home. My mother just had to learn to cook after a fashion. She cooked with diligence and admirable devotion; she also cooked the most abominable dishes ever concocted by man.

Father – so fussy once upon a time and such a great connoisseur of food – said, and perhaps even believed, that my mother was the best cook he could dream of. He said he preferred Mother's cooking to anybody else's. Sometimes the result of her efforts was so awful that Mother hesitated to put it on the table. Father tasted it and declared that it was delicious. Occasionally Mother burnt the supper – she might be watching a soap opera on television and forget all about it – and suggested that they should go out or to a restaurant. Father would taste the dish, admit that it was slightly burnt but insist that Mother had a special way of burning things which made them even more delicious.

Then I realised that Baucis may have been fond of Philemon; Abélard may have fancied Heloïse; Romeo, perhaps, had an eye for Juliet. But Father *loved* Mother. (But the table, even in Hicksville, Long Island, had to be laid with heavy silver and slightly more elegantly than tables are laid at the Waldorf Astoria.)

There was a series of books on Little Cecily (*Cilike*), very popular during my mother's childhood, or perhaps a little later. The books were for girls, so I never read them, but Little Cecily became a by-word and a well-known folkloristic figure, rather like Billy Bunter – an utterly different character – was in Britain. Cecily was sweet, well-meaning and extremely likeable but very accident prone and all her well-intentioned moves turned into minor disasters. Mother was a Little Cecily of real life.

A Physicians' Travel Association flourished in Budapest. Groups of doctors used to make journeys together, usually disguised as a medical conference – a ruse not utterly unknown in our own days. These journeys were often slightly overshadowed for my parents by the fact that Mother invariably forgot to pack something essential so that Father would have to beg to enquire why he had no shirts, or why she brought one black and one

Maturity?

brown shoe instead of a pair. Good points, on the whole, but the humble enquiries made Mother more and more nervous and less and less deft as a packer.

They were about to go to Zakopane, in Poland, a skiing resort in the Tatra mountains. The Hungarian doctors were to be greeted by the Polish doctors, with their customary hospitality and generosity, and Father was designated to reply to the toast. It was a black tie affair and Mother was absolutely determined not to fail on this grand occasion. A dinner jacket in those days was more complex a garment to wear than it is today. The shirts had to be starched; collars had to be fixed on by the wearer, using little shirt-studs, there were further studs – often made of gold – for the front of the shirt; then there were the cufflinks, the tie and further tiny details, all terrible pitfalls for a not too proficient packer. Mother checked and rechecked everything a million times. In the end she was satisfied: no small accessory was missing.

Indeed, no small accessory *was* missing. On the great day, Mother put out the socks, the shoes, the tie, the studs and the cufflinks: they were all there. Only a big accessory was missing: the trousers. In despair, she tried to substitute a pair of dark blue trousers for the missing ones, hoping that it would pass unnoticed. It did not. Father noticed it. They tried to borrow a pair from a waiter but the waiters all had to wear their trousers so that wasn't any good either. So it happened that every guest appeared in his dinner jacket with the single exception of the main speaker. My father was not amused.

Not much later, the family travelled up to Vienna for a few days. Father – in order to gain an extra working day – followed us by air; the rest of us, three children and Mother, went by boat. The journey up-stream on the Danube took twenty-four hours. We had one cabin for the four of us and the journey started inauspiciously. Tibor and Hédy quarrelled as to who should sleep in the upper bunk (one of the two upper bunks was occupied by me, this was not disputed) and could not agree. So they drew lots. Hédy won. Tibor, however – not yet the perfect gentleman he is today – refused to accept the verdict of fate and as a revenge took out the bolts of Hédy's bunk. As a result the bed

How to be Seventy

collapsed in the middle of the night, Hédy rolled off, finding herself on the floor between the two bunks, shrieking like mad, Tibor was laughing his head off and Mother ringing for a steward in panic. The whole scene was not only somewhat peculiar but rather noisy, too, and failed to enhance our reputation or our popularity among the passengers.

Worse was to follow. In Vienna, we stayed in a hotel in Maria-Hilferstrasse, the Oxford Street of Vienna. Father duly arrived. There was a terrific heat-wave on and he had a bath after his arrival. He never slept in the afternoon, he hated the very idea, but on this occasion Mother persuaded him to lie down: he had a tiring journey, there was this terrific heat, he was on holiday after all, etc. Her solicitude was not prompted by her otherwise undoubted devotion to her husband, but by the fact that while he was having his bath she had noticed that this time she had forgotten to pack any underpants for him. It was a Sunday, so she could not even rush down and buy a few pairs in a nearby shop. But she was a resourceful woman and worked out a plan. While Father was asleep, she would wash his one and only pair of pants – the pair he was wearing – and in this heat they would dry in no time. And on Monday she would be able to buy as many pants as she pleased. Father agreed to rest, and she washed the pants according to plan. In order that they might dry even more quickly she put them out on the balcony. At that time all Vienna was praying for a little breeze and God granted the wishes of these pious people: the breeze came, lifted Father's pants from the balcony and landed them on the top of a tree underneath. Father's one single pair of pants were gone. My mother panicked easily but her spirit was indomitable. In the room was one of those rods with a hook at the end, used for opening and shutting sash windows. Armed with this she went out to the balcony to fish for pants. The operation took a long time and needed great patience. In the end she hooked the pants. It looked for a second as if she was to drop them again, this time right down to the street – but she managed to retrieve them. All would have been well except that at this moment enthusiastic cheers broke out. Mother had failed to notice that a crowd had gathered in the street to watch the lady pants-fishing. The generous people of Vienna now

Maturity?

signalled their appreciation. Their cheering woke Father who soon enough realised what had happened. Faced by the cheering populace as well as his heartily laughing children, he did not start his customary vociferous enquiry but simply murmured a few words, among which '*Zakopane*' was clearly discernible.

We were a slightly crazy lot but not really crazier than any normal family.

My school was now the 'gymnasium' in Budapest, and after the Cistercians of Pécs I did not find it too strenuous. Manners here were very different from those in Pécs. There we were reasonably polite to one another, sex was never even hinted at and the equivalent of four-letter words were never uttered. In Budapest boys were, to say the least, more informal to one another; sex was the main subject of conversation and obscenities and dirty jokes filled the air. Quite a few boys boasted constantly of their sexual prowess and adventures and at first I felt like someone who had moved from an elegant country mansion to a Metropolitan brothel. In the Madách gymnasium in Budapest all the boys used the familiar '*tu*' to one another from the start. I used the formal '*vous*' to most, keeping '*tu*' for those who formally encouraged me to use it by uttering the word '*servus*' and shaking hands. This habit of an awkward and timid country boy created, as it turned out, quite a craze, first in my form and then in the whole school. They all started addressing one another as '*vous*', and mock courtesy became the order of the day.

Being a provincial among sophisticated urban adolescents made me as unhappy as I am capable of being. I wanted to become a true metropolitan lad, a true son of Budapest, like all the other boys in my form. I tried to shed my Transdanubian accent. Transdanubian is one of the two nicest accents in the language, so I am not sorry that I did not succeed in my endeavour and that I failed to pick up the awful accent of Budapest. (My brother was only four when we left Siklós, yet he – miraculously – preserved a much stronger Transdanubian accent than myself.) But in most things I was a quick learner. I picked up the obscenities in record time, although I could never

How to be Seventy

be rude and rough – that is not really my nature. I probably lost a good deal by my desperate efforts to get rid of the country bumpkin. I still love cities and dislike the country as a place to live. I once wrote somewhere that I preferred the smell of petrol to the smell of daffodils and this is true, even if not literally so. I trained myself not to recognise trees, plants, flowers and birds because only country boys are clever at such things, the sons of Budapest are idiots. With a considerable effort I succeeded in becoming a super-idiot. I can now tell a sparrow from an ostrich, but that is the limit of my ornithological accomplishment.

The general level of teaching in Budapest was lower than in Pécs. The Cistercians were monks, they had no families and no worries. Their main interest in life was their pupils. In Budapest, a number of worried and harassed men, often the fathers of too many children, were struggling to make ends meet. At Pécs if a boy did not come up to the mark, he was mercilessly failed and had to leave school; here the masters – with a few exceptions – were much more lenient and leniency meant the lowering of levels.

I had no difficulties at school. My interest in school subjects was genuine, if rather perverse. I loved the Magyar language and poetry – a passion I shared with quite a few others. But I had a definite passion for grammar, too. All grammars. Latin grammar I loved most, and even today I am quite willing to study the grammar of languages I do not intend to learn, just for the fun of it.

My passion for Latin grammar disgusted many a friend. I had been one of the best Latinists even at the priests' school, where Latin was *the* most important subject of all (seven Latin classes a week). Latin at the Madách was child's play. Later, when we started learning Greek, I got into trouble because of my love for Latin. The incident was vaguely reminiscent of my stealing – or rather not-stealing – paper from my father's office, an episode which has left an indelible effect on me. *Then* I was not guilty of the charge brought against me but I was guilty of *something*; now I was quite innocent. What happened was this. I sat down and translated about thirty-five lines of the *Odyssey* into Latin hexameters. I was rather pleased with myself and handed over

Maturity?

the result of my labour to Mr Farkas, the Latin master. He read it and asked me where this translation came from. I told him – rather hurt – that it had come from me, I had translated it. He read it through more carefully and repeated the question, very sternly. I repeated my answer. He told me that there were four translations of the *Odyssey* into Latin hexameters and he had them all at home. He would check and if I had copied from one of them there would be dire consequences. I told Mr Farkas that I knew nothing about rival translations: this was my own work. Next morning I received a handsome and generous apology. But my zest for showing off was damped.

Mathematics was another love of mine, but an unrequited love. I was fascinated by its pure beauty, almost poetry; by its logic, its brilliance, its power to prove and disprove things, but whenever I tried to penetrate its mysteries, I always failed as soon as I left the surface. Even today I cannot forget my hopeless love for the subject, indeed my infatuation with both my childhood loves. Every now and then I try to read a Latin author, only to find that my knowledge has become rusty and the effort would be too much – to go on with it would be hard work and no enjoyment. And occasionally I pick up a book on mathematics, take paper and pencil, make up my mind to work hard and not to be discouraged by difficulties . . . but half-way through – indeed often much earlier – I have to acknowledge defeat.

In those days a *one* was the best mark you could get. A *two* was still good, a *three* was a pass, and a *four* meant failure. I usually had *ones* with a few *twos* thrown in. The *twos* were frowned upon by Father but were tolerated. *Threes* were absolutely out of the question and they never cropped up except on one disastrous occasion – disastrous for me and also for Hédy. Our troubles were not connected in any way but they cropped up at one and the same time.

'General behaviour' was regarded as a subject and we were marked on it. Usually everybody got a *one*, indeed this almost went without saying. A *two* would have been shame and disaster. Hédy got a *three*. I cannot recall the heinous crime she committed to achieve this, but according to Father the world had come to an end.

How to be Seventy

At the same time I, for the first and last time, got not one but five *threes*. And something even worse. It was noted in my midterm report that my performance in Latin – Latin! – was especially feeble. Father did not understand the reasons for this sudden decline. But I knew it only too well.

My grandparents still had their own flat and employed a good-looking, black-haired maid who was fun to talk to. We became great friends although she looked extremely ancient, about twenty-five. I was fifteen. We started some horse-play when opportunity offered, and suddenly I saw the chance for going farther. My parents were about to give a party and I had to spend the night in my grandparents' flat. They, of course, would be out, at my parents' party. So I was to stay alone with Bözsi who, no doubt, was regarded as a baby-sitter. But I had different ideas about baby-sitting. On the day of the party, at three p.m., I went to a school-mate, called Pauncz, because I knew he was the proud possessor of a condom. These commodities were freely available but I was too shy to go to a pharmacist and ask for one. I might have been thrown out, although this was unlikely – business was business. Pauncz, fully aware of the value of his possession, refused to give it up, but in the end, having extorted various promises as well as speedy repayment in kind, he parted with it at 7 p.m. Soon afterwards I dashed over to my grandparents' flat where Bözsi gave me dinner. After dinner I went to bed and started reading a book, admittedly not fully concentrating on the narrative. Bözsi came in, lay down next to me – fully dressed – and declared her great interest in my book. I made love to her. She did not resist. She knew I was a virgin and must have been amused. The whole exercise did not last more than a few seconds and I found it extremely disappointing, a wildly overrated pastime (a view I subsequently revised).

The immediate result of this adventure was the disastrous decline of my school performance. Perhaps it was not the result of the physical effort exerted or the energies wasted, but of guilt. I spoke about it to no one except Pauncz: a fully detailed report was one of his stern conditions. Although I tried to make my story to Pauncz as pornographic as I could, I remained disappointed and disillusioned, and made a vow not to go near a

Maturity? woman until my *baccalauréat* – called *maturity* in Hungarian – was over. A vow I kept.

Our bad school reports caused a major explosion. Father was proud of our generally good performance at school and this he regarded as a personal insult to him. In those days we went to a dancing class and it so happened that the final evening – a kind of small ball – fell on the day we received our school reports. I was sure we would not be allowed to go. As I hated dancing and was pretty bad at it, I did not mind much. I was keenly interested in one of Hédy's school-mates and would have regretted missing meeting her, but this blow could have been borne. To our amazement nothing was said about the evening. We dressed and were allowed to go. However, hardly had the evening begun, when Father – accompanied by a slightly trembling and deeply embarrassed Mother – appeared and in full view of all our friends and many strangers ordered us to go home. After our shameful school-reports, he declared, we did not deserve to go out and enjoy ourselves. We left, feeling like criminals in hand-cuffs.

I shrugged my shoulders as I do in most cases, but Hédy was deeply hurt. Father was a sadist, she maintained. It was all right to punish us since we both deserved it, but it was nasty to humiliate us. To make it nastier still it had all been carefully planned and thought out. That was Hédy's opinion, and she was right.

Father died many years later in New York where, by then, Hédy also lived. She was a generous and dutiful daughter, a much better child than I, and she made her parents' last years as comfortable as she could. In other words, she fully deserved a *one* in 'general behaviour', and her father must have forgotten her bad mark years ago. But she never forgot the incident, and she never forgave her father for that night at the dancing class.

Choosing a career was never a problem either for me or for Hédy. There must have been a period when I, too, wanted to be an engine-driver but I fail to recall it. As far as I remember, I always wanted to be a writer and a journalist – the two were more or less inseparable. My real father used to write and he remained

How to be Seventy

my hero. I wanted to follow in his footsteps. My decision met the fiercest disapproval for a number of reasons. Journalism was not a profession for a 'gentleman', my mother told me. That increased my desire to be a journalist. I was under the influence of Bernard Shaw at the time, and did not want to be a gentleman in the sense she intended. She and the rest of the family decreed that I should become a doctor like my step-father, and in due course take over his practice – one of the largest private practices in Budapest. But this was not on as far as I was concerned. I thought cutting people up, removing infected organs, examining excrement, etc a filthy profession. It has to be done, no doubt, like sewage work, but not by me. All my life I have disliked doctors – an oedipal reaction to my step-father, perhaps, I do not know. I dislike their authoritarian ways, their posing as the knowers of all secrets, and I find them, on the whole, rather stupid. This antagonism is quite unjust and unjustified. And considering how much I have loved many of the doctors in my own family and how well I get on with numerous doctor friends, it is probably downright stupid. But all prejudices are stupid, why should mine be exceptions?

It was kept a secret from me that my real father started off as a medical student but gave it up during the first semester because anatomy classes turned his stomach. My mother suggested that if I would not be a doctor I should become a lawyer. She argued convincingly that if I wanted to follow my father, that's what I ought to do, since he, after all, had been a lawyer not a writer. 'You can try your hand at journalism for a year or two,' she told me, 'in order to get connections and to get to know people. Journalism can be an excellent spring-board.' I told her I did not want to spring, I wanted to become a journalist. Hédy, on the other hand, *wanted* to become a doctor. As a rule Hédy supported me in all my endeavours, but she too was against me this time.

'You can't be a writer,' she warned me. 'What if you run out of subjects to write about?'

This was a curious line of attack.

'What if you run out of patients?' I asked her.

'Don't worry. As long as humanity exists there will be sick people.'

Maturity?

'And as long as there are sick people there will be subjects to write about.'

One would have thought that the solution was evident. I did not want to become a doctor. Hédy did. So why couldn't I do what I wanted to do while Hédy trained to take over her father's prosperous practice? But not at all. Father did not want *Hédy* to be a doctor. Hédy maintained that the sole reason for this objection was that she *wanted* to do so, but Father's explanation was that the medical profession was all right for a man but not for a girl: a curious argument, even in those days.

In the end we reached one of those famous Hungarian compromises. Hédy could go to university to study medicine provided she became a medical researcher (biochemistry was one of her main interests) and not a practising physician. I could try my hand at journalism provided I did so while I was studying law at university. (Law students in Hungary could easily do things on the side: attendance was not compulsory, as long as one passed one's exams one was all right.) All this, however, was still in the future. There were two big hurdles before me: I had to pass my *maturity* and I had to get a place at a university.

There was a *'numerus clausus'* at the universities which meant that only five per cent of places were allotted to Jews. This was their percentage in the population, but as they were primarily middle-class people, excluded from many jobs – the civil service, the army, nearly all public services – they could only get along in the professions and commerce. In theory sixty-six per cent of university places were reserved for peasants – *their* proportion in the population – but as they did not claim any seats at all, or very few, this was a ludicrously unfair arrangement. I was not unduly worried. I wanted to become a journalist and if I did not make the university, the pressure on me to become a lawyer would cease. But there was one snag from my point of view. All Jewish pupils who passed their *baccalauréat* with distinction were assured a place at a university. (A stupid rule. It meant that only the cream of Jewish students got in and as a result they seemed to be better and more successful than the other, unselected students. This appeared – inaccurately – to prove the superiority of the Jews, and thus increased anti-Semitism and ill-feeling.) I was obviously

How to be Seventy

heading towards a *baccalauréat* with distinction – but I did not have to do well, after all: I was free to do as badly as I needed. But then Father made me an offer. He knew I had set my heart on a European journey after the *baccalauréat*, and that although I had made some money towards it by tutoring some other boys, I did not yet have enough. He offered me 300 pengoes if I passed my maturity with distinction. This put me into a quandary but the desire to travel was too strong. The danger of becoming a lawyer could be faced later. Besides, I was only against becoming a lawyer and not at all against studying law which, in fact, interested me very much.

I have a head like a sieve, not very good for anything else perhaps, but excellent for passing exams. I could fill it with the necessary knowledge – well, with unnecessary knowledge, if you like – very quickly, be fluent and articulate at exams (mostly verbal) and then forget almost everything as fast as I had learnt it.

I thought Father's offer over carefully. I discussed the matter with Hédy (Tibor was still too small). We decided that I should accept Father's offer.

So I condescended to pass my *baccalauréat* with distinction.

The previous generation of middle-class people in Hungary spoke fluent German, almost without exception. Even Hungarian peasants had to learn, willy-nilly, some German. They had to serve three years in the Army, and in most units the word of command was German. There were some Honvéd regiments in which the word of command was Hungarian but these were few and far between. This word of command business was, by the way, one of the most explosive and acrimonious issues of the Austrian-Hungarian Empire. Hungarian patriots were incensed: why should our boys be compelled to learn a foreign language in order to serve their country? Or were they serving foreign interests? There were vociferous debates in the Hungarian Parliament, demonstrations in the streets, pitches of near-hysteria were reached and few people realised how happy the country was whose main problem was not more serious than that.

Maturity?

The Austrians insisted on a unified language in the army and it had to be German. You could not expect Austrians to learn Hungarian. The Hungarian peasant-boy – in retaliation and self-defence – murdered the German language.

The one dubious advantage of our losing the 1914–1918 war was that Hungary became independent. That meant that the Hungarian sergeant major could now bawl '*Vigyázz!*' instead of '*Habt acht!*' when calling the recruits to attention. And we children – reaching school-age just after the war – did not have to learn German. We were immensely proud of not knowing German. We boasted of this lack of knowledge. It was a distinguishing mark; perhaps we regarded it as a token of our national independence; perhaps it was just interesting. We would not have been prouder of speaking seven languages fluently than we were of not knowing German. Hungary's so-called independence did not last long: the country became first a German, then a Russian satellite. The only lasting gain seems to be that I – and a few like myself – did not learn German. It was hardly worth fighting a world war for that.

After my *baccalauréat* Father told me that not knowing an important European language was not such a dazzling achievement as I rated it and suggested that I should go to Vienna to learn it. Studying German did not appeal to me very much but going to Vienna was real joy. The family council decreed that in September 1929 I was to go to Vienna, and that I would return in the spring of 1930 to prepare for my first law exams in Roman Law and Constitutional History.

I had a wonderful time in Vienna. I became a student in the *Hochschule für Welthandel* – High School for World Commerce – but as I did not intend to take any exams there and was not in the least interested in World Commerce, I could do as I pleased. There were a number of pretty Lithuanian girls there, studying German as well as World Commerce and speaking Russian among themselves. As a result of this I made much greater progress in Russian than in German – indeed, a few months later my Russian became quite fluent.

I was infatuated with one of these Lithuanian girls and she suggested that we should go to the Opera. Not being mad about music – being, in fact, tone deaf – I was not irresistibly drawn to the opera, but I would have gone anywhere with that girl so we climbed up to the fifth – or seventh? – floor of the gallery (standing only) and listened to *Der Rosenkavalier*. She was enthralled; I was bored stiff. I did not like standing, and found the piece interminably long. *Der Rosenkavalier* was the death blow to a budding romance. I never saw the girl again.

But I did see *Rosenkavalier* again. In London, before the war, I got an invitation to spend an evening with some very nice friends. I was instructed to wear a black tie because we would go to the theatre before supper. The theatre proved not to be the theatre but the opera. We went to Covent Garden. The opera performed was *Rosenkavalier*. I made a vow never to see it again – a vow I failed to keep. In 1961 Brigitte Lohmeyer, Cultural Counsellor to the German Embassy in London, invited me to go to Berlin to see the newly built horror, the Berlin wall. I went and took my son Martin with me. We were given an official guide – a pleasant and intelligent student – who was as glad to get rid of us as we were to get rid of him. But on the fourth day of our visit he informed me that I was to go to the Opera. What was on? I asked, suspecting the worst. *Der Rosenkavalier*. I refused to go, but he was adamant. It was quite impossible to refuse, he explained. The invitation was a great honour, people were fighting for tickets and many of them failed to get them. Well, would it not be wiser then to offer our tickets to people who were keen on getting in? No, this would be an insult to my hosts. I asked Martin if he wanted to go instead of me. He declined with thanks and a grin. He was off to the cinema to see a film with Rita Hayworth. I sighed and went to see *Der Rosenkavalier*.

A few years later the same Brigitte Lohmeyer invited me to Glyndebourne. I was delighted, as I had never seen that lovely place before. On the road to Sussex I found out that we would see *Rosenkavalier*. This put a great strain on my friendship with Brigitte but as our friendship survived that strain, it will survive anything. By then I was in despair. *Der Rosenkavalier* seemed to be my curse, my misfortune, my evil dispensation. But at Glyndebourne I had the surprise of my life. I started *enjoying* it. I knew it quite well by now and started discovering its beauty. I still have not seen any

Maturity?

other opera, but I have returned to *Der Rosenkavalier* – quite voluntarily – several times. I have seen it on eleven occasions, all told. When in good mood, I whistle a gay aria from the second act of *Rosenkavalier* – out of tune.

But back to Vienna. Having dropped Lithuanian Girl Number One, I fell in love with a Lithuanian Girl Number Two, called Fenya. Her mother tongue was Lithuanian, not Russian, so we had to speak German. She was a gentle, sweet and affectionate creature. She never dragged me to *Der Rosenkavalier*.

Suddenly I received a telegram from Budapest. I thought at first that it was congratulations for my birthday, although it arrived a few days too early. But it was no congratulation. Father informed me that my grandmother, Róza Mama, had died and ordered me to return for the funeral without delay. I was furious with Róza Mama. I bade an emotional farewell to Fenya and we wept all night. I was very unhappy. I had hoped to stay till April and about ten weeks of happiness had been stolen from me. Just like Róza Mama, I thought. She was always a bore and now I deeply resented her choice of the date of her death. Her funeral was on my birthday – a final insult. I was sullen, morose and peevish at the funeral but as I was not expected to be hilarious or frolicsome my last feeble protest passed unnoticed.

Malice in Wonderland

'I should like to speak to the Editor-in-Chief, please,' I managed to get the words out. This was the first time that I had appeared in the editorial offices of a newspaper and I was overawed by the occasion.

'Whom may I announce?' asked the nice-looking and kind secretary, Kató, obviously amused by my acute embarrassment.

'Mr Miklós Lázár,' I replied.

'No. That's the name of the Editor-in-Chief. I mean your name.'

'I was told to mention the name of Dr Szilágyi,' I said.

The secretary smiled, very patiently, and asked me for the third time: 'What's *your* name?'

I told her my name and she disappeared behind a huge, padded door. A few seconds later she came back and told me to wait. But almost immediately afterwards a very short and fierce-looking man, quite bald, with his glasses pushed up on top of his head, came out and told me: 'Come in.'

He faced me. We were both standing.

'Yes?' he asked ferociously. Later I learnt that this ferocity was a pose on such occasions, to compensate for his short stature.

'I was told by Dr Szilágyi to come along today at nine o'clock, sir,' I said, and was pleased with myself for having been able to utter a coherent sentence.

'And what do you want?'

'I should like to become a journalist.'

'Why?'

'I've always wanted to become a journalist.'

This did not answer his question at all but he nodded.

'Very well, then,' he said. 'Sit down somewhere.'

I left the inner sanctuary, went out to the big room and sat by

Malice in Wonderland

an empty desk. I did not explain anything to anybody and no one asked me any questions. If questions had been asked, I would not have known what to answer. I had no idea what my status was now. I had been told to sit down and I sat down. I sat at that desk for several hours without anybody paying the slightest attention to me, with the exception of Kató (she was Lázár's niece, as it later turned out) who sent encouraging glances in my direction from time to time.

The paper whose offices I had invaded was *A Reggel* ('The Morning', probably copying the French *Le Matin*), a Monday morning paper, equivalent to our Sundays. (On Sundays the dailies produced large editions. It was on Sundays that the printers did not work, so there were no daily papers on Monday mornings. The 'Mondays' filled that gap.) *A Reggel* was a lively and well-written paper and I was an avid and admiring reader of it. Its editor-in-chief and proprietor was Miklós Lázár, a political animal, a Member of Parliament for the famous wine-growing district of Tokay, a late successor of the great Lajos Kossuth, one of the great national heroes of 1848. A friend and patient of my step-father's, Dezsó Szilágyi, a lawyer, knew Lázár, and promised to put in a word for me. The result was this visit.

Slowly I understood what the position was. Sunday was, of course, the main working day and it was the boss, Lázár, who was the first to appear in the office. He had given me an early appointment because he was free and alone at that time. Later the others started turning up. The big boys, the important members of the staff, walked into Lázár's room without being announced and without knocking; the smaller fry sat down at desks, started reading the papers and threw curious glances at me. Some made telephone calls, others ordered cups of black coffee from the café downstairs, all flirted with the secretaries. I was full of admiration for all of them. Can I really become one of them? Shall I flirt one day with those secretaries as their equal? Shall I one day just lift the receiver and order black coffee for myself?

I knew Lázár's name but as his field was politics, he did not really interest me. The man I was hoping to see was the famous, even notorious, Zoltán Egyed. He was the theatrical critic. His pieces were witty, scurrilous, scandalous but always amusing and excellent reading. He also wrote the two most famous gossip columns of the country (one in this paper, the other in *Szinházi Élet*, Theatrical Life) and many thrilling articles about scandal in high society. I thought he was a knight in shining armour (which he wasn't) and an exciting and brilliant journalist (which he was). Many people were coming and going and I wondered if Egyed was among them. But when he arrived I had no doubt that it was him. The door was flung open with wild and theatrical ferocity. Someone said, '*Szervus*, Zoli,' but he paid no attention to the greeting. His face was set, hard and angry, and he stormed into Lázár's room. No one paid much attention to him, this was obviously his customary entrance. A few minutes later he came out, picked up a paper and started reading, without sitting down. One or two people asked him polite questions but he ignored them. Then he threw down the paper and stormed out of the room without acknowledging anyone's existence. One day, perhaps – if I am permitted to stay here – I shall have to meet him and talk to him. I was trembling at the very idea of it.

Soon a milder looking man arrived, greeted the girls and the other minor editorial characters lounging about, and entered Lázár's room. He was Dezsö Kiss, the economics editor. A few minutes later Lázár came out and looked round. He seemed a little surprised when he noticed me – he had forgotten all about me. But he spoke to me: 'My boy, go and get a *Györi Hirlap* for Dr Kiss.' And he went back to his room.

The *Györi Hirlap* was a provincial newspaper, published in the western town of Györ. I had never heard of it, let alone seen it. But I knew that to buy a *Györi Hirlap* on a Sunday morning in Budapest was no mean task. I tried hard but the newsagents all looked at me as if I were barmy. Then I had a brainwave. I took a tram and went to the main railway station. I would get it there or nowhere, I thought. *Nowhere*, was the answer. I failed in my first journalistic assignment. I returned to the office but did not even get a chance of reporting my failure to Lázár as he was engaged with some bigwig. He and everybody else had completely forgotten about the *Györi Hirlap*.

I went back to the desk. Lázár came out with his visitor, Istvan

Malice in Wonderland

Friedrich, a former Prime Minister – and noticed me again: 'Go home now. In the afternoon we work at the *Népszava* printing plant. Be there.'

He walked away. Then turned back and added: 'Be there early.'

I had no idea what 'early' meant but this order sounded as if my being a little late would endanger the publication of tomorrow's paper.

I went home for lunch. Father and Mother asked me what had happened. I wanted to ignore their questions in the best Egyed fashion but did not dare. So I said that I found being there very interesting and was told to go back to the printing plant.

'So you got a job?' my mother asked.

'I don't know. I was told to sit down at a desk in the morning and I was told to go to the printers' this afternoon.'

And I added gravely: 'Early.'

During lunch and while walking over to the printers' I kept thinking of my hero, Egyed. I was longing to meet him but was also terrified. Our first encounter did not turn out to be very auspicious.

Our paper was printed then by *Népszava*, the Social Democratic daily. The plant was a huge building, situated in the most notorious red-light street. Typesetting went on in a spacious central hall and our offices were scattered all around that hall. I saw Lázár arrive and settle in an office at the far end of the hall, and later Egyed settling at the other end, near the entrance. I was hanging around in the hall, watching the printers.

Lázár came out with some manuscripts in his hand and looked round. He caught sight of me and handed the manuscripts to me: 'Take this over to Egyed,' he said.

This was a great moment. I was going to face Egyed himself. I suddenly remembered a book I had once read about newspapermen. The writer explained that a novice must behave modestly. Indeed, even to introduce himself to seniors was presumptuous and arrogant. He must wait until his existence is noticed and that – according to the author – took at least six months. So I decided to be modest. I walked into Egyed's office and found him sitting at his desk, smoking a cigarette – as always – and making notes. I handed him the papers: 'The Editor-in-Chief told me to hand these over.'

He looked at me with murderous eyes: 'And who the hell are you?'

I told him my name.

'Can't you introduce yourself, properly?'

I did not answer.

'And what are you doing here?'

I told him that I was allowed to be here and hoped to become a journalist one day.

He stood up and offered me his hand: 'I am Zoltán Egyed,' he introduced himself and rushed out, to Lázár's office. After that Egyed did not seem to notice my existence for weeks.

I hung around from half past two till seven, watching how the paper was put together. A few unknown people came and chatted with me, some giving me a word of encouragement, others just showing off, and most of them offering me cigarettes.

Mr Vértes, the chief sub, came out from his office with some notes in his hand and looked round. He asked for two or three people but was told that they were not available, doing other jobs. His eyes fell on me.

He called me over. He said that the house of a school-master had been burgled. The story was that the whole family, about five of them, were at home, listening to the radio, while the burglars ransacked the house and took away everything movable, including pieces of furniture. He gave me the address: 'Go and find out what happened. There may be a story in it.'

I rushed towards the nearest tram stop. But my departure was delayed because my nose started bleeding profusely. I had to dash into a nearby public lavatory and quite a time elapsed before the bleeding stopped. It was sheer excitement. I never had such a nose-bleeding experience before or since.

I got my story. I wrote it up and handed it to Vértes. He read it, then, without looking at me, stood up, called a typist and completely rewrote it, using my material but not my words.

I had no idea whether I had succeeded or failed. I was driven

Malice in Wonderland

slowly to the conclusion that I had failed because for weeks after that I was given no jobs at all, was not even sent out to buy a *Györi Hirlap*. I turned up on Sunday mornings in our office, on Sunday afternoons at the printers'. I got to know most of the people and liked nearly all of them, but I was given absolutely nothing to do and Egyed did not even reciprocate my greetings.

Then, perhaps in the fourth week, Lázár called me in and sent me to a beauty contest for dogs. I returned with a longish piece. He read it, changed a word here and there and said nothing. My piece appeared in the paper and he put my name under it.

I do not think that anything I have written in the subsequent fifty years gave me as great a satisfaction and filled me with as much pride as my piece on the dogs' beauty contest.

My mother, too, was inordinately proud. Slowly she resigned herself to my becoming a journalist and started giving up all hopes of my ever becoming a gentleman.

One Sunday, during the slack period when the paper was ready and we were waiting for the machines to start, I was hanging around in the central hall. Egyed came out. I was used by now to his looking through me as if I were made of thin air. But this time he came up to me, put his arm around my shoulder, asked me a lot of personal questions, enquired after my university studies and my family and then offered me a job. The job was strictly non-journalistic. It was for a law-student, as he put it.

He explained to me that he knew a lady called Ilona Titkos. (She was a great, beautiful and sexy star and the whole of Hungary knew that Egyed was her lover.) Her tax affairs were in a mess and I was to sort them out. He offered me a splendid salary. It would be misleading to say that it was more than I received from the paper because from the paper I had as yet received nothing. My piece on the dogs was paid for, that was all. I was overwhelmed by Egyed's offer. I was delighted that he had noticed my existence and, apparently, trusted me. I was overwhelmed by the idea of meeting that famous and beautiful star – or at least I hoped I would meet her.

Next day I was told to meet Miss Titkos and Egyed for lunch, in a restaurant opposite the Vig Theatre, where Miss Titkos was rehearsing. She was a charming yet very formidable woman. She was the *femme fatale* of Hungary. No great beauty, perhaps, but she had a wonderful figure, a tremendous personality and a great deal of what was called sex-appeal in those days. She devoured a host of men. Some of them went bankrupt later but she kept their gifts: a villa on an elegant hill in Buda, a silver Lancia car, dazzling and valuable jewellery and so on. She was a shrewd, level-headed woman of working-class origin with a tremendous amount of common sense, and she was also a talented actress. My duties often took me to her villa or to her dressing-room. When in a hurry, she would change in my presence. There she would stand stark naked, discussing tax matters with me. Not that she wanted to impress or seduce me. Far from it. I just did not count.

I was no great tax expert but it was not very difficult to reduce chaos into normal disorder. She was pleased with my work.

Hardly had I started on my new job, of which I was immensely proud, when Lázár called me in: 'I've heard Egyed roped you in to work for his lover,' he said.

'I am trying to sort out Miss Titkos's tax affairs,' I replied diplomatically, but feeling uncomfortable.

'You have to give up that job immediately.'

I was stunned.

'Look,' he continued, 'you seem to come from a respectable family and I am sort of responsible for you. I can't really allow you to become the private secretary of a whore.'

I was speechless. Lázár seemed to be on the friendliest terms with Egyed. Egyed was the main pillar of his paper, its greatest asset. And to refer to that great actress – however she may have acquired her villa and her silver Lancia – in such terms reflected a certain lack of respect.

'You give up that job today. You've heard me. Not tomorrow: *today*.'

I left the room.

I did not leave the job on that day or the next. I kept it. The subject was never mentioned again.

I had many reasons for wanting to stick to my so-called private secretarial job, one of them being the splendid salary. But there was one snag about that splendid salary. I never saw a penny of it. Having worked for eight months for Ilona Titkos, one day I went to have lunch with them again in the same restaurant opposite the Vig Theatre. I made my report on various matters, then Miss Titkos unexpectedly asked me: 'I say, Gyuri, do you get your salary regularly?'

Before I could reply, Egyed told her, in the tone of someone deeply hurt: 'Ilona, please . . . This is a matter between Mikes and me.'

But by then I had been with them eight months. I had written a large number of pieces – mostly unsigned reports but quite a few signed pieces too. I had breathed the air of the editorial office and was losing the dew of my innocence, so I told her quietly but firmly: 'As a matter of fact Mr Egyed has overlooked this matter lately.'

'Do you know how much you have received? The exact sum?'

'Yes, I know. I have received nothing.'

She opened her handbag and paid out my eight months' salary. In later life, every now and then – not often enough, but every now and then – I managed to collect tidy sums. But never again did I feel so rich as then, having that unexpected windfall of eight months' salary in my pocket.

After two years' hard work I left my job with Ilona, but I remained friendly with both of them. Egyed, of course, remained my boss, but I often visited Ilona. When I had to study for my law exams, I took my books early in the morning, went up to her villa and studied in the beautiful garden till two or three in the afternoon. Then Ilona and Zoli got up and joined me in the summer house. As a rule they had champagne for breakfast and offered it to me, too, but I declined with thanks, sticking to coffee and cold meat. After breakfast they moved back to the house and I could, once again, concentrate on the beauties of international private law or the rules of criminal procedure.

Zoli Egyed remained my hero although I found out soon enough that he was not exactly the knight in shining armour, the cavalier of impeccable probity I had imagined.

He most certainly was a brilliant journalist and his reports as well as his criticism were compulsively readable. He could turn the dullest subject on the earth into exciting reading. He was also one of the most corrupt men I have ever met. 'My friends write good plays, my enemies write bad plays,' seemed to be his guiding aesthetic principle. The same went for actors. If he had an eye on a pretty budding starlet and hoped to get her to bed he praised her lavishly and could make her famous overnight; if she refused to oblige or had a quarrel with him later on, her name was mud in no time. He was a great power in the theatrical world, he could make or mar a play or a reputation. His vanity was overwhelming. He was a pugnacious man, always involved in quarrels, and he fought innumerable duels – a great vogue in Budapest before the war. He would go and visit a bank director or a rich industrialist and demand money from him, telling him that unless he paid up he would mention in his gossip column the affair he was having with his secretary or with somebody else's wife. He was not even ashamed of this. He regarded it as a healthy redistribution of wealth: these bankers were robbers in the first place and it was their duty to help poor artists. He was the Robin Hood of Hungarian journalism. He got the money from the banker or industrialist, put it in his pocket and, if half an hour later he met a needy actor or a penniless old journalist, he gave him the lot.

On one occasion I met him in a café. As he was coming away from a bank, I had little doubt what his errand had been. He seemed satisfied; he looked like a tiger who had just devoured a gazelle. An actor came over to our table and regaled Egyed with a horror story. His mother had died and now he had no money to bury her. There she lay, the poor, emaciated old woman – his one and only mother – unburied in a cold and dark flat. What difference the coldness and darkness made to the emaciated corpse was not quite clear, but it added gruesomeness to the story. Egyed took out a large wad of money from his pocket and handed it to the actor.

'Go and bury your poor mother,' he said.

The actor thanked him and left in a hurry.

'What a world . . .' Zoli remarked. 'That a man should not be able to bury his own mother . . .'

Malice in Wonderland

'Terrible,' I agreed. 'Even more terrible than you think. That a man should not be able to bury his mother *once*, is awful enough; but not to be able to bury her *twice*, is too horrible to contemplate.'

'What are you talking about?' he asked in the uncertain voice of a man who starts vaguely recalling something.

'A few months ago you gave a pretty large sum to the same chap to bury the same mother.'

Now he remembered it all. He jumped up: 'I'll kill him!' he shouted.

'Don't,' I told him. 'You may have to pay for *his* funeral, too.'

But he rushed out to catch and kill – or at least beat up – the actor . . . who had not, naturally, lingered in front of the café.

On his next appearance in a play he was unfavourably reviewed by Zoli.

Zoli was unscrupulous and a blackmailer – after all not everybody agreed with his theory that it was the duty of rich bankers to support poor journalists, or that *he* was the poor journalist they had to support. He was a great womaniser, and his many escapades were not always in the best taste. (He lived for a while in the Grand Hotel on Margaret Island and once hung a sign on his door-handle: DO NOT DISTURB BECAUSE I AM FUCKING MISS . . . and here followed the full name of an operetta star whose husband adored her and was madly jealous of her. An earth-shaking scandal ensued. Three years later the husband had a literary evening, introduced by Zoli Egyed. The husband referred to Zoli as his best and most trusted friend, and Zoli, in turn, rhapsodized about the talents of the husband.) But, as I have said, Zoli was also a dazzling journalistic talent. He was also a brave man, a much-decorated soldier in the first war. He had the courage plus the vanity of a man who was determined to become a hero. He could be good-hearted and generous to a fault; and he embraced many a good cause, disregarding his own interests and peril. He was happy when he took on the whole establishment; happier still when he took on the whole world.

In the mid-thirties he fell in love with an operetta prima donna – a great beauty who eventually became well known all over the world. That was Zoli's doing. He met Mr Mayer (Metro-

How to be Seventy

Goldwyn-Mayer's Mayer) in Karlsbad, Czechoslovakia (I was there with him) and persuaded him to give a contract to a dazzling beauty and world-shaking talent. She got the contract. She begged Zoli to follow her to Hollywood, and Zoli, after some hesitation, agreed. There were farewell dinners, banquets, innumerable speeches and articles: Zoltán Egyed is to leave Budapest for good, to become a script-writer in Hollywood. He went. On arrival he found that the lady had become the lover of an MGM director and refused to see him. Hired thugs told Zoli to leave Hollywood, or else. He left without even seeing his former lover who had begged him to follow her and for whom he had got the contract. Such an adventure would have broken many a strong man. But not Zoli. Three weeks after his departure for good he was back in Budapest. He did not sneak in, furtively; he came home as a conquering hero.

This mercurial and incalculable man was invariably kind and helpful to me. Once he pinched a girl-friend from me but he regretted it bitterly. It was not his conscience that bothered him, but the change that came over that naïve and modest little girl who had been a good pal to me. In Zoli's hands she became a greedy gold-digger who cost him more money and trouble than a dozen prima-donnas, opera-singers and international film-stars put together. Apart from that one slip, he was always a true friend. He fought with Lázár – rather a mean man – on my behalf, to get me a proper salary; and when he saw that I was doing a large part of *his* work, he gave me – voluntarily – a considerable part of his own income from the film-page. His spontaneous sacrifice made me quite a large earner. He even defended me behind my back.

One day the telephone rang at home and it was a well-known *diseuse* who wanted to speak to me. She said: 'All right, I apologise to you most humbly.'

I was flabbergasted.

'What for?'

'Please don't pretend,' she said. 'You know perfectly well.'

But I had no idea. The following facts emerged. She sang songs on the stage of a small theatre. She sang well, I was a fan of hers and often praised her in my reviews. On the last occasion,

Malice in Wonderland

however, the rest of the programme was unusually good and while I liked her performance, this time I failed to mention her. I was not even aware of this omission but she – needless to say – was. And she concluded – as all paranoid actors do – that I had some dark reason for trying to harm her. She complained to Egyed, telling him that I had offered her some songs, written by me, and as she refused to sing them, now I had revenged myself on her by leaving her name out of my review. Egyed became very angry. He replied that I was an honourable man and until she apologised to me, her name would not be printed in our paper. Hence the mysterious telephone call and apology – without a full explanation, however, because she knew perfectly well that I was not writing songs at all, for her or anybody else.

Egyed acquired a very unpleasant illness during the First War – I think *erysipelas* is its medical name, commonly known as St Anthony's fire. From time to time he fell terribly ill with great pain and high fever. He knew how to treat himself – he had all the instructions and the appropriate medicines at home – and never even asked a doctor to come and see him. He just treated himself and after a week's absence returned to work.

During World War Two he stood up to the Nazis. He despised that vulgar and illiterate lot and said so. He was quite ready to pass an anti-Semitic remark on a banker who refused to pay him ransom but he regarded the Nazi persecution of the Jews an outrage. For this, during the Nazi terror period in 1944, he found himself in the worst military prison of the country, at Sopronköhida. The humiliation, the kickings and beatings half killed him, and the job was nearly finished by his old illness which he could not treat in prison.

He survived the war but was a human wreck. He had no illusions about himself. A friend of mine who served with the American army visited Budapest soon after the war and met a number of Hungarian journalists in one of the inevitable coffee-houses. They introduced themselves in the Hungarian manner:
'I am X.'
'I am Y.'
'I am Z.'
Then Zoli introduced himself.

How to be Seventy

'I used to be Zoltán Egyed.'

I visited Hungary in 1948 and looked forward to seeing him again, but it was not to be. His untreated illness had returned with a vengeance. His attacks became worse and more frequent and he was slowly losing his mind. In his last days he was reduced to crawling around in his room on all fours, uttering inarticulate howls, shrieks and moans.

His many friends, sycophants and lovers had deserted him. He died alone. A victim of the Nazis, unsung by the Communists.

Perhaps he was not a great character. Perhaps he was not a good man. Perhaps he was not the right idol for a young man wanting to become a journalist. But the memory of Zoli Egyed still warms my heart.

Budapest in the thirties was a city and a society far removed from reality: a city and a society which fiddled while Rome burnt. It could not have influenced events in any case, so it might just as well fiddle.

Hungary was no universal Paradise. Far from it. The hungry thirties were even hungrier there. There was no dole. A man who lost his job – as tens of thousands did – or just lost his capacity to work, earn, borrow or steal could not keep himself and his family. He might as well jump into the Danube from one of those beautiful bridges. Many did.

Wages were low, strikes hardly ever attempted. The regime was nationalist, irredentist, anti-semitic and semi-fascist – getting nearer and nearer to three-quarters and eventually to full fascism and nazism. The Communist party was banned after the escapade of 1919. The Social Democratic Party existed but was banned from recruiting among the peasantry and consequently divided between those who accepted the prohibition and those who regarded the abandonment of the peasantry as a betrayal of the proletariat. Parliamentary elections were open, secret ballots were only introduced in the large cities. It was explained that this openness suited the open and frank nature of the Magyar nation. Tremendous pressure could be exercised on voters – peasants were intimidated – and the ruling government party won all the elections before the war. There were noisy scenes and acrimonious debates in Parliament and these created the impression of free speech. The government, in fact, was not totally oppressive and did tolerate criticism, but certain subjects were taboo. Freedom of speech compared favourably with totalitarian Italy or Germany but compared with a real democracy it was a sham. Miklós Horthy, the Regent – a former aide-de-camp to Francis Joseph and a former Admiral of the Austro-Hungarian Navy – was a revered figurehead and also one of the stupidest men in charge of the destinies of a European nation. Yet above all this misery and deception, there was a happy-go-lucky and well-to-do (often extremely rich) middle class and aristocracy, witty, funny, cynical, self-seeking people fiddling loudly on the roof of Europe while the furnace in the basement was getting hotter and hotter. For the lucky ones Hungary was a delightful place while the party lasted – a fool's paradise. In the early days of Nazism, Germany courted the Hungarian regime: it needed all the approval and support it could gain and it saw a possible ally in Hungary. So, we concluded, there was no need to worry.

Women were beautiful, food was excellent, wine was abundant, gossip was rampant, high society balls were as elegant as anywhere, gipsy band-leaders played soft, romantic Magyar tunes in the ears of visiting foreign ladies courted by slim Magyar dandies: in short, for the lucky ones as well as the tourists, Budapest was one of the pleasantest, most amusing and most intriguing cities in a turbulent Europe which was hoping against hope, but which knew at the bottom of its heart that the carnival would not last. In Budapest itself, unemployed bookkeepers and managers of bankrupt firms went on jumping into the Danube, but the splash of water was suppressed by the nostalgic sobbing of the gipsy violins, playing in those elegant hotels on the banks of the river.

Fundamental to the peculiar Budapest culture were the coffee-house and the joke. The coffee-house as an institution came from Vienna, which is surprising. After all, coffee was brought into Central Europe by the Turks who occupied Hungary for 150 years but could never conquer Vienna. Be that as it may, the coffee-house habit did come from Vienna. The coffee-house was

How to be Seventy

not just a place you dashed into for a cup of steaming and strong black coffee or a snack, it was a way of life. It was *weltanschauung*, way of looking at the world, for those who did not want to look at the world at all. It was a second home for people who very often preferred it to their first one. They loved its smell, its moist heat, its stale air. The coffee-house habitué, as a rule, was no addict of sporting life, he was no health-maniac, no fresh-air fiend. Indeed, he declared: 'The coffee-house has two great advantages: you are not at home and still you are not in the fresh air.'

Every profession, every sect had its own café, with its regular habitués and regular tables where no stranger was allowed to sit without being invited. Every shade, faction or sub-group within each profession had its own coffee-house. There were coffee-houses for writers and artists – these were the most famous because these people were not only the most interesting but also the most articulate – but there were also coffee-houses for textile salesmen, scientists, horse-dealers, pick-pockets and politicians. Journalists wrote their articles in coffee-houses and playwrights their dramas; businessmen held conferences there. Having ordered one single black coffee, you were entitled to sit there for hours on end, read the daily and weekly papers – both foreign and local ones were available on large, wooden frames – and you were given glasses of fresh, iced water every half hour or so.

People called on you in your café and if you happened to be out the headwaiter always knew when you would be back. You received phone calls there, and your more confidential mail – and occasionally the most innocuous and innocent letters, as well, because although an acquaintance might not know your home address he would certainly know the coffee-house you frequented. The headwaiter, by the way, while seeming to be extremely polite, almost servile, was a figure of authority, an avuncular being, an advisor and father confessor. He gave you credit and even loans when needed, and some of the great headwaiters of that era are more vividly remembered than a few obscure prime-ministers.

The joke was another speciality of Budapest. Jokes, of course, were not invented there – not even all the Budapest jokes. (I have written a great deal about jokes and do not intend to repeat here

Malice in Wonderland

what I have said before, but during my previous researches I was struck by their ubiquitousness. The first appearance of one joke was traced to the Paris Commune in 1871. It was resurrected in modern guise in Hungary and Poland in 1945, and was being told in China in the late '70s.) Budapest prided itself on its jokes. Whatever the event, the comment was a joke, very often witty and to the point. But as Budapest regarded itself as the city of jokes, which *had* to respond with a joke to everything that happened, occasionally the jokes were forced or dull. A joke in a semi-fascist regime is the equivalent of a leading article, a political protest, a strong view expressed with force and conciseness; in a totalitarian state it is an act of rebellion, a nail in the tyrant's coffin, and a cry of despair as well as a ray of hope. In the early days of Nazism such jokes were current in Budapest.

A storm-trooper in Berlin eyes an old orthodox Jew with side-curls, in a long kaftan and a small, round black cap. The man goes up to him and asks: 'What are you looking at me for? ... Haven't you ever seen a Swiss citizen?'

Or: A young and dandified Prussian lieutenant and an old Jew are standing in front of the statue of General Moltke. The old Jew cannot read whatever is written at the base of the statue and asks the officer: 'Excuse me, sir, but is this General Moltke?'

The lieutenant replies, imitating the old man's Jewish accent: 'Yes, this is General Moltke.'

The old Jew looks at him and tells him: 'Don't imitate *me*. Imitate *him*.'

The spirit of these jokes reflects a lack of reality, the cloud-cuckoo-land atmosphere so characteristic of those times. The Nazis are being treated as paper tigers, rather comic figures who would not dare to harm a Swiss Jew; they struck heroic attitudes, they could be rude to an old and defenceless Jew, but were most certainly unable to imitate General Moltke.

It was a witty, happy-go-lucky and malicious atmosphere which permeated this sinking wonderland. A man hesitated to leave a coffee-house table because he could be sure that he would be discussed – his financial affairs, his sex life, his failures – in the most entertaining and cruel way. Women, and particularly actresses, were regarded as fair game. The aim was to take a

How to be Seventy

woman to bed and then boast of the achievement. If you could not make the conquest, you could always lie. A stage designer had been trying his best for years with one of the greatest actresses and, at last, succeeded. Hardly was the act over than he jumped out of bed and started dressing. The actress asked him: 'Why the hurry? Where are you going?'

'Down to the coffee-house. To tell the boys about it.'

The journalists' club, the Otthon, was the source of many famous stories. Here is a typical one.

A priest (for some reason or another there were always priests there, playing cards) was losing heavily. He could ill afford it. Once again he seemed to be in trouble. His opponent had four kings, a combination which could only be beaten by four aces – an extremely unlikely hand to have. The priest kept the cards close to his chest, opened them with agonising slowness and realised, to his delight, that he did have four aces. He exclaimed: 'There *is* a God in Heaven!'

Such were the moments when Hungarian priests in the '30s were relieved of their tormenting doubts.

When there was no other target, the self was always good enough, a proof, at least, that Budapest could laugh at itself.

Ferenc Molnár – one of the wittiest men of his age – spent the various seasons in different towns: winter on the Riviera, spring in Venice, summer in Budapest, autumn in Vienna and Paris. He always said that he had a six-room flat: one room in Cannes, one at the Danieli in Venice, and so on. (In Budapest he had a *two-*roomed flat, hence the number six.) He was engaged to a famous prima donna, Sári F., whose many virtues did not include sexual fidelity or abstinence. When Molnár returned to Budapest after a prolonged absence, his so-called friends ('If you have a Hungarian for a friend you need no enemies') told him that while he was away Sári had behaved disgracefully. 'I wouldn't upset you if it had just been one or two . . . but she really has been going outrageously too far. She went to bed with dozens, scores, perhaps hundreds of people.'

'That's all right,' replied Molnár.

'All right? How can it be all right?'

'She goes to bed with all that lot because she loves them. But

Malice in Wonderland

for money — only with me!'

I was, and still am, amused by these (and hundreds of other) stories. But I notice that nowadays there is a shade of disapproval in my tone. I seem to be speaking as a man who shakes his head at Budapest's caddish, cynical and slightly destructive morality. This may be the result of my prolonged sojourn in England. I certainly did not shake my head in those days. I became a fully fledged member of that society, sharing its morality, laughing at its jokes and chasing all its chaseable women.

When a bus or a tram passed a church, most people raised their hats in respect. A few did not: the sprinkling of atheists and the Jews.

I was not entitled to raise my hat and that irritated me so much that I decided 1. not to wear a hat and 2. to get baptised.

I do not say that it was my only, or even my chief, reason. My main motive — with hindsight it looks ridiculous — was that I was a Hungarian, I felt myself to be a Hungarian, I wanted to be a Hungarian. My culture, my background, my language were Hungarian and the only factor which divided me from the rest of the people — *my* people, I felt — was my religion, which did not mean anything to me. I wanted to eliminate that one dividing factor. It seemed very simple.

I went through the formalities and was baptised in the Roman Catholic Church at the Square of the Roses. My godfather was a journalist colleague of mine, Dr Pál Bernát. A brief religious fit — the only one in my life — followed and I had no idea what had hit me.

I was now entitled to raise my hat to churches so I acquired a hat for this very purpose. I did my hat-raising with as much casualness as any old parishioner. I also started visiting churches. I paid many visits to churches, crossing myself on entering and also on leaving, in order to show the other worshippers: look, I am a Christian, one of many, just like you. Then a mystic feeling gripped me. I started murmuring Our Fathers and Hail Maries (so recently learnt), reading books on religion and believing in the divinity and resurrection of Christ.

How to be Seventy

This phase was about a month old when I was invited to dinner by Pista Vértes, the chief sub-editor of our paper, who had a charming house in Buda and often asked me to be his guest. One of the others was a well-known Catholic columnist. He and I left the house together and took a long walk in the night. I told him about my conversion and he decided to strengthen my faith, using mostly mystic arguments. Now, mysticism was one theme which I could never swallow; it amused me rather than terrified me. I have a prosaic and matter-of-fact brain. As he went on, more and more seriously, I began to see my whole behaviour and so-called belief as grotesque and a self-deceiving sham. Suddenly I saw through myself. I had been trying to convince myself that I was a more honest person than in fact I was. I had been trying to persuade myself that I had not converted for purely practical reasons, for the sake of convenience, which had nothing to do with religion, but because of honest conviction. Forgetting, most conveniently, that *first* came the conversion, *then* came the conviction. The conviction was a lie. I said good-bye to my friend, thanked him for his well-meant words and decided to stop lying to myself.

I have remained a Roman Catholic till this day. But I am a lapsed Catholic.

I lapsed four weeks after my baptism.

I lapse fast.

Early in 1934 I became a Doctor of Law.

The final ceremony at the University was quite an impressive one. We candidates had to wear tails – or at least it was customary to do so. (Many years later I took part in a debate of the Cambridge Union and an undergraduate told me during the preceding dinner: 'I am really very broadminded and I do not dislike foreigners. But I do despise people who wear tails in the morning. Don't you?' 'No,' I replied. 'I despise people who eat marmalade with their afternoon tea.') We, despicable people clad in tails, were called one by one to the huge desk behind which sat the highest dignitaries of the university, the Rector and the Deans of the four faculties, wearing the ancient chains of their office.

Malice in Wonderland

The Rector sat in the middle and the four Deans were placed in order of seniority: the Dean of Theology on his Right, the Dean of Law on his left, the Dean of the Medical Faculty on his far right and the most junior Dean, that of Philosophy, on his far left. We had to shake hands with all of them, going from the Rector down, in seniority, stepping left and right and then far left and far right. In our excitement some of us made mistakes and that always caused childish merriment among the spectators. The Rector and the Deans shook us by the hand and murmured the magic words we had worked for four years to hear: 'I accept you as a Doctor of the University.'

My parents were present and so was the entire editorial staff of my newspaper, led by Lázár and Egyed, although the ceremony occurred on a Saturday, at the time of our weekly news conference. I was glad that studying was over. My parents were pleased too: I was among the first to qualify, mostly because I wanted to get rid of my obligation to study and meant to fulfil my promise. I never regretted having studied law. In fact, I am delighted and grateful that my mother forced me to do so because it is a beautiful subject and a marvellous discipline. I am still very much interested in it, I read law books whenever I have the time, and the way of thinking acquired at the university has stayed with me for a life-time. How often have I heard the exasperated cry from wives, girl-friends and other opponents: 'You are a bloody lawyer!'

Everyone was pleased but no one more so than the headwaiter of the café Bucsinszky. In a coffee-house everyone was addressed by some title, usually undeserved. A young actor was 'Mr Artist' (which sounds, I must add, less foolish in Hungarian than it does in English). Every clerk, anybody with a job was 'Mr Director' or 'Mr Director-General' and every young journalist was 'Mr Editor'. I once heard a young man tell a headwaiter: 'Don't call me Mr Director any more. I've got a job.' Perhaps it was this remark or, maybe it was just inverted snobbery, but I never permitted the waiters or anyone else to call me 'Mr Editor'. 'I have a name,' I told them, 'and I'm no editor.' They knew I had a name, but to call someone simply 'Mr Mikes' meant that I was the lowest of the low and this degraded the establishment. Now they

How to be Seventy

were all smiles and received me with a chorus of 'Mr Doctor', but their pleasure was short-lived. I asked them to do me the favour of reverting to the old way. I thought it silly that a writer of light articles and theatrical and cinema criticisms should be called 'doctor'. I only signed myself *doctor* on legal documents and when in trouble over some article I had written, trying to impress the other parties. But on a few occasions being a 'doctor' served me well and gave me real pleasure. I wrote a long report for my paper, revealing wide-spread corruption in one of the counties. It caused quite a sensation and scandal. Next day an angry gentleman was announced. He was the Lieutenant of the county concerned and he demanded to see the writer of the article. He was led in. I stood up to greet him but he brushed me aside: 'I don't want you. I want your father . . .'

'No sir,' I told him coolly. 'You want me. My name is Dr George Mikes.'

The moments in life when you can deliver such satisfactory lines are few and far between. The only vaguely similar occasion – less good because it did not cut anyone down to size – occurred here in London. I was sitting in a bus, holding one of my books, taking it somewhere. A kind gentleman sitting next to me noticed what the book was and said with a smile: 'You read him too?'

'No sir,' I replied. 'I write him.'

I did every kind of work on the paper with the exception of politics and sport. About sport I knew nothing and, in my case, that was a completely separate department. Politics interested me but not madly. The empty bombastic patriotic slogans of official propaganda rather repelled me – no, worse: made me laugh. General Gömbös (a captain, really, who as Prime Minister promoted himself to the rank of general) was a loud-mouthed bully. A former white terrorist of the post-war years, he 'revised his views' vis-à-vis the Jews, in order to gain liberal support, but in the end he revised his views once again and it was he who laid the foundation of the Nazi alliance. His one claim to fame is that he invented the phrase the 'Rome-Berlin axis', from which the name of the Axis Powers derived. He was an uneducated lout, whose speeches were full of ridiculous mixed metaphors. I could not possibly support a man who mixed his metaphors.

Some friends of mine tried to persuade me to join, or at least to sympathise with, the Communists. But my friends, determined to recruit me, were too persuasive, too intense, painted much too rosy a picture of the Soviet paradise and I did not believe them. The Nazi danger was not yet imminent in Hungary and I did not accept the argument that the Communists were the strongest bulwark against the Nazis – as indeed 1939 proved them not to be. Perhaps I was a coward, too. Communist connections might have harmed or ended my career. But the truth was that I was not a Communist. I am one of the few of my generation who have never been. Had there been an election, I would have voted Social Democrat but I had no chance of voting in Hungary.

I was deeply involved with the theatre. Many of my friends were actors; even more were actresses. Every theatre in Budapest has a 'salon', a kind of common-room or rest-room. Actors, between scenes, come in for a chat, a cigarette, or a cup of black coffee. There are always a few visitors hanging around too: actors from other theatres, theatre administrators, journalists and others. There was good conversation in those salons and one could always pick up some news or gossip.

One evening I had to go to a ball as a reporter and I had to wear a white tie once again. Before the ball I had to visit the Vig Theatre where there was a first night. I went through the stage door and walked into the salon which, to my surprise, was almost deserted. Only one person was pacing up and down nervously: the author of the play. He was Dezsö Szomory, a famous and distinguished man, one of the great eccentrics. He regarded himself as king of Hungarian literature and he insisted on being addressed as 'Your Excellency'. He loved organ-music and had a huge organ built in his house and it was known that he was fond of playing the organ stark naked, with a royal crown on his head. He was not naked now; he was wearing tails, too. I stopped at the door and hesitated for a moment. I had never met Szomory before and was keen on meeting him, but this moment, I thought, was not very suitable for a relaxed chat. I was about to withdraw when he caught sight of me. He stared at me and stood still for a few seconds. Then he walked up to me and said abruptly: 'Will you do me a favour?'

'Certainly, if I possibly can.'

'Of course you can. Otherwise I wouldn't ask you. Look here. The first act of my play is about to finish in five minutes. That stupid audience in there will howl: "Author, author!" They expect me to go out and take curtain calls.'

He stopped. I waited.

'I hate it. I just hate it.'

I still had no idea what all this had to do with me.

'Go out and take a bow instead of me.'

That was pretty unexpected.

'I?'

'Yes. You.'

'But, excuse me, sir. I haven't written the play. They want to see you.'

'You are in tails,' he said firmly, 'and they are all fools. They don't see a man, only his white tie. They won't notice a thing.'

'But one or two of them *might*,' I objected meekly.

'So you refuse... I never expected anything else from you,' he said contemptuously and resumed his nervous pacing up and down in the room.

Here are two anecdotes of the theatrical world which I think not only funny but also very wise.

Laszlo Beothy was a famous director and producer. A young man's first play was being rehearsed by one of Beothy's young directors. The great man himself came down to see one of the final rehearsals as was his habit, to judge the work of the director. He listened carefully and kept interrupting the rehearsal with remarks: 'Cut that line...' 'That should be out...' 'Oh no, that exchange is out.'

When it happened the umpteenth time, the young playwright gathered enough courage to interfere:

'I really must protest, Mr Beothy... You are cutting out much too much of my play.'

Malice in Wonderland

Beothy turned to him and replied: 'Remember, young man, that no play has ever flopped because of the lines that were cut out; only because of the lines that were left in.'

The other story concerns Ferenc Herczegh, the prince of official literature, the darling of the nationalist and right-wing establishment – an able and remarkable novelist and playwright in spite of this love of officialdom. He wrote a new play and it was performed, like almost all his plays, in the National Theatre. Jeno Rákosi, the editor of a daily paper of the same establishment and a great friend and supporter of Herczegh, gave it an absolutely stinking review. Budapest was stunned because it went without saying that Rákosi's paper found everything Herczegh wrote a masterpiece. Next day, for the second performance, both men sneaked back to the theatre to take another look at the play. They both waited until the audience was seated, meaning to slip unrecognized into a box. But both needed to go to the loo first, and to their dismay they found themselves peeing next to each other. Rákosi felt that he had to say something.

'I say, Feri,' he said, 'you know that I have the greatest respect for you. I think you are our most outstanding author. I am truly sorry that I felt obliged to say a few unfavourable words on this new play of yours and I hope it will not impair our friendship.'

Herczegh looked at him and said: 'That is perfectly all right. There is only one thing I should like you to observe in the future. Next time please *offend* me in the lavatory and *apologise* in the newspaper.'

I was happy with my paper, *A Reggel*. The only minor bore was that Lázár was an inveterate walker and an even more inveterate frequenter of the Turkish bath. When he caught one of us hanging around in the office, he asked us to accompany him and very few excuses were accepted. I hated the walks and even more intensely the Turkish bath. When we smelt the danger, we scampered or withdrew to safe rooms but, at regular intervals, we were each caught.

One day he caught me again and suggested: 'Come with me, we are going to visit Simi Krausz.'

How to be Seventy

Now, that was a very different kettle of fish, a truly attractive proposition. Simon Krausz was a legendary figure: a former banker, once upon a time a multi-millionaire and probably the richest man in Hungary. And, unlike most rich men, he was recklessly generous. Perhaps, as a new rich, he was insecure and felt that he had to buy people's admiration and affection but, whatever his reasons, he threw his money about with reckless generosity. His friends and lovers were all rewarded in a royal fashion (Miss Titkos's lovely villa in Buda was a gift from him); a commissionaire who helped him with his coat received a tip the equivalent of £10 in today's money. The gossip columns were always full of Simi Krausz stories – I had written quite a few of them myself. One day he went bankrupt and was completely finished. The papers reported that he was living in penury. I was much interested to see him although I was afraid of an endless walk to the outlying, cheaper suburbs, where, I presumed, his dismal bed-sitter must be situated.

Hardly had we walked ten minutes, when Lázár stopped in front of a most elegant villa in Andrássy ut, the best part of Budapest. We entered the villa. I saw a huge, black Packard in the garage. A uniformed chauffeur was fiddling with the engine. We were received by a butler. Lunch – caviar and venison and chocolate soufflé – was served by two footmen and obviously there must be at least one cook in the kitchen.

On the way back I said: 'I thought Simi Krausz was poor.'

Lázár sighed. 'Desperately poor. He's miserable.'

'But he lives in one of the most elegant villas in Andrássy ut.'

'Oh yes, because there is so much debt on it that it is simply not worthwhile for his numerous creditors to put it up for auction.'

'He has a huge car.'

'An old wreck.'

'And a staff of five. Maybe more.'

'Poor bastard. He owes so much money to these people that they cannot afford to leave him.'

'And the meal he gave us . . .'

'What is a meal? Do you expect him to starve?'

Lázár, I realised, was genuinely sorry for the man. Simi Krausz, however, *did* live in an elegant house in the most

Malice in Wonderland

expensive part of the town; *did* have a huge car and a large personal staff; and *did* wash down his caviar with the best Moselle followed by red Burgundy for the venison. I remarked that when a rich man gets ruined he is still much better off than a poor journalist who gets rich. But Lázár strongly disagreed. I was supposed to shed a few tears for poor Simi Krausz.

The long walks with Lázár were bad enough. The Turkish bath – the *Rudas* – was worse. I disliked the heat. All my life I have hated heat and found it hard to stand. I also disliked those sweating and palpitating naked old men, with their pot bellies. But, every now and then, when caught, to the *Rudas* you had to go.

In the mid-thirties I was offered another job – an additional one, as I never thought of leaving *A Reggel*. There existed an extremely successful picture-magazine called *Szinházi Élet* (*Theatrical Life*). Its owner and editor-in-chief was Sándor Incze, its editor Gyula Lukács. The magazine was very skilfully put together – it was witty, vivid, full of good photographs and the best writers could be persuaded to write for it from time to time. Many people loved it; others thought it was abominable; but everybody read it. I contributed occasional articles to it and then, unexpectedly, I was asked to take over the gossip column, called *Intim Pista*. That notorious column – originally started by Zoli Egyed – was a byword, usually referred to with the utmost contempt, which I shared. I had never – not once – read it from beginning to end. It was, however, the only part of the paper in which Incze, the owner, was really interested. The magazine appeared on Wednesdays and I had to deliver my piece at lunchtime on Tuesdays, the last manuscript to be sent down to the printer's, to assure that it was up-to-the-minute. I was told – when offered the job – that I was to discuss the column with Incze every week. That was nice, he was amusing company (later an emigré in America and a great friend). In those days I was supposed to regard this close personal contact as a great honour. But there was a snag. Every Monday morning at 9 o'clock Incze's chauffeur came to fetch me and took me to the *Rudas*, the Turkish bath. Sometimes I met Lázár there with another victim from *A Reggel*. I was invariably there, with Incze, every Monday morning

How to be Seventy

for years. I acquired a life-long loathing of Turkish baths. After that period of my life was over, I visited a sauna once in Finland – that was professional duty – but apart from that I never saw the inside of a Turkish bath ever again. Perhaps it was the Turkish bath element which prevented me from really warming to that column. It was very popular, I was well paid, but somehow it was the first and last regular commitment in my life I did not really relish.

On one occasion I heard a hilariously funny piece of gossip on a Tuesday afternoon, just after I had delivered my manuscript to Lukács, the editor. It was foolish even to hope that it would keep till next week but as it eminently suited my column I decided to take a chance. I scanned anxiously all the papers and weeklies – including Egyed's column in *A Reggel* – and I was incredibly lucky: I did not see the story anywhere. Next Monday – in the Turkish bath – I told the story to Incze who was delighted. I put it at the end of my piece and handed it over to Lukács, expecting warm praise. But he crossed it out angrily and told me to put another story at the end.

'But why?' I protested. 'It's a very good story.'

'Damn it!' he thundered. 'Of course it is a good story. It is such a good story that I put it at the end of your *last week's* column and the whole town was greatly amused by it. Don't you read your own bloody column?'

I straightened myself up and said with dignity: 'I am paid to write this column, not to read it.'

My answer did not carry much weight. The only extenuating circumstance was that Incze had not read his own magazine, either; not even that column in which he took such great personal interest.

Soon enough I got a third job, too. It was offered to me by my friend Laci Héthelyi. When, for the first time in my life, I was sent to a political meeting, I felt very shy sitting at the press table among experienced colleagues who threw inquisitive and derogatory glances at me. When the meeting was over, a robust – well, let's not mince our words, a fat – young man came to me and asked me: 'Who are you?'

'I am Mikes from *A Reggel*.'

Malice in Wonderland

He gave me his hand: 'I am Héthelyi,' he said and told me the name of *his* paper. From that moment to this we have been close friends. Today, Laci Héthelyi Hervey is a high-ranking civil servant in – you will never guess – Jamaica. (We shall come to that later.) Laci Héthelyi has one of the sharpest, quickest and most original brains I have ever come across. Also the most wicked.

In those days it was impossible to get a licence to publish a daily paper. Before the first war, Hungary was quite a liberal country. In 1914 Parliament enacted a press law which was a true model of high, liberal principles. According to the provisions of that law, anyone could start a paper without special permission. All he had to do was to inform the mayor of his city of his intention and deposit 5,000 crowns as a cover against possible libel damages. The law was in operation only for a few months when war broke out and it was suspended, by a government order, based 'On Special and Temporary Powers' given it by Parliament – for six months only. The war, however, lasted longer than those optimists expected and the 'Special and Temporary Powers' were extended for many more six months. This became quite a habit of subsequent post-war administrations. Every six months Parliament was asked to vote for a new extension. It did so, without debate. The procedure became automatic, no one paid any attention to it.

Laci wrote a letter to the Mayor of Budapest and informed him that – according to the requirements of the Press Law of 1914 – he was going to start a daily paper and enclosed the mid-thirties equivalent of 5,000 crowns, eight shillings in English money of the day. The Mayor returned the eight shillings and drew Héthelyi's attention to the fact that the 1914 Press Law had been suspended by the Special and Temporary Powers, renewed – and he gave the innumerable dates when it had been renewed – the last being a few months before. Laci appealed to the Court of Administration, the highest tribunal for such cases which ranked with the Kuzig, the supreme court. He listed eleven grounds why the Mayor's refusal was misconceived. The first of his grounds said that it was ludicrous to exercise 'Special and *Temporary* Powers' based on emergencies created by a war which ended eighteen years before. The Court decided that Laci's first

How to be Seventy

argument was valid so there was no need to examine the other ten. The appeal was allowed and Laci was in possession of a licence to start a daily paper – an almost incredible feat. Gyula Gömbös's semi-fascist government rushed through legislation to prevent others from emulating Laci.

He managed to find the necessary financial support to start his paper called *A Nemzet* (The Nation). Later it became *Magyar Nemzet* (Hungarian Nation) and it is the only paper which has survived the ravages of war and Rákosi's tyranny and exists even today. I became the editor of its theatrical page and was – sometimes, as a stand-in – in charge of the foreign pages. There were two chief correspondents writing on foreign affairs. The Spanish civil war was in progress and one of the two was violently anti-Franco, the other equally violently pro. I kept receiving pieces, often on the same subject, flagrantly contradicting each other, even giving the facts differently. I tried to merge them into a reasonably fair and balanced piece but occasionally pressure was too much and I failed. So every now and then General Franco was pictured as a hero and a saviour of Spain in one column and a blackguard and a murderer in the next. Some readers may have been puzzled!

I led a busy, interesting and satisfactory life and saw no reason why it should not last forever. There were grave troubles in Austria during February 1938 but it seemed that Schuschnigg, the Austrian Chancellor – although deeply humiliated at Berchtesgaden – had ultimately outwitted Hitler: he ordered a defiant plebiscite and there was no doubt that the people of Austria would overwhelmingly vote against the Anschluss (union with Germany). We laughed aloud with delight when the plebiscite was announced. Clever Schuschnigg, that will teach Hitler. One day in March I went to the first night of a play when other journalists – coming straight from their offices – arrived and told us that the plebiscite was off and the German Army had started marching into Austria.

I can't say that after that very clear warning Hungary woke up. But I did. I knew that the Carnival was over.

* * *

Malice in Wonderland

My theory – primitive but right – was: as long as Austria was free, Hungary could get away with it. Now Austria is being swallowed up and is becoming to the unvoiced annoyance even of the Austrian Nazis – simply a province of the German Reich.

Nazi pressure increased on Hungary and anti-Jewish legislation was announced by Darányi, Gömbös's successor (Gömbös had died in hospital, in Germany). The anti-Jewish laws were mild measures compared with what was yet to come, but they were, of course, discriminatory, turning Jews into second class citizens. Among other measures a Chamber of Journalists was to be established and only its members would be allowed to go on working. It was quite clear – indeed, this was the aim of the exercise – that Jews would find it extremely difficult to get in.

I mentioned my fears to Lázár who reassured me: 'Don't you worry. I guarantee that I'll get you in.'

Lázár was a baptised Jew himself and I was too polite to ask him: and who guaranteed that *he* would get in? (In fact, he never did and later his paper was banned too.)

This, serious though it was, happened to be only my second worry. My other anxiety seemed to me more pressing: the authorities would look into our papers and it would become public knowledge that I had lied, even to my closest friends, about my origins. Denying that I had been a Jew was not only dishonest but also extremely stupid. Budapest was a village and everyone knew everyone else. I am sure that everybody around that table in the coffee-house knew the truth about me and laughed at me. I knew that they knew; they knew that I knew that they knew. Yet I went on trying to keep up this ludicrous pretence, and they acted as if they had believed me. Only once did a Jewish actor tell me: 'It's easy for you . . . you don't need to worry.' He knew perfectly well that I had every reason for worrying, he was pulling my leg with a straight face. Still, I went on playing the part of the benevolent liberal, who feels strongly about these barbarous injustices about to be committed but who was not personally affected: I felt the situation strangling me. This was all wrong, I knew. But I think I was even more concerned at the prospect of being made to look a fool. That was my main reason for leaving the country of my birth.

How to be Seventy

I told Lázár that I had decided to go to France.

'Why France?' he asked. 'Go to England. I assure you that you are foolish to go at all. You have nothing to fear. But if you do go, put that little stretch of water between you and the Germans.' He added that if I went to London, I could become the paper's correspondent there. An old, avuncular friend of mine, Robert Lukács, a lawyer, also favoured England. He – although a secret Communist – adored the English and admired their institutions. 'Perhaps,' he said, 'the English will save Europe. If they don't, nobody will.' (The English did save Europe but they could not save Robert Lukács. During the siege of Budapest – the Russians were already fighting at the outskirts – some Arrow Cross thugs shot him and threw his body into the Danube.)

Laci Héthelyi also dismissed the Paris idea.

'Why do you want to go to France and not to England?'

'Because I speak good French and only lousy English.'

He brushed this argument aside.

'We'll go to England,' he declared. 'And we'll go together.'

I agreed. Very well, we shall go to England. I accepted my friends' advice and Laci's decision and did absolutely nothing about it beyond saying here, there and everywhere that I was going to London as correspondent of my Sunday paper. The Editor of *Nyolc Órai Ujság* (Eight O'Clock Journal – named thus because it appeared at two thirty in the afternoon) got in touch with me and suggested that I should be their correspondent, too.

This sounded excellent. Now I had a daily paper and a Sunday paper. No financial worries and quite a promising start. But I also had a charming girl-friend in Budapest and – Nazis or no Nazis – I was very reluctant to leave. So – as so often in my life – having made a firm, quick and manly decision, I then did nothing about it. Indeed, I rented a flat in Buda and ordered furniture to be made.

I met Laci one day and he asked me how my preparations for departure were proceeding. 'I have decided to emigrate to Budapest,' I told him.

'How d'you do that?'

'Look, I've lived here all my life as a citizen, now I shall live here as an exile. All right, I shall be a second class member of society but I would be a second class member of London society, too. I need no visa to get here. I speak the language fluently. And I have many friends who will help me – it's a far better idea.'

Both Laci and Hitler were against this concept. Hitler claimed Czechoslovakia and the threatening and warlike noises became more and more deafening. Prague was in deadly danger, yet it was obvious that the final decision would not be made in Prague but in London.

The editor of the 'Eight O'Clock Journal' called me in.

'You are going to London tomorrow.'

'Tomorrow?' I asked, taken aback.

'Yes, tomorrow. I want a correspondent there *now* and not when you will send me evergreen reports on Speakers' Corner and Madame Tussaud's.'

'But excuse me, sir . . .' I stuttered. 'I have no passport, no English visa. I have rented a flat and ordered furniture and . . .'

He interrupted me: 'That's why you are going tomorrow. Otherwise you would be going today.'

I was, of course, used to the ways of editors and knew that it was useless to argue.

'Very well. I'll go tomorrow.'

He relented a bit.

'You go to cover this crisis. You'll be back in a fortnight or so, to settle your affairs.'

I agreed with him. Indeed, I looked forward to it. It would be an exciting fortnight. Next day Laci and I left for London. That was more than forty years ago.

Some fortnights are longer than others.

LIFE THREE
London

Lala

'What date did he stamp into your passport?' Laci asked when I emerged from the Immigration Officer.
I examined my passport.
'No date.'
'You are lucky. He let you in unconditionally.'
Laci, as usual, was primarily interested in the legal aspect of things. He had explained to me all about the Immigration Officer's great and often sinister power. Countless refugees were determined to get into Great Britain, and who could blame them for trying to save their lives? The British, while anxious to keep up their humanitarian traditions, were equally anxious to stem the flood – and who can blame *them*? We heard innumerable stories about the cunning of refugees, frustrated by the even more devastating cunning of Immigration Officers. A German refugee put all his fortune into a Stradivarius and tried to bring it in duty free as a personal chattel. The Immigration Officer asked him: 'Do you play the violin?'
'Yes.'
'Who is your favourite composer?'
'Mozart.'
'Do you play Mozart a lot?'
'Quite frequently.'
'Do you play Mozart well? I mean, do you play Mozart better than you play any other composer?'
'Yes, I think so.'
'Then play a little Mozart for me,' said the Immigration Officer.
The man was petrified. 'What, here?'
'What's wrong with this place?'

How to be Seventy

'Nothing's wrong with the place . . . But all these people around . . .'

'Just play. A few bars from the Fourth Violin Concerto. Or from the Missa Brevis in F. Or whatever you like.'

The poor chap did not even know how to hold the violin properly. He was refused admittance for trying to mislead the Immigration Officer. Many similar stories were in circulation and the Immigration Officer cast a long shadow over the future of would-be refugees. But I was not afraid of the bogey-man. I regarded myself as a *bona fide* journalist – which I was – and refused to admit to myself that I was also a refugee. Although Laci did his best to bring this truth home to me. When we were travelling through Switzerland and I was looking out of the window, admiring the mild hills, wild mountains, noisy waterfalls and peacefully grazing cows, he jumped up and pulled the curtain down angrily. When I looked at him puzzled, he told me: 'Lest you should think you are a tourist.'

We missed our train from Dover to Victoria. We had to take a slow train about forty minutes later which took us to Charing Cross. We arrived at midnight on a Saturday. The newsvendors were selling early editions of the Sunday papers and we bought the *Sunday Times* and the *Observer*. We took a taxi and were driven to a boarding house called Green Court Hotel in Prince's Square, Bayswater, where Laci had booked rooms for us.

As soon as we reached our respective rooms, we sat down and started working, trying to concoct despatches for our papers based on the two English Sunday papers. Next morning at eight we were rung up from Budapest and gave the latest crisis news from the London angle. After that we went in to have breakfast.

A waiter, glum and wearing dirty tails, came to me and asked if I wanted porridge, cornflakes or prunes? I had no idea what he was talking about. On Laci's advice I asked for prunes. 'But what is porridge?' I asked.

'If you're lucky, you'll never find out,' he told me curtly. I haven't been quite so lucky. I did find out.

Everything about me was strange and fascinating. I felt almost at home in England from the first minute, yet I knew that I would never be really at home here. Only a few weeks ago – after forty-

Lala

two years of sojourn in this country – a friend asked me why I did not buy a little hut or peasant house in the Vaucluse, in France. I explained that I had several reasons for that, one among them being that I didn't want to. 'But don't you want to live abroad?' he asked. 'I *do* live abroad,' I told him truthfully.

On that first day I was drinking in those rich first impressions, watching people's ways of dressing, talking, walking. So that's England and these are the English! I looked at a man sitting in the corner of the small breakfast room and could hardly believe my eyes. One knew that Italians were fond of gesticulating and quarrelling, that the French were logical, that the Spaniards were proud and that cats were shrewd. But every now and then you expected to meet a quiet Italian, an illogical Frenchman or a naïve cat. That phenomenon in the corner ... no one could really be quite so true to type. He looked as if he had escaped from a *Punch* cartoon of 1908. He was tall and thin; he wore a checked tweed jacket; he was smoking a pipe and was reading *The Times*. I found it disappointing that the English resembled their own caricatures to such an extent.

This archetypal Englishman stood up and came over to us. He addressed us in Hungarian: 'Excuse me, gentlemen, but I could not help overhearing that you were speaking Hungarian. I am Captain András Szunyogh.'

We introduced ourselves, somewhat reluctantly.

He was a retired hussar officer and the former owner of Die Drei Hussaren (Three Hussars) – a famous Hungarian restaurant in Vienna.

'I am in temporary difficulties, gentlemen,' he said after a brief chat. 'I wonder if you could oblige me by lending me half a crown.'

Laci gave me a sign which meant: 'Don't start this sort of thing!' but I found the Captain fascinating and did lend him the money. Captain Szunyogh became a feature in our early life. He was here in order to establish an English version of the Three Hussars but spent most of his time shootin', huntin' and fishin' with the aristocracy. He had arrived with a few excellent letters of introduction. People regarded him as the incarnation of the wild and romantic Magyar, just as we had regarded him as the incarnation of the typical Englishman – and he was indeed a charming and amusing man, so every weekend visit produced three new invitations for grouse shooting or whatever.

We spent a lot of time together. Every morning he bought a red carnation for sixpence – very often his last sixpence – and then we walked together through Kensington Gardens and Hyde Park to Piccadilly. At night we often played ping-pong or darts in the basement till 3 a.m. He knew a great deal about horses and every now and then won vast sums at the races. Then he invited us and lots of others to luxurious parties at the Dorchester, spent his money like a maharajah gone mad and handed out fabulous tips. On other occasions he borrowed half-a-crown on which, as a rule, he bought a dozen oysters for his supper. He never opened his restaurant in London but his skill in ping-pong – not speaking of his style – improved beyond recognition during his stay in England.*

We settled quickly into a routine. Every weekday, at noon, we went to the Foreign Office for the daily press conference. Our questions always concerned Hungary, which puzzled or even irritated the spokesmen. After all – they seemed to imply – this is a world crisis, not a local, provincial Central European affair, even if Czechoslovakia happens to be in Central Europe. We were correspondents of Hungarian papers, fully aware of the fact that official Hungary (and Poland, both acting with suicidal folly) were hungry jackals waiting for the dismemberment of Czechoslovakia. The issue of war and peace seemed less important to the Hungarian and Polish governments than the prospect of getting a share of the spoils.

Today I condemn Munich roundly. But in those days I could not make up my mind whether I wanted war or surrender – called, euphemistically, appeasement. I dreaded the consequences – it needed no great acumen – of letting the Czechs down. A German triumph would mean the extension of German influence and Hungary would become a Nazi satellite. Yet a war postponed

---

* Should any reader be interested in this flamboyant and attractive Magyar gentleman, he should read my story about him, 'Twice Lucky', in *How to Unite Nations*, Deutsch, 1963.

Lala

might mean a war avoided. Laci had more insight and foresight than I had. War was inevitable, he said, and the later it came the better the Germans would be prepared for it. One day – when the letting down of Czechoslovakia was obviously on the books – he threw himself into an armchair and declared with a grim face: 'The angels of war are being threatened by the evil forces of peace.' We thought this was a *bon mot*. However, when Churchill delivered his famous – but then extremely unpopular – post-Munich speech in the House of Commons, he heartily agreed with Laci, without mentioning him by name.

My job kept me pretty busy but I had plenty of time left for my private life. Soon enough I acquired an English girlfriend, whom I am going to call June – and she was largely responsible for my English education.

There was first of all the little problem of the English language. I described my trials and tribulations in an earlier book* and this is the gist of what I said there.

When I was sent to England I thought I knew English fairly well. In Budapest my English proved quite sufficient. I could get along with it. On arrival in this country I found that Budapest English was quite different from London English. I found Budapest English much better in many ways.

In England there were two difficulties. First, I did not understand people, and second, they did not understand me. It was easier with written texts.

The first step in my progress was when people started understanding me although I still could not understand them. This was the most talkative period of my life because I could only conceal my shortcoming by going on and on, keeping the conversation as unilateral as possible. The next stage was when I began to understand foreigners speaking English, but not the English or the Americans. The more atrocious a foreign accent, the clearer it sounded to me.

June took me in hand. She never corrected me. She never 'knew' anything, but whenever I made a mistake and asked her

---

* *Shakespeare and Myself*.

How to be Seventy

whether it was right, she 'rather thought' that most people 'might' put it somewhat differently. However atrocious my English was, she always praised it and emphasised that it was incomparably better than her Hungarian – how clever I was! I always had a million questions for her. One of my perversities is that I love grammar but she refused to consider any enquiry relating to grammar. My second problem was where to place the emphasis in individual words. Although she knew the language well and spoke it beautifully, I often succeeded in confusing her to such an extent that she managed to forget her own mother-tongue. Once I asked her how the word *obligatory* was to be pronounced. 'Where do you put the emphasis?' I asked. 'Do you say *ob*ligatory, ob*li*gatory, obli*ga*tory, or obligat*ory*?'

By that time she was completely lost. She thought a bit and told me: 'You just say: compulsory.'

I discovered at an early stage that it was much easier to learn the long words of Latin and Greek origin than the original Anglo-Saxon words. *Egocentric* was a natural, *selfish* had to be learnt; *ambivalence* was self-explanatory, but speaking of two conflicting feelings was much more complicated. When I spoke of a *philatomane* (a non-existent word, by the way), I impressed June but betrayed the fact that I could not have described a maniacal stamp-collector in any other words. I sounded in those days like an early Victorian headmaster, showing off his knowledge of Latin and Greek. And June, indeed, was impressed. One day I told her: 'I have notalgia.'

'You mean you are homesick?'

'No. I have a pain in the back.'

At that point she'd had enough. She burst out: 'Look, Mikes' (she always called me by my surname, considering the extremely English 'George' ridiculous for a Central European in a long overcoat, while Mee-cash sounded all right) – 'look Mikes, the time has come for you to forget the long words and start learning the short ones.'

(Perhaps I'd better explain. I made up the word *notalgia* for backache from the Greek *notos* [back] and *algos* [pain]. I admit it is not a word in common usage. In fact, checking up on it just now, I could not find it in any of my numerous dictionaries including

Lala

the vast *Shorter Oxford* – but the word does exist. To my delight and amazement I finally discovered it in Nuttall's, 1938 edition.)

One beautiful autumn day June came in her car to pick me up and asked me where I wanted to go. I had absolutely no idea where I *could* go.

'Esher?' she suggested.

'Yes. Esher.'

So to Esher we went, and we were walking towards the village green when I noticed people clad in white, two of them holding peculiar wooden implements, playing a ball game I had never seen in my life. It slowly dawned on me that it must be cricket, the national mania of the English. June confirmed that indeed it was. We stopped. We had watched the game for barely two minutes when one of the batsmen was hit by a ball and collapsed with a profusely bleeding forehead. An ambulance had to be called to take him away. It was no good telling me afterwards that this was a chance in a million. I had seen it happen after watching cricket for two minutes, and for a long time the game remained fixed in my mind as a sport slightly more savage than bullfighting and I refused to go near a cricket ground for about twenty years. The next occasion when I went to watch cricket was with Vicky, the cartoonist. I shall come to that episode later.

June was a lovely woman, as English and as county as they come. She was married to a solicitor who hated foreigners (with every reason) but who also hated the Irish, the Scots, the Welsh and most of the English people he knew, including his wife. His sentiments were heartily reciprocated, yet the forms of respectability had to be maintained. On their wedding night – June was a virgin – he did not touch her, saying that he was tired. A week later he braced himself to the ordeal and made love to his wife once. And never again. He was lucky though, because she became pregnant and they had a pretty child. June came to see me every single weekday afternoon. I asked her how could she manage to get away. Her reply (recorded above) was:

'Nanny is looking after the baby . . .'

'That's not what I mean,' I told her. 'What explanation do you give your husband?'

'That I go out shopping.'

I was flabbergasted.

'But isn't he suspicious?'

'Why on earth should he be suspicious?'

'You go out shopping five times a week, you stay away for hours and hours, and yet you never buy anything. What sort of shopping is this?'

Now it was her turn to be surprised.

'I'm afraid, darling, you will remain a bloody foreigner forever. Shopping has nothing whatsoever to do with *buying* things.'

Then one day June asked me quite casually if I were a Jew. I told her that I was not.

'It doesn't matter if you are,' she reassured me. 'I like Jews. It's Roman Catholics I can't stand.'

I remained silent. But she went on: 'As long as you are not a Roman Catholic it's all right with me.'

Good God, I thought, now I should deny that I am a Roman Catholic. So I told her I was. That was a painful piece of information.

'But you are not a practising Roman Catholic?' she asked me at last.

'No, I'm not a practising Roman Catholic.'

'Then that's all right, I suppose.'

It was obvious that I belonged once again to the wrong minority. Yet I was pleased. In England I was regarded as a Hungarian –something I could not achieve in Hungary – and I was not only a Roman Catholic, but a *persecuted* Roman Catholic. Quite an achievement.

In a long life you cannot help gathering a little wisdom. One thing I have learnt is that should someone begin a sentence by saying 'I am not saying this because . . .' then it is always worth listening. Nearly always he will reveal his innermost thoughts and true motives. He says: 'I am not saying this in order to blow my own trumpet . . .' or 'I am not saying this just to harm him.' You may then rest assured that he *is* saying it in order to blow him own trumpet and that he *does* intend to harm him. Another piece

Lala

of wisdom is that whenever I feel very strong – unreasonably strong – disapproval, then I ought to examine myself, knowing that I must have been touched on the raw. Something may indeed be wrong about whatever I am condemning; but something must also be wrong with me.

It is not always easy to apply this last piece of wisdom in practice.

I have always been irritated beyond measure by certain modish words and phrases, particularly by the way people go on nowadays about 'identity'. 'What is "identity"?' I asked myself sarcastically. You are what you are and it does not matter a bit to what clan, tribe, race, religion, region or class you belong. The unit of humanity is the human individual and that's all that matters.

Slowly it dawned on me to apply a bit of self-examination: why do I object so strongly to this expression? In the end I understood that I was trying to brush it under the carpet because it has always been the central issue of my life.

In Hungary I am the 'chap who became an English writer'. In Britain I am 'the Hungarian'. I am probably neither. An English writer should be born in Stratford on Avon and should go to school there or thereabouts; a Hungarian, on the other hand, should write in Hungarian. The same goes for religion. I am the atheist who first refused to be a Jew, then refused to be a Christian.

I tried to ridicule this question of identity because I was unwilling to face it. I did not like the idea that I was neither fish nor fowl, that I belonged nowhere. Now I know that *nowhere* is quite a pleasant place to belong to. Looking always *in* – as an outsider must – deprives you of the warmth of the kennel, but it clears your views about the people and places you observe from without.

Now I realise that leaving Hungary – the place where they did not allow me to be really at home – and settling among strangers, where I found a real home, was the most exciting adventure of my life.

Take my name. Had I known that my visit to Britain would be such a prolonged one I would have added an *h* to it. Then people would have *believed* that I pronounce it Mee-cash. Now they know

How to be Seventy

that it is not Mikes (to rhyme with likes) but many cannot remember what it is. In addition to Meeks, My-keesh, and Mee-keese, my name has another seventy-seven variations. My favourite is the Scottish version: McAsh.

'Have you heard of a chap called Noël Coward?' Lala asked me.
'Yes, I have.'
'Is he somebody? I mean, does he matter?'
'Yes, he is somebody.'
'Is it worthwhile ringing him up? Can he help me?'
'If he wants to he can help you a lot.'

This conversation took place at Trafalgar Square Underground Station. Lala had just arrived from Budapest *via* Paris where he had met Coward.

'In that case I'm going to ring him,' he said. 'Wait a minute.'

He went into a call box. I explained to him how to use that cumbersome 'Press Button A' system. He took out a little address book from his pocket, looked up the number and dialled. He talked for about twenty minutes. I could not hear him but I could see him through the glass. Sometimes he was earnest, sometimes listening with deep attention, sometimes he smiled, occasionally he roared with laughter. At last he finished and came out.

'He invited me for a drink for tomorrow afternoon. It's all your responsibility. I want to make a career and I do not want to waste my time.'

We came up from the station and then a sudden thought occurred to me: 'What language did you speak? You don't speak one single word of English.'

'Oh no. He speaks fluent French.'

'*He* does. But you don't speak French either.'

'That's true,' he agreed and went on speaking of something else.

It was late spring in 1939. Lala Básti (his first name is to be pronounced as in *ooh la-la* in French, except that the emphasis is on the first *la*) was a new arrival in London. He was an actor, a matinée idol of Budapest, Romeo on the stage and in private life a male beauty, a heart-throb.

Lala

He was six foot tall, blond, a little too Teutonic looking perhaps, with a tremendous amount of charm and a laugh that could be loud and neighing. (He only laughed in this neighing fashion when he did not find something funny; when he was really amused, he laughed like a normal human being.) He only had to look at women and nine out of ten fell on their backs. But he was a devoted artist, perhaps even taking his art a shade too seriously, particularly when strangers were present. From his friends he would take anything with a grin. We often told him that actors were the lowest species of creation and that he himself occupied a pretty low rank even among actors. It became his permanent excuse for everything: 'I'm only an actor . . .' Lala was very intelligent and well read. He was ambitious and determined to make a career in England.

He had several letters of introduction. (Talking of letters of introduction, I had several, too. Among others one to Alex Korda, who received me kindly. The former director of the Hungarian National Theatre, Sándor Hevesi, gave me letters to his two great friends – in whose houses he stayed when in London – Granville-Barker and Bernard Shaw. The Granville-Barkers invited me to some parties but I did not dare to face Shaw with my poor English. By the time I deemed my knowledge of English sufficient to face Shaw, I could not find Hevesi's letter. That is the brief and exciting story of how I never met Bernard Shaw. But let us return to Lala.) He had an introduction to some distinguished society lady and on his first night in London took her out for supper. He spent his very last penny on this occasion, but such trifles never worried him.

'Did you make love to her?' I asked him next day.

'Oh yes,' he replied.

That surprised me.

'Did she take you back home?'

'No, she wouldn't do that.'

'Then where did you make love?'

'We were walking through some park after dinner. I put her up on the stone part of the railing and made love to her.'

'Wasn't she surprised?'

'A bit.'

How to be Seventy

Two days later he showed me a cheque-book. He had struck up a friendship with a charming playboy whose millionaire father owned a bank or two, and who had opened an account for him in one of his father's banks.

'But you had absolutely no money to start an account with,' I said.

'Of course. But Dickie arranged it for me and they allowed me a 300 pounds overdraft to begin with.'

I am quite sure Lala interpreted this phrase 'to begin with' differently from his bank manager.

I had to teach him how to write out a cheque. He asked me. 'Do you want a hundred pounds? Do you want two hundred? Or do you need the lot?'

He meant it. When I had some money – after receiving my last salary from Budapest – he had no scruples whatsoever about spending my last penny on a sumptuous dinner or on some silly gift for a girl. But if I asked for his last penny, he would give it to me without even asking what I needed it for.

'I had a chat with Noël,' he reported to me one day. 'There was a chap in his house called David O. Selznick. I talked to this Selznick about you. I told him that you had an absolutely magnificent play ready. A world-beater.'

'Did you?' I asked with a faint surprise, as I had no play ready, world-beater or otherwise. Indeed, I had not even begun to write a play. Once I had mentioned to Lala a vague idea for a satirical play about Hitler and his regime.

'You have to sit down and write it,' he told me. 'Selznick promised a large advance if he liked the first act.'

'In that case we might as well forget about the whole thing. I cannot write a play in English.'

'You just write it in Hungarian and leave the rest to me.'

But this was not good enough. I asked him to whom could he show my version because, as far as I knew, neither Coward nor Selznick was fluent in Hungarian.

'For goodness' sake, stop this stupid pessimism. Sit down and write that first act. I told you to leave the rest to me.'

The idea of Lala's translating my work did not attract me. His English was somewhat peculiar. He had a marvellous ear. When

Lala

he repeated a sentence he had just heard, he sounded as if he had been born in Surrey and just graduated at Oxford. I had no doubt that he could perform on the stage and sound practically accentless. But when it came to making up sentences of his own, it was quite a different story. He was the only person I knew who could achieve a sentence with more mistakes in it than words.

'You know,' he told me one day, 'if George Tarján turned up in London – and alas, there is no hope of that – the three of us could conquer the world.'

George Tarján turned up in London a few weeks later and the three of us did not conquer the world.

But, under Lala's guidance, we made a reasonable attempt at it.

Lala had a tremendous admiration for Tarján whom I knew, too, but only vaguely. I noticed him – as many other critics did – when he was still a drama student and later when he started playing small parts in the National Theatre. He was of remarkable appearance: a tall, thin man, with a rather ugly, horse-like face – yet he looked likeable and intelligent. He was an able actor with a beautiful voice. Soon after graduating from the drama school he became a stage director. As the youngest director of the National Theatre he was an immediate success. He was told that Gizi Bajor would star in his first major production, whereupon all his colleagues and rivals had a good giggle. Miss Bajor was undoubtedly one of the great actresses of her age, but she did not suffer fools gladly and made experienced directors tremble in their shoes. Tarján – with courtesy coupled with firmness – tamed her in no time. She was turned into a little lamb. The simple truth was that being a true professional, she recognised and appreciated real talent and imagination when she met it.

I had met Tarján here and there but we had never become friends. I knew his fiancée, later his wife, Etelka Dán, a young and successful actress, a little better. We often met and chatted at the covered swimming pool at Margaret Island. Tarján never came to swim.

Now he arrived in London without his wife, to look around. He stayed with a relation of his, a Hungarian woman married to an Englishman. Lala put him to work without any delay. We discussed the subject of my play. Tarján gave his general approval and some excellent criticism which inspired me to produce new ideas. After four days the whole project looked much more promising and I had no excuse for not sitting down to work.

The translation of the play into English – even into bad English – seemed a grave problem to me; but not to Lala, who repeated that I should leave it to him. He used his invariable and infallible method: he found a rather ugly but extremely literate girl and worked on her in all senses of the word. Julia (which was not her name) fell madly in love with Lala in no time and would do anything for him. They worked together on the translation for long hours every day. Lala's English was shaky, Julia's Hungarian non-existent. Lala used a dictionary but that was unsatisfactory. So he had to describe notions, ideas, synonyms, finer shades of meaning with movements, grimaces, animal noises, leaping across the room on all fours, chirping like a bird, roaring like a lion, hooting like an owl. After tea Julia was sent home to avoid meeting the next female visitor.

Complications, however, inevitably arose. One evening I was in my room when a sobbing girl appeared at my door. She had come to see Lala but had found a girl – Julia – in his room. I explained to her that she had no reason to doubt Lala's loyalty: Julia and Lala were simply translating a play. 'Then why were they naked?' she asked. This was a relevant question and I could not think of a really convincing reply.

The girl was in distress and needed consolation. I consoled her so successfully that she became my girl friend for the weekends, when June was busy with her family.

For another month everything went on smoothly, but then exactly the same disaster occurred, except that this time it was Julia who found another girl with Lala. She was deeply wounded and left us in disgust. I reproached Lala for losing our valuable translator.

'In any case,' he replied, 'I didn't like her style.'

I was not quite sure what style he had in mind.

* * *

Lala

Things were happening fast. First everything went like a dream. Lala spent all his weekends with Coward, in his country-house in Kent, and saw him frequently in his London house in Gerald Road, behind Eaton Square. I, too, was invited on two or three occasions to the London house, to parties. I was a rather timid onlooker but saw enough to realise that Lala – the charming, romantic and eccentric foreigner – was the centre of attention.

Coward planned a film in which there would be a part for a Continental prince. He offered the part to Lala who – not surprisingly – accepted the offer. He also told Noël that he was temporarily a little short of cash, so could he instruct his agent to give him an advance. He came home with a cheque for several hundred pounds. Soon I delivered the first act of the play, in Julia's and Lala's joint translation. The script was handed to David Selznick at one of Coward's parties. A few days later Selznick told Lala that he liked the play although it had to be adapted and put into proper English. Lala replied that he saw no difficulty in that, adding that momentarily I was a little short of cash, so could Mr Selznick give me an advance. He returned home with another large cheque.

Soon after Lala's arrival he decided it was silly to stay in digs. We found a lovely furnished flat in Nottingham Place, near Baker Street, and Lala, Laci Héthelyi and I were about to move in. Then Laci unexpectedly left for Budapest without giving us any indication about his return. We did not want to lose the flat but it did not seem easy to find a third person to pay one third of the weekly rent of three pounds. Tarján, the obvious candidate, was staying with his relations and was not prepared to leave them in order to pay rent – he was not the most easygoing man with money at any time. We knew a lovely girl – a great beauty, indeed, formerly an actress in Budapest – who was staying in a boarding house near Swiss Cottage. We knew that she was fed up with that sort of accommodation so we suggested that she should move in with us. She was a bit doubtful: to move in with two men? We told her that in a boarding house she was living with more than two men and here, at least, she would share the bathroom with only two people, not with twelve. She was easily convinced – she was a sweet and easy-going girl – but told us that there was one snag.

How to be Seventy

She had a boyfriend and he might not like this arrangement. A day or two later she informed us that she had talked the matter over with her boyfriend who would come to have a drink with us on Sunday morning and if he found us respectable enough, she would move in. So it was up to us. We were rehearsing respectability for the rest of the week. The man – a well-to-do, successful but rather dumb businessman – turned up on time. Lala was the very incarnation of seriousness, sobriety, respectability, dignity and courtesy. His paternal care for Eve was touching. For about twenty minutes we talked trivial rubbish in the best English tradition and then I stood up and said that I had to go to Church now. Lala – not to be outdone – looked at his watch and said: 'God, we nearly missed it . . . What delightful company can do . . .' We departed. Eve moved in the next day.

Our slightly bohemian household became more and more bohemian as the weeks passed. Eve fitted into the set-up perfectly. We – even Lala – treated her as a sister and neither of us made any advances to her, which probably contributed to an almost excessive informality. Eve would often burst into the bathroom while one of us was using it, declare 'I'm sorry . . . but I'm in a hurry . . .', undress, have a bath, put her dressing gown on and leave. To start with we found this refreshing though strange. Later we paid no attention to her comings and going, naked or otherwise.

Tarján, on one occasion, was truly shocked. He was a true puritan, a sober and dignified man, absolutely faithful to his wife (still in Budapest), to whom he wrote a letter every day: Girls – our secret allies – tried all sorts of tricks to seduce him but they all failed: Tarján remained a rock of marital fidelity.

He had a key to our flat and one morning he turned up to have breakfast with us, as he usually did. He found neither of us in our respective rooms, so he went to the bathroom and knocked. There was no reply, so he opened the door. There was Eve, naked.

'Don't come in!' she shrieked.

Lala

Tarján was deeply shocked. First, he was not interested in naked women, however beautiful. Second, the idea that she thought his intrusion deliberate was painful to his prudish soul. He stammered his apologies and added his explanation: 'I thought that George and Lala were in there.'

Back came Eve's stern and unforgiving reply: 'So what? George is having a bath and Lala is on the loo.'

Twenty years later Tarján was still telling this story with horror in his voice.

In our flat we had a vast kitchen. It seemed a sheer waste. We asked Eve if she could cook but she could not. 'I can cook,' I told the others, 'but only scrambled eggs.'

This statement was well received. What was wrong with scrambled eggs? For three weeks – except on the rare occasions we had a meal out – we had scrambled eggs and tinned pineapple, twice a day. We loved pineapple, it was an exotic food for us, unavailable in Hungary. After three weeks we all started itching. We complained to a doctor friend who, after a few appropriate questions, hit upon the obvious reason: our diet of scrambled eggs and tinned pineapple was lacking in vitamin C, or B, or D or whatever. We ought to eat proper food.

'Very well,' declared Tarján, always the stage director even in real life, always the chief organiser, 'we shall cook proper food.'

'But you told us you couldn't cook,' Lala reminded him.

'I can't. But if all those silly women can cook, then we shall cook better.'

I suddenly remembered that I owned a cookery book. When I went to say a hurried good-bye to Incze, the editor of the theatrical magazine, he had given me a generous farewell gift, a tidy sum of money. He had also given me a cookery book.

'I don't cook,' I told him.

'Not yet. You will.'

I assured him that I did not have the slightest inclination to learn how to cook.

'In London sooner or later everyone will learn to cook,' he said. 'Just take the book.'

This sounded barmy to me but as he had just given me a decent sum and seemed to be determined on my taking his silly book I decided to oblige him. Now it took me a long time to find the book.

'We'll make a goulash,' Tarján announced.

He studied the recipe and added: 'Not bad. But we shall improve on it . . .' We begged him not improve on it but he was an ambitious man.

And he did improve on it. At his first attempt at cooking he made a goulash any experienced cook could be proud of.

That's how my life-long hobby of cooking started. Today my cooking is not bad at all (as any true Englishman puts it when he wishes to boast), not bad at all but – like my speech – it still has a strong Hungarian accent.

People kept arriving from Budapest, mostly refugees although their official status varied, at least on paper. Our circle of friends grew and our flat became a popular meeting place. As a rule, we had between ten and twenty people for breakfast, discussing the world situation and the news from Hungary, pulling one another's legs and, on the whole, having a great time.

Eve had a friend, a former Budapest actress called Ági. She was married to Emeric Pressburger, the film-writer, and Ági and I went one day to the Tower. I saw her home, went up to have a drink and that was the first time I met Emeric who has remained my closest friend to this very day. On that particular day, however, as soon as I got home, I received a slightly puzzled and irate call from Emeric who asked me what the hell had I been telling his wife. I had no idea what he was talking about. Ági had told Emeric, as soon as I had departed, that never in her life had she met a man of such wide culture and dazzling erudition as I. I only had to look at a spear in the Tower and I was able to tell her who made it and when; at a shield, and I could explain which king carried it in which battle. What sort of joke was that? I told Emeric that on this occasion I was innocent. I had simply been translating the little notices affixed to the various objects and was not aware that Ági had failed to realise that fact.

We admired Emeric very much. He had come to London a few years before us; he lived in a nice flat of his own; his circumstances were obviously settled and he had a job with Alexander Korda. He was generous, helpful and a wonderful cook. He invited us for magnificent dinners and gave us mountains of food which terrified us twice: first when we saw that pile on our plates and second when we realised that we had eaten it all. It was one of Laci's standing jokes that after a vast dinner – when we could hardly move or even breathe – he would declare that he was still a bit hungry and asked Emeric if he could have a piece of bread and butter. On one occasion Emeric gave us turkey – he was the first ingenious man to discover that turkey is a good dish at any time of the year, not only at Christmas, an unheard of idea in those days. About six of us polished off a huge bird and were in a state of stupor when Laci, as usual, told Emeric that he was a little hungry and could he, please, have a piece of bread and butter.

'But why bread and butter?' asked Emeric most politely.

He went out to the kitchen and half a minute later returned with another turkey, freshly roasted, steaming and smelling most appetizing.

'Have a little more turkey.'

Laci looked at the huge bird, turned yellow, then red, then green and rushed out to the loo to be sick.

Another new arrival was Béla Iványi, a professor of history at Budapest University. He was a charming and witty man, with a sharp mind; he was also the untidiest and worst dressed man I ever met, and my own sartorial eminence is pretty low. His clothes just hung upon him as if someone had thrown them at him with a pitchfork. His shirt was often dirty and smelt strangely. He hated the countryside, just loathed it with a quite unreasonable hatred. He was the most undomesticated of men but he had a passion for ironing. We shared a flat later and to my astonishment he moved in with one single suitcase plus an ironing board. He hardly ever washed his shirts but he kept ironing them. After some years he married an English lady. From one day to the next Béla became dapper and neat, always carefully dressed and well groomed. They moved to Suffolk – a prospect which really terrified Béla. But another metamorphosis occurred: he fell in love with country life to such an extent that he felt unhappy when he had to come up to London even for a day.

How to be Seventy

Mundi Gál (later Gale), my mother's cousin, arrived too. He was a gentle, lovable and funny man. He was what the Austrians call a *pech-vogel* – the champion of the losing game, the man who always slips on a banana skin, the anti-Midas – and he took it all in good part. In the early thirties he decided to move to Vienna. He arrived and got a room in a block of workers' flats called the Karl Marx Hof. A few days later Dollfuss, that malicious fascist dwarf, decided to break up some disturbances by force and ordered the Austrian artillery to open fire on that block of flats. Mundi changed his mind about Vienna and moved on to Paris, where he was unable to leave the Gare de l'Est because the French artillery was bombarding it. So on he went to Spain. A few days after his arrival the Andalusian revolt, a precursor of the Civil War, broke out. He was sitting in front of a café in a street in Barcelona, when people started shooting from one end of the street to the other – he being in the middle. But as he had to stay *somewhere* he made up his mind not to move on from Spain. He moved to Madrid where he started an office-cleaning business. It was flourishing merrily when the Civil War broke out. One day six Republican militia-men came into his office, each carrying half a dozen hand-grenades conspicuously displayed in his belt. Their leader asked Mundi if he had ever thought of donating his firm to the community. He looked at the grenades and replied that he had often thought of it. 'Your decision is quite voluntary?' asked the leader who was a stickler for legality. Mundi counted the hand-grenades and replied that his decision was indeed voluntary. The man was pleased and told Mundi that he could stay on as manager but Mundi declined with thanks and came to London without a penny. He had a very hard time, but eventually he seemed to have struck some luck: he told me with delight that he had been appointed the sole English representative of a Polish umbrella factory. The thing was bound to be a success: in Britain everyone carried an umbrella and the Polish umbrellas were good and cheap. Mundi's contract with the Polish firm became valid on the 1st September, 1939, the day when Germany attacked Poland. During the war Mundi became a soldier in the British Army, serving in the Pioneer Corps, also known as His Majesty's Own Enemy Aliens. One military disaster followed another, and neither the High Command nor Churchill himself knew the real reason for it. The reason was simple: Mundi had become a soldier. Eventually he was invalided out of the army. A week later the Battle of Alamein was fought and won.

Mundi told me a story which, I think, is a good one and has metaphysical implications, touching on the essence of Truth. When is Truth Truth, and when does it begin to be or cease being Truth?

In his Pioneer Corps unit he was the only Hungarian, the others were all Germans. Most of them were German Jews, but they were as typically German as any so-called Aryan. Once, when they thought that Mundi was asleep, they started discussing him. They all agreed that he was a very nice chap but he had, they decided, two bees in his bonnet: one was that he had been an officer in the Austro-Hungarian army during the First World War (which he was, I once saw him in uniform and limping after being badly wounded on the Russian front) and the other was that Britain would win the war. Next day they started grilling him about it: how on earth could Britain possibly win the war? France was lost, Britain had no ally, half of Europe was under Nazi occupation, half of the British army had been lost at Dunkirk: so please would he give them just one reason, however fantastic, for believing that Britain could win the war? Mundi replied that he could not give them any reason for believing that Britain was going to win, but he had full confidence in the British and felt it in his bones that that's what was going to happen. Upon which he gained the nickname of 'Gale, the Idiot'. Everybody still liked him, but Gale the Idiot he remained for all of them because he thought it possible Britain might win the war. Some time after he was invalided out of the army, in February 1945, he met in the street one of his former German comrades from the Pioneer Corps. This man was delighted to see Mundi, embraced him and exclaimed quite emotionally: 'Gale, the Idiot!' But Mundi would not have it. 'Wait a minute,' he said. 'Why do you call me Gale the Idiot? Who is winning the war?' The German pushed this argument aside. 'Anyone can see *today* that we are going to win the war. But *then* only an idiot could believe it.'

Another arrival – the last I want to mention – was a young chap called André Deutsch. He used to go to school with my younger brother and I did not pay much attention to the little boys who came to swap stamps or play tiddly-winks with Tibor. I was seventeen then, they twelve – an enormous difference in age at that time. When André telephoned me in London, I remembered his name but was not at all sure which of those little boys had been André Deutsch. He came to see me and I liked him (which was easy; he wasn't my publisher yet). When the first, mild anti-Jewish laws had been enacted in Hungary, young Jews were encouraged to learn a trade or craft, instead of becoming doctors, lawyers and company directors. His father gave André some money for this purpose. He spent it on learning to recite Hungarian poetry. He became the pupil of a great artist and did quite well, but neither the law nor his father had this type of skill in mind. His newly acquired art did not help him much in increasingly anti-Semitic Budapest, so he decided to come and try his luck in London – where reciting Hungarian poetry, however beautifully, was – if possible – even more useless than in Budapest. So he got a job for himself as a van driver for a patisserie firm. He used to come to dinner with us and always brought wonderful slices of cake which had been reduced in price to fourpence each. We always insisted on paying him back because he was hard up. We liked him but this poor little van-driver with his wild enthusiasm for Hungarian poetry and his cheap pieces of cake was a slightly pathetic figure. One day he told me that he would like to become a publisher in London.

'Or Lord Chancellor,' I suggested.

His chances of becoming either one or the other seemed about equal.

Our lives went on but dark clouds had started gathering on the horizon.

Lala's consumption of women grew to an incredible degree. He thought he conquered them but in fact they made him work hard; they picked him as one picks a rose, wears it in a buttonhole for a day, and then throws it away. 'You think you are an irresistible Don Juan,' Tarján told him, 'but in fact you are a slave labourer. Women exploit you.' At that period Lala's normal consumption was three women a day.

Suddenly he fell into a deep depression. At first we thought it was a piece of play-acting but soon we had to realise that it was something serious. He did not get dressed all day, but wandered about in his dark red dressing-gown without uttering a word. He refused to shave and began to resemble an American film-gangster.

At last, after four or five days, he burst out and explained: 'I was sleeping here with a woman. In the middle of the night I woke up and felt a body next to me. Who was she? I racked my brain but could not remember. Was it Miss A? No, she had been here the night before. Mrs B? No, she had been here during the afternoon. Very well, then who the hell? I just could not recall. I tried to remember how I spent the evening but my mind was a blank. I could not fall asleep again, I went on tossing around for hours. I had to wait for the light of dawn to find out who she was.'

He held a little dramatic pause.

'What sort of a man am I if I can't even remember who the girl in my bed is? I am a whore . . . I am a whore . . .'

'But who ever suggested anything else?' asked Tarján, genuinely astonished.

'And in any case,' said I, 'what does it *matter* who the girl was?'

But it was no use. Lala remained buried in his gloom for another two or three days. Then he shed his depression, put on a well-cut suit, shaved and everything went on exactly as before.

Another event of those days might have had more serious repercussions. Lala came home from a weekend with Nöel Coward, plunged into deep gloom once again. He called Tarján and me and told us glumly: 'He wanted to make love to me.'

He gave us the details: 'He came into my bedroom wearing his dressing gown. He sat down on my bed and talked about homosexual love. Heterosexual love-making, he said, was crude, primitive and unsophisticated. The ancient Greeks – the most accomplished human beings who ever lived – loved women *and* men, were ambidexterous, at least. He did not try to touch me, not even to hold my hand, he is much too civilised and sophisticated for that. But he asked me to reflect upon the

How to be Seventy

subject. This is terrible. This is an ultimatum. The message is clear. Unless I agree, I shall lose my film-part and he won't help with the play either. Indeed, he will tell Selznick to drop me. I don't know what to do.'

What indeed? We started playing a cruel joke on him of which I am not too proud today, but we thought it hilarious at the time.

'What do you mean, you *don't know what to do?*' said I. 'It's quite clear what you have to do.'

Tarján joined in: 'After all you have a conscience.'

Lala looked at us with grateful eyes: 'Your duty is clear,' I went on. 'You can't let the play down.'

'What do you mean?' Lala asked suspiciously.

'You've got to go to bed with Noël.'

He was horrified. Tarján, the puritan, added all his weight: 'Look, Lala, you are a bit of a whore, you must admit it . . . You did admit it a few days ago. You've gone to bed with hundreds of women. Perhaps with thousands of them. Surely, one single man won't make any difference?'

We went on in this vein. Making love to all those women was pleasure – or so we supposed. Making love to Noël was a sacred duty. Our future depended on it.

'Sacred duty?' Lala tasted the phrase.

'Sacred duty,' Tarján repeated firmly.

We spent the rest of the week discussing the situation. Lala, of course, began to see the joke but he also realised the seriousness of the situation.

'I'll do what I can . . . Yes, I'll do my best . . .' he repeated many times, and looked determined.

We gave him a big send-off next Saturday morning. On Monday he returned like a thief, he sneaked in and hid himself in his room. When we entered, his head was buried in his hands and he exclaimed: 'Shame on me . . . Shame on me . . .'

Both Tarján and I were terrified. Surely we had not made him turn himself into a pansy whore?

'Shame on me . . . I couldn't do it. I let you down. I meant to do it, honestly I meant to . . . But I just couldn't.'

We forgave him and felt relieved. Coward forgave him, too, which was more important. Lala's refusal made absolutely no

Lala

difference, Noël remained as helpful, generous and friendly as ever.

June kept telling me that we ought to go on holiday together. The idea sounded strange to me. I had, of course, been on holidays before. As a child I was taken to Lake Balaton, as a teenager I went with Hédy and Tibor to Austria and to Italy – but a holiday as a must, because I 'needed' one sounded nonsense to me. Or it sounded English, which was the same thing. I have never really liked holidays: if I was working on a book in Japan it seemed all right to spend a few days sightseeing in Kyoto; or if in Jamaica spending two days (maximum) in Montego Bay. In any case, that was part of the job. But lying on the sand sunning myself always seemed a loathsome idea.

I had been working hard ever since arriving in London. As I was employed by a daily and a Sunday paper, I was busy seven days a week. But I was certainly not overworked and I thoroughly enjoyed London as well as my work. London was the diplomatic capital of the world; my despatches, as a rule, appeared on the front pages; so my work was satisfying.

June, however, was determined that a holiday we must have, so we hired a car and June, a girlfriend of hers, Lala and I drove off to Scotland. We spent a day or two in the Lake District and then proceeded north.

A minor episode which stuck clearly in my mind occurred while we were still on this side of the border. We stopped at a small hotel in Cumberland and while we were having breakfast the proprietor went round the diningroom asking people whether anyone had lost a wallet. I asked June what a wallet was and when she had explained, I realised that I had indeed lost mine, with £32 and some membership cards and other documents in it. I was given the wallet back. It was soaking wet. The proprietor explained that he had fished it out of the loo. I had been stupid enough to let it fall in and was grateful to get it back. Later I checked its contents: all my documents were intact but £16 of the £32 were gone. The finder had taken half of my money as his reward but had returned all my documents which were no use to him. I did not say a word to him but the event made a deep impression on me as the second greatest example of the English gift for compromise. The first greatest example of it, of course, was the Munich Agreement.

I loved Scotland and found it pretty exotic. On the tenth day of our fortnight's holiday, I switched on the car radio and heard the news of the Hitler-Stalin Pact. I stopped the car and turned round, explaining to my companions that I had to return to London without delay. They tried to laugh it off, saying that I was a jumpy journalist, over-reacting to every bit of news, that these crises had been going on all the time, etc. etc. I asked them to take me to Edinburgh railway station and carry on with their holiday but they decided to return with me. Having driven through the night, I was on the phone to Budapest next morning.

A few days later, on Sunday morning, June, Lala, Eve and I went over to Berkeley Court, near Baker Street Station, to the flat of some friends to listen to Chamberlain's speech at 11. The phrase: '. . . and consequently we are at war with Germany . . .' still rings in my ears. Then our host, true Englishman that he was, poured out gins and lime – the fashionable drink of the day – lifted his glass and said: 'Well, well, well.'

We lifted our glasses and I was racking my brain to find something equally momentous to say when the sirens started howling. 'Just like those bloody Germans,' our host remarked.

Leonard, our hostess's brother, a doctor, was interested in Eve and asked her if she had her gas-mask with her. She said she had not. In fact, none of us had our gas masks but Leonard felt sure that the Nazis would start this war with a devastating gas-raid on London, so we were told to rush home to get Eve's gas-mask. And our own, too.

The streets were empty, except for a few people hurrying to the shelters. There were a few air-raid wardens around, completely bewildered, yet enjoying their sudden eminence. They stopped us and said we were not allowed to be in the streets. Leonard said that we meant to get our gas masks and lived quite near. The warden was inflexible, he told us not to argue and ordered us to go down to the shelter.

So down we went to the air-raid shelter of Berkeley Court. It

Lala

was half full of bewildered people. There was no panic at all, people just found the situation irritating and boring. A few men made uncomplimentary remarks about the Germans. A few women worried about the Sunday roast in the oven and found the time of the raid most inconvenient. Others again – perhaps most of them – just sat on the benches in silence: a raid was not sufficient reason to start talking to neighbours whom one had been avoiding most carefully up to now. Then a rebellious and wrathful man was hustled into the shelter by a zealous warden. We heard no bombs and no gun-fire and we started wondering whether all this fuss wasn't unnecessary, but we could not be sure as we had no experience of air-raids. The newcomer grew angrier and angrier. He kept looking at his watch and trying to leave but the warden stationed himself at the entrance and would not let anyone go. Then the man looked around and said, still huffing and puffing: 'Will someone explain to me what the hell that Polish corridor is?'

I meant to oblige but before I could open my mouth, the all-clear was sounded. We had survived somehow, even without our gas-masks.

But the phony peace had ended; the phony war had started.

All the theatres of London were closed by the government in those early days of the war, because of fear of air raids. All film-making stopped too. Lala – who had lost all hope of his two parts, one in Coward's film and the other in my play – felt terribly frustrated. But he was not easily defeated. Coward told him that he was still ready to help him any way he could – but what *could* he do? He offered Lala money, just to help him out, but Lala refused. He happily accepted advances; he did not accept gifts.

Then Lala suggested to me that we should go to America. Selznick was back in Hollywood and was probably still interested in my play. I told him that this was pure nonsense: why should the world's leading producer, in happy, rich and neutral America, be interested in the play of a Hungarian writer in London – a play written in bad English on a purely European subject? Besides – I explained – a lot of rich Englishmen were trying to escape to the United States and would be pleased to pay vast sums for an American visa if they were on sale. With our wretched green Hungarian passports we would not even be let into the Consulate to *apply* for a visa, let alone to get one.

Lala was listening to me but – very unusual for him – remained silent.

He settled down to write his memoirs and read us a few remarkably vivacious, colourful and well-written chapters describing his childhood on Lake Balaton.

One day I was alone in the house when the door-bell rang. There were two sinister-looking strangers outside. They told me they were detectives. I asked them to come in and sit down.

'We had reports,' said the senior man, 'that there were enemy agents in this house.'

'Yes,' I nodded.

'Do you think that's possible?'

'Yes, it is possible.'

'You do?'

'I don't know anyone else in the house. Perhaps *all* the others are enemy agents. I only know the housekeeper and his wife.'

I suddenly realised that it must have been the housekeeper's wife, an obsequious but malicious busy-body, who had reported us.

'Are *you* an enemy agent?' the man asked me.

'I am not. On the other hand . . .'

'What "on the other hand"?'

'On the other hand I would say I wasn't even if I was.'

The two men were no fools, of course, and they felt uncomfortable. The senior man explained: 'We have received an anonymous report. In normal times we would throw such information into the waste-paper basket. But the times are not normal and we have to investigate.'

'Do you want to search the house?' I asked.

'Oh no.'

'Do you want a drink?'

'Oh yes.'

We had some whisky together, then the senior man went on: 'There is another gentleman living here. Is he in?'

Lala

'He is not.'
'When will he be in?'
'After seven.'
'Is he an enemy agent?'
'I don't think so. He never mentioned a word about being an enemy agent and we are close friends. I think I can state definitely in his name that he is no enemy agent.'
'We must ask him personally.'
They came back soon after seven. Lala told them that he was no enemy agent either. We had a few more whiskies together. End of story.

During the next few days Lala bustled off to see Noël Coward even more frequently than before, and one day in January, 1940, he told me that we must go to the US Consulate to pick up our visas. They are waiting for us. Next morning we went to Grosvenor Square (to the old building) and at the moment we sat down opposite the Consul, the air-raid sirens went off. That was the second air-raid warning of the war. The Consul jumped up and instructed us to follow him. He hurried to the Embassy shelter where we sat down and waited in silence. Nothing at all happened and a few minutes later the all-clear was sounded. We trotted back to the office and official business started. We mentioned our names and Lala began to elaborate on our stories when the Consul interrupted him: 'I know about you. We have received a number of cables from Mr Selznick telling us that you are badly needed in Hollywood. We have also received good references. Fill in these forms and may I have your passports in the meantime?'

An hour later we left the embassy with our visas stamped into our passports.

Lala was jubilant.

'In Hollywood – or in New York – we won't hear these bloody air-raid sirens,' he said.

I did not reply. We were walking home. A few minutes later I felt that I had to speak out.

'Lala,' I said, 'I am not going to America.'
He did not believe his ears: 'What did you say?'
'I said: "I'm not going to America." I am sorry.'

How to be Seventy

We stopped in the street to talk it over. I had to repeat for the third time that I wasn't going. He simply did not grasp it.

'Do you think it will be pleasant here?'

'No. I am sure it will be very unpleasant.'

'Do you owe anything to this country?'

'Nothing really. Or perhaps I do. After all, I am here and not at home.'

'I see. You are grateful for being in war-time Britain instead of being in neutral Hungary?'

'That's it.'

He thought for a long time and then asked: 'Why did you come to collect your visa?'

'Because I was absolutely certain that we would not get it. Besides, *you* need *yours*. You must go.'

'I won't go without you.'

I tried to persuade him, but in vain.

'Very well. Then you will stay here. But I think you are mad not to go.'

'I am madder than you think. I am not going to America without you but neither am I going to stay here. I'll go back to Hungary.'

Now it was my turn to be flabbergasted.

'Why on earth?'

'I need the stage. I am an actor. I want to be on the stage. Here the theatres are closed; in Budapest they are open.'

Why did I not go? I don't really know. There was no heroic pose in it. I could still send cables to my paper – I could not phone any more – and I did think that I ought to do my bit, however small a bit it was and however futile it was likely to prove. But I do not know my real reasons for not going; only that I did not hesitate for one single moment and that I never regretted my decision.

One day, at the end of January 1940, we all – Tarján, Laci, Eve and I – drove with Lala to Victoria Station. We handed him a set of keys to the flat at Nottingham Place, and told him that he would always be welcome back and he would always have a home as long as we had one. He travelled by train across allied France and neutral Italy. About a fortnight later a picture postcard

Lala arrived from him with an Italian stamp.

'I am in the railway restaurant in Milan. It has places for almost a thousand people. I am the only guest but all the chandeliers are blazing. Having an omelette. It is a pity that you missed the chance of a lifetime.

Yours ever,
Lala.'

I felt no regret about that missed chance; I felt great regret about Lala.

Murder

At midnight, a day or two after my twenty-eighth birthday in 1940, my telephone rang. It was Feri Aldor, a publisher, who said that he wanted to see me urgently. I murmured something about 'first thing tomorrow morning' but he cut me short. 'Urgently means now,' he said. 'I'm coming along straight away.'

A few minutes later he arrived and asked me if it was true that I had interviewed some ex-prisoners from the *Altmark* in the Ministry of Information. I told him that this was so and that I had kept in touch with one of the sailors, called Thomas Foley.

'Very well,' he said, 'I want you to turn a long interview into a book for me. It should be written in the first person singular, in the name of Foley.'

The German ship, *Altmark*, used to be an auxiliary to the *Graf Spee* but after the *Graf Spee* was sunk by three British destroyers in Montevideo harbour, she was used as a prison-ship for captured British seamen. The Admiralty believed that about three hundred British prisoners of war – sailors from sunken ships, picked up by U-boats – were on board. On February 14 the *Altmark* was sighted by British aircraft in Norwegian territorial waters, heading southward. If the Admiralty's information was correct and the ship was really carrying British prisoners of war, then she was violating international law by using Norwegian waters, and Norway was doing the same by allowing her to use them. If she was not carrying prisoners, then the British would commit a grave crime in international law if they intercepted or boarded her. Winston Churchill, the First Lord of the Admiralty, instructed the Captain of the destroyer *Cossack* to seek information. The Norwegians explained to Captain Vian that they had searched the *Altmark* twice and the ship was unarmed and was carrying no prisoners. Churchill remained convinced that there *were* prisoners on board and ordered Vian to free them. Vian's men boarded the *Altmark* and bitter hand-to-hand fighting ensued on the decks. Four Germans were killed and several others wounded. Vian's men liberated 299 British prisoners who were hidden in every nook and cranny of the ship. They also discovered that the *Altmark* carried two pom-poms and four machine-guns. These, of course, could have been hidden from the Norwegians, but how a thorough search – in fact, *two* searches – could have missed 299 prisoners in a smallish ship remains a mystery. (Or perhaps not so much of a mystery: the Norwegians were in a delicate, indeed, alarming situation.)

The glorious British rescue operation caused boundless excitement. Captain Vian and his men became national heroes; the cry of the British captives: 'The Navy's here!' was echoed in every headline and was on every lip in the country. The action, a few weeks after the sinking of the *Graf Spee* in South American waters, was clear proof that Britannia still ruled the waves. National interest was focused on the liberated British prisoners.

The idea of writing a book excited me. I had written innumerable articles but I was haunted by every journalist's delusion that a book is more permanent than a newspaper article. (Some are, some are not.) So I was pleased to accept Feri's suggestion. His main problem was: how long would it take me to write the book? I told him that I was a quick worker and interviewing my man and writing the book would not take more than four or five weeks. He laughed heartily. This was a book of reportage on a current event which might be forgotten in a very short time. He needed the manuscript in *three days*. Before I could protest, he explained how we would work. He would send a stenographer to my house at 5 p.m. on the next day. I would interview Foley in the morning and early afternoon and dictate the first day's material to the stenographer in Hungarian. I would have three days to do the whole book. I could leave the rest – transcription and translation – to him. About a week after our midnight chat my first book, *I Was an Altmark Prisoner* by Thomas Foley, was on sale. My name did not figure on it, not even in the usual 'as told to' formula. The book was sold out in a few weeks and a French edition was also published about a fortnight after ours. It all seemed very easy.

How to be Seventy

I first met Feri Áldor in a friend's cottage in Chorley Wood. Someone mentioned an unflattering remark made about him upon which he banged his fist on the table and exclaimed full of indignation: 'Whobody said so?' This word, *whobody*, made a lasting impression on me. Even in those days I knew that it did not exist; I also knew that it ought to exist.

Arthur Koestler mentions Feri in his autobiography and describes him as an evil genius. I have no doubt about either his evil nature (*evility* – he might have supplied another missing word) or his dazzling – and misused – abilities. Whether he was rich or nearly bankrupt, he always lived like a millionaire. He paid me something for the work I did for him – he paid me badly but paid me, and paid Foley, too. I was, however, to receive another five pounds (yes, I repeat: five pounds) for the French rights, and that he did not pay. He refused even to discuss the matter. One evening I visited him in his luxurious little palace in Mount Row, Mayfair. He was playing bridge for very high stakes. He was a bridge-player of world class and one of his permanent partners was Imre Alpár, a former world champion. I watched the game for a while and saw him put his winnings of £128 in his pocket. I reminded him that he owed me five pounds and asked him to pay me. He laughed it off. Oh no, he would not pay. But he had just won a large sum, I protested. He could pay me easily from his winnings. He would be still £123 the richer.

'That has nothing to do with it,' he shouted. (He always shouted – even when he meant to whisper.) 'I never said that I couldn't pay you. I don't pay you because I don't recognise "obligations". I don't "owe" anything to anybody. If you are broke and need money and ask me humbly, I may lend you – or give you – fifty pounds. You can have it as a gift. But you can't have it as a payment of a debt.'

I was young, foolish and proud. So I did not ask him humbly to give me just five pounds. I told him that I only wanted my dues and would see to it that I got them.

Years later – by then there was no contact between us – he rang me up out of the blue early one morning and asked me to go and see him. First I refused but he was very insistent so I agreed. (I am a lousy practitioner of the art of saying *no*.) It was about ten in the

Murder

morning when I arrived. He told me his story.

'Last night I met a well-known film director at a party. I told him a story-idea of mine and he became quite excited about it. He asked me to give him a written synopsis and he is coming to collect it at three o'clock this afternoon. I can invent but I cannot write. So I am going to tell you the story now and I want you to put it down on paper – about three or four pages, that's all.'

'I am not interested,' I replied with studied coolness.

'I'll pay you whatever you want.'

'A hundred pounds,' I told him – an outrageous sum for so little work in those days.

He took out his cheque-book and wrote out a cheque for a hundred pounds.

'Very well,' I said. 'You tell me the story and I'll make notes. Then I walk over to your bank round the corner and cash the cheque. If it is a dud – that's the end of the story. I mean *our* story. If it is paid, the synopsis will be in your hands before three o'clock.'

The cheque *was* met. The story was based on an excellent and original idea. The film was never made but the basic idea was used in another film made by the same director. I arrived at Feri's house a few minutes before three and on leaving I ran into the film director and his secretary (or wife? or girlfriend?). Feri took his visitors into his magnificent drawing-room and then came back to see me off. He had nearly closed the door when he opened it again and told me with a broad grin: 'But I still haven't paid you your five pounds. And I never will.'

He never did.

Soon afterwards I wrote another book of war reportage, this time for Hutchinsons. The pattern was the same as the *Altmark*, the source being once again the Ministry of Information. It was strange, but this story was also connected with Norway. In April 1941 the Germans occupied that country. According to Churchill's memoirs the German decision was made on December 14, 1940 but he adds: 'The incident of the *Altmark* no doubt gave a spur to action.' Soon after the occupation of Norway the British raided

How to be Seventy

the Lofoten Islands – a group of islands north-east of Iceland – and brought back with them a number of Norwegian resistance fighters and a bunch of quislings, as well as some German prisoners of war. The whole episode has been forgotten but in those days it was celebrated as a splendid British victory – and we badly needed some splendid victories. I concocted a little book based on interviews given by the Norwegian patriots, telling all about the Nazi invasion and life under the Germans, about the British raid and about their coming to Britain. The little paperback book sold like hot cakes and to my utter surprise it was mentioned among the 'Recommended Books' in *The Times Literary Supplement*. I have always been an intellectual snob – still am – and was delighted, yet at the same time my conviction grew that this writing business was much too easy. By the way, I wrote that book in Hungarian and translated it into English myself.

My name appeared on the cover as Dr H. George Mikes. The *H* was a typographical error. I had meant to cross out the *Dr* and did this in Continental fashion by two vertical lines, crossed by a horizontal one which admittedly look like an *H*. I have never lived that *H* down. In many library catalogues – including that of the British Museum – I am still listed as Dr H. G. Mikes.

This sudden and unexpected tie with Norway was further enhanced by a third book – written in fact between the two mentioned. It led to the worst literary and indeed common crime ever committed in my life. It is connected with the only cold-blooded murder I have ever committed.

I got a telephone call from Paul Tabori, who was another Hungarian writer-journalist. He came to London in the mid-thirties, so he was very much at home here when I arrived. He was a remarkable character: to paraphrase Chesterton's opening sentence of *The Man Who Was Thursday:* Paul was not a novelist, he was a novel. A serious man with a wide knowledge of contemporary literature, a likeable fellow and a good friend, he was also a maniac for hard work. Later, when we worked together in the BBC's Hungarian Section, I often saw Paul writing his next novel, completely unaware of the surrounding chatter. He typed at breathtaking speed, never even slowing down. Then a news item was brought in. He tore out the manuscript of the novel from the typewriter, translated the news item – as soon as this was done, put back the manuscript of his novel and went on typing at dazzling speed. One of his eyes was short-sighted, the other long-sighted, so when translating he could read the English text with his long-sighted eye and the Hungarian text in the typewriter with the short-sighted one, without wasting any time looking from one to the other. Paul had serious ambitions and was an honest man but he certainly had germs of the hack in him. Because he was such a glutton for work he could not refuse anything. His self-confidence and daring were limitless. A few days after Pearl Harbour he wrote a long and learned essay about Japanese secret societies about which he knew as much as the average Japanese journalist knew about the problems of Hungarian maize-growing. When television came into the vogue in a big way, he went to the United States to *teach* television writing although at that time he had never written a television play in his life.

This time he told me that he had made a contract with a publisher for the life-story of a Norwegian patriot. The man escaped in the nick of time from Oslo, after the arrival of the Germans, and was now in London. The story of this man had to be written down, as I had done in my story about the *Altmark* – and as he, Paul, was extremely busy, he wanted my help.

I was only too pleased to offer it and asked him where I could meet that Norwegian in order to start interviewing him straight away.

'That's the snag,' said Paul. 'There is no Norwegian. I have invented *him*, you have to invent his story. That is the essence of collaboration.'

In those days very little material was available on Norway. We had great difficulties even in finding a name for our hero. Once in my life I had met a Norwegian and his Christian name was Ejnar. Paul had been in touch with a publishing firm in Oslo and the publisher's surname was Dybwad. So our hero became Ejnar Dybwad. I rushed to Colindale, to the newspaper library of the British Museum, and spent about two mornings there concocting Ejnar Dybwad's odyssey, mostly from news item culled from the *Daily Telegraph*. I dramatised all the news items and set them down in the first person singular, as if Ejnar Dybwad had witnessed all the events. The manuscript was duly delivered after four days and a few weeks later our paperback, *I Saw the Invader* by Ejnar Dybwad, was on sale in all the worst bookshops.

While the book was being written, Paul delivered the manuscript bit by bit to the publisher who was so much impressed by Dybwad's courage, resourcefulness and strength of character that he expressed his desire to meet him. Paul tried to fob him off with excuses but the publisher was insistent. What could I do? I had to get rid of him. I just *had* to kill him and dump his body in the sea. In the last chapter Dybwad expressed his determination to return to Norway and fight for the freedom of his country. On the way home his plane was shot down and he perished in the waves.

About a year after the publication of this little book, I met a minister of the exiled Norwegian government at a reception and, to make conversation, I mentioned that I was one of the authors of the book, *I Saw the Invader*. He was not amused. His face grew dark and he told me grimly: 'That book did more harm to Norway than the German invasion.'

In September, 1939, the BBC started broadcasting in Hungarian. I knew nothing of these broadcasts being organised and was not among the Section's original members. Tarján got in a few weeks after the start, just as a newsreader – an 'auxiliary voice', as he later put it – but rose, throughout the years to be first head of the Hungarian Section and eventually of the whole Central European region. My missing the boat was a rather painful blow because my financial situation was becoming more and more precarious. I was still sending daily despatches to Budapest but my salary arrived at irregular intervals, if at all. All the same, I was never really worried. First of all it is not my nature to worry. Secondly, the war was so absorbingly interesting that I could not focus my attention on such an insignificant detail as my personal fate. Finally, in the last minute something always turned up: a book, an article on Hungary for an English paper or magazine, or some money seeping through from Budapest, as occasionally happened.

Murder

And, although I did not have a job, the BBC too started becoming a source of income. I started writing talks, and later features, for the Hungarians. I wrote a feature, called *Killer Boy*, the story of an originally decent German youth who became a Nazi bomber pilot and was shot down over Britain and died for a bad cause. This feature became a great hit. For quite a while I could hardly ever switch on the European Service without hearing in one language or another the solemn and grave funeral speech of an English clergymen over the dead German boy. After *Killer Boy* I was invited to write features for the French, and a little later I became a regular contributor to the Italians, too.

In these features there was always a wicked Nazi, so the Italian Section needed someone who spoke good Italian with a strong German accent. A young monitor called George Weidenfeld was eminently suitable for these parts, and he played many of them.

Years later I was invited to one of his parties and Tom Driberg remarked that I must have known George for a long time.

'Oh yes,' I replied happily. 'I met him first in his capacity as an actor. Once upon a time he used to play Nazi villains in my features.'

If looks could kill I would have dropped dead on the spot. Apparently I had put my foot in it, for which I should like to offer my belated apologies. I had no idea that my host was not proud of, and amused by, his rise in the world and that he tried to conceal the fact – or at least hated to be reminded of it – that he was not the twelfth Lord Weidenfeld.

The BBC soon decided that I was earning too much money, which just would not do in wartime. They wanted to offer me a job and I was only too keen on getting one in the Hungarian Section; but there were no vacancies there. So how could they stop me making too much money?

One day an assistant from the manager's office called me and asked if I spoke German.

'Very little and very badly.'

The girl-assistant replied coolly, in the manner of a skilful cross-examining counsel: 'I am told that *all* Hungarians speak good German.'

'I am the exception who confirms the rule.'

How to be Seventy

'Never mind,' she went on imperturbably. 'Be in Broadcasting House at 9 o'clock tomorrow morning.'

I duly appeared and realised that they were determined to give me a job as a German monitor at Evesham, Worcestershire. In those days all foreign broadcasts had to be jotted down in shorthand and transcribed, then translated into English. I was led to a room where eight professional German stenographers were sitting around the table, listening to a programme broadcast by the German Forces Station. When they heard my strange accent, they raised their formidable eyebrows and looked at me with undisguised contempt. Then the martial music stopped and the reading of the German news began. It was mostly about the German-Finnish war, full of interminable Finnish names, and I failed to understand half of it. Neither could I put down the other half in longhand (I knew no shorthand). So I gave up and watched the others. They were making efficient little squiggles with supercilious ease and with plenty of time to spare. The news bulletin, at last, came to an end and then a miracle occurred. The German announcer declared that now he would repeat the whole thing at dictation speed, for the forces' newspapers. And so he did. Whenever he came to a long Finnish place name – or to a short German one, for that matter – he spelt it out. So I wrote out the whole text, accompanied by the murderous glances of the German shorthand-writing champions, who were sitting around the table with folded arms. I translated the stuff into English and two days later I was called into the manager's office and offered a job as German monitor. I told him that I was not really up to it. He brushed this aside. I had told his assistant that I could not speak German and yet I was the best in the whole group, particularly my translation into English was the best of the lot. I explained what had happened. He replied that it was the result of the test that mattered and he was not really interested in details. He was growing very annoyed by my reluctance. He told me that I was earning too much money; in wartime – if I was really loyal to the British cause – I should not pick and choose among jobs, I had to accept a 'job of national importance' (as the phrase went) even if it meant a financial sacrifice and even if I had to go and live in Evesham. He threatened me with stopping my contributions

Murder

to the European Service altogether if I refused a job offered to me. But, for once, I remained adamant, explaining that I was prepared to accept any job – however ill-paid and wherever it might take me – but that I could not take on work I was unable to do and a job from which I would be dismissed after twenty-four hours – and rightly so. He repeated his threats about stopping my work altogether but I stayed in London and went on working for the BBC as before.

I got an invitation from a little literary magazine to meet H. G. Wells (the other 'H.G.') for lunch at the Dorchester Hotel. There was a pretty secretary in the Italian Section, Isobel was her name, and I asked her if she wanted to come with me. She told me that she was very much interested in H. G. Wells because Wells was a diabetic and so was she, since the age of twelve. A strange reason for being interested in Wells, I thought. I found out soon enough, however, that Isobel was no fool, far from it, and indeed Wells's diabetes was not her only interest in him.

We went to the Dorchester where we found that Wells had been conned. The editor of the magazine had asked him to come to the lunch to discuss some interesting international project with a few friends. Instead of the few friends he found an audience of four hundred who expected him to make a speech. He made an angry speech, denouncing the editor and all the guests present (his likely accomplices), denouncing our Government, the direction of the war, the Nazis, the Americans and the whole world. Then he predicted the impending doom of humanity and went home, probably to forget the whole episode quickly. But I did not. A few weeks later I married Isobel.

It was she who popped the question, after a brief period of friendship. I said that, quite frankly, I had never thought of marriage, but it might be an amusing experience. I told her that my livelihood was rather precarious, the Italian Section was a source of only a modest income, and that while I would be able to buy her a ring – a wedding ring, not an engagement ring – I could bear no further expenses. That was all right, she replied, the licence did not cost much. Whether it cost a little or a lot, I could not bear *any* further expense. Very well, in that case she would get the licence. She produced the document next day and invited me to dinner at her parents' place.

The dinner was excellent, a lot of *wiener schnitzel*, an almost unimaginable luxury in war-time. Isobel's mother, a charming French-speaking Swiss lady, just to make conversation, asked me about my gastronomic likes and dislikes.

'I like everything,' I told her, 'with the single exception of rabbit which I cannot swallow.'

'And what do you think you are having a third helping of?'

Wiener schnitzel was followed by some sweets – made with Isobel's special diet in mind – and during that course Isobel, seizing on a short pause in the conversation, butted in: 'By the way, George and I are getting married on the 17th.'

There was another short pause. Then Isobel's father – a tall, bearded and very English Englishman – turned to me and said: 'I suppose I ought to ask you now whether you can support my daughter?'

'I can't,' I replied.

'You can't?'

'No, I can't. But Isobel said she could support me.'

He meditated on that for a few seconds and then gave his verdict: 'That's all right then.'

This happened at the beginning of December, 1941. Quite a lot of things occurred between that dinner and our wedding day.

The Hungarian (formerly and subsequently Czechoslovak) town of Kassa, or Kosice, suffered a light air-raid from German planes, disguised as Russians, upon which mighty Hungary – a Nazi satellite by then – declared war on the Soviet Union, Britain and, for good measure, the United States. As next day the Japanese attacked Pearl Harbour, Hungary's declaration of war was somewhat overshadowed, but it was not overlooked by the British authorities. Hungarians became enemy aliens and about a hundred of them were interned and dispatched to the Isle of Man. Sixty of the people interned were Hungarian sailors found on the high seas, the remaining forty amounted to an odd

Murder

mixture, a rather haphazard selection. Among them there were a few notorious black marketeers and other shady characters, but there were also some perfectly respectable people with no conceivable stigma on their past. And all – the shady characters as well as the respectable ones – were devotedly loyal to this country.

André Deutsch had given up his job as van-driver for a patisserie firm because he suspected – rightly or wrongly – that the stuff he had to deliver included black-market goods. Soon after that he came to visit us (I was still sharing a flat with Béla Iványi, the historian) and informed us with a grin that he had got a new job. He had become a receptionist at Grosvenor House. He had to stand behind the counter, wearing a morning coat. He lived in the hotel and had excellent meals in the staff dining room, served by waitresses. He was very pleased. But one morning, in December, he was taken away by the police, and packed off to the Isle of Man. It took the hotel a long time to recover from the shock. The authorities realised quite soon that André was as innocent as could be and, in fact, he was the very first person to be released from internment.

Feri Aldor, the non-paying publisher of *Altmark*, was also whisked in. So were a few of his bridge-partners and so were a lot of others, Laci Héthelyi among them.

On December 17 I married Isobel as planned. Returning home from St Marylebone Registry Office and the subsequent reception, I found a congratulatory telegram from Laci, sent from the Isle of Man. It read: 'I prefer internment.'

My Political Career

Hungary, having slowly slipped into the pocket of the Nazis, became a belligerent Axis Power in 1941. Antal Zsilinszky, the First Secretary of the Hungarian Legation, resigned from his post and – with a number of friends – founded a free Hungarian movement called the Association of Free Hungarians in Great Britain. I became first a member, later a Committee Member, later still Hon. Treasurer and in the end Hon. Secretary. We tried to arrange lectures and discussions, make public statements through letters to editors or articles and, generally, to voice the views of Hungarians who were in a position to speak freely.

During the course of one lecture Béla Iványi – whose pronunciation of English was not one of his major assets – trying to describe the condition of poor peasants, reduced to being 'landless beggars of Hungary', kept referring to 'three million buggers' and assuring his audience that in our country every fourth person was a bugger. This amazing statement created a greater impact, at least in some circles, than all our other activities put together.

Antal Zsilinszky, after a short period as President, committed suicide. His reasons for killing himself were purely private but our enemies (and the small world of free movements was full of intriguers) tried to make the most of it, spreading vicious rumours that Zsilinszky was a Nazi spy, a Russian spy, an embezzler (from whom?) and so on. All this was pure invention: Tony Zsilinszky was an unhappy man but an unhappy man of absolute integrity. His successor was Andrew Révai, an arts publisher. He had rather unfortunate, prickly manners and was full of mannerisms and inhibitions. It took me some time to discover that he was not only a brilliantly clever man but also a warm-hearted although extremely shy one; but once this had

My Political Career

been discovered we became close friends.

Our Association represented the anti-fascist bourgeoisie. We had a lovely house in Manchester Square, with a good Hungarian restaurant, and our excellent chicken paprika helped to recruit many followers to the cause. We, however, represented only one narrow layer of society, and other movements also sprang up. One was headed by Count Michael Károlyi who represented the non-Communist left, and the third movement was formed by the Communists – who, however, would never call themselves Communists.

I am not going to delve into the intricacies of Hungarian emigré politics. We suspected – even if now and again we were carried away by false hopes – that, on the whole, like all emigré politicians, we were pretty ineffectual. All the same, we also knew that it was our duty to speak up for our compatriots and that we must do our best.

In those days, however, I met several fascinating and memorable characters, well worth recalling.

My own contribution was more literary than political, particularly at the beginning. Tarján organised various Hungarian performances and I contributed to them. There was one evening arranged in the Royal College of Music for which I wrote a little comic opera (Matyi Seiber composed the music). It was called *Balaton* and it satirised the political situation in Hungary. The little opera was quite well received, and was later broadcast by the BBC and, after the war, even by Budapest Radio. (The broadcast was arranged during the short liberal era of post-war Hungary but by the time the records got to Budapest, Rákosi's take-over was in full swing, so Hungarians were not to be reminded that Britain, too, had played a part in winning the war. They did not actually reject the agreement to broadcast *Balaton*, but it was put out at 6 o'clock in the morning.) We also formed a regular group and performed political songs, little plays, and sketches describing emigré life in London. We performed both at Manchester Square and at the Communist Club at Pembridge Square. Tarján and his wife (who – obviously – had arrived in the meantime) played the leading parts; Jani Strasser, the chief co-repetiteur of Glyndebourne, was our principal singer and Paul Ignotus – a

How to be Seventy

highbrow literary critic and a witty and incredibly absent-minded man – was our compère: an essential figure in the Hungarian political cabaret tradition. I wrote the whole programme and Matyi (Mathias) Seiber composed all the music. Many of my songs, little verses and sketches as well as Matyi's music were eventually published in book form, with drawings by Peter Lambda.

Matyi Seiber, a tiny man with a small moustache, was an excellent – even great – musician. I often hear his name mentioned on Radio Three and I am told that his serious music is still being performed all over the world. When I first visited him near Swiss Cottage, numerous sheets of music were placed all over the table and on other pieces of furniture or on the floor in the vast room and Matyi, while chatting with us, went from sheet to sheet, putting little squiggles on each.

'What are you doing?' I asked him.

'Oh, nothing.'

'But you are doing *something*.'

'Just orchestrating my new violin concerto. A dull job. It's mechanical work, once the actual composing is done.'

That was a strange world to me. It seemed even stranger to learn from Matyi that he hardly ever used the piano for composing. 'What for?' he asked, quite amused. He just sat down and wrote, as a writer does. 'But don't you want to *hear* it?' I asked. 'But I *do* hear it,' he told me. Matyi looked an austere, almost forbidding little man, but his wry humour and sharp wit shone through both his personality and his music. He was a fragile man, always sick. A breeze was enough to give him a cold, a single flake of snow to give him pneumonia and a pinch of spice enough to cause grave stomach cramps. He was always on a diet – sometimes he brought his own milk to the BBC because he could not trust the canteen milk. We always told him that he would survive us all because he looked after himself with special and loving care. This might have been so but for a stupid quirk of fate.

Matyi had a great admirer in South Africa who repeatedly invited him to visit him there. Matyi refused on several occasions because of his dislike of South African politics, but he liked his friend and in the end he accepted the insistent invitation. All

My Political Career

went well: his friend's family was not only very hospitable but also very rich. Matyi lived in great comfort, conducted several concerts in the big towns and was treated like a VIP everywhere.

One day they went to visit the National Park. There were four people in the party: Matyi himself, his friend's father, the friend's fiancée and the chauffeur who was driving a brand new Bentley. They admired the lions, giraffes and monkeys and just before leaving the park, Matyi's host declared that he would like to drive his new car for a bit. They changed places: Matyi and the father – who had been sitting in the back – occupied the front seats while the chauffeur and the young lady moved to the back. They were just outside the park – driving at low speed – when the steering went. (How the steering of a brand new Bentley – or any other car – can 'go' is not clear, but this was the phrase I heard.) The steering went and the car hit a tree. Matyi died on the spot; the father remained an invalid for the rest of his life. The chauffeur and the fiancée escaped unhurt.

Back to London and the war. I was on friendly terms with the two other movements. It was Bandi Havas who took me along to Count Károlyi. Havas used to be a refugee in France and after the French collapse he managed to escape to Morocco, with a group of friends including George Faludy, the brilliant poet. Havas was a hopelessly impractical man and, on his own, he would never have reached the coast or dared even to ask for a place in one of those overcrowded boats. Yet, he was an incredibly brave and tough man. Before the war he was caught by Horthy's police distributing Communist leaflets in front of a factory, on the outskirts of Budapest. He was arrested and tortured in a most inhuman manner but he did not squeal. Where many a tough giant broke down, the little Spec (as Koestler describing this scene in his novel, *Arrival and Departure*, called him) stood firm.

Havas was one of the ugliest men I ever met. He had flaming red hair, horrible, spotted skin, prominent horse-like teeth and protruding eyes. Yet he was a sweet man, a gentle soul and a sensitive poet. He had suffered a great deal because of his ugliness – children and young girls laughed in his face – and his ugliness played a part in turning him into a devout Communist. Many anti-fascist intellectuals sought salvation in the Communist

How to be Seventy

Party in those days of Fascism, even if they had a much pleasanter appearance than Bandi Havas. But for him the Party was a special magnet. The Party was the 'family'; the one place where he was not laughed at and teased because of his Caliban-like appearance but was accepted, respected, listened to and used for serious jobs, such as distributing pamphlets. There was never any doubt that he would do any job entrusted to him; and there was no doubt either that he would bungle it and be caught at the first attempt.

After the Hitler-Stalin Pact he – a shattered man – left the Party and felt like an orphan. After arriving in London he became the devoted and loyal secretary of Michael Károlyi.

There is no former head of any state with whom I washed up so many dirty dishes as I did with Count Károlyi. He was a remarkable man, a source of endless fascination for everybody who knew him. A member of one of the richest, most aristocratic, landowning families of Hungary, he divided his own land among the peasants in 1918. A man with a horrible impediment in his speech, he became one of the greatest popular orators of his day during World War One. A great liberal and radical, he became the last Hungarian Prime Minister to be appointed by a Habsburg and then the first President of the Hungarian Republic. Once the richest man in Europe, now – in his sixties – he had to carry up the coal to the third floor of his house in Church Row, Hampstead. He was not bitter about this, he found it quite amusing. He was broad-minded and generous, yet simultaneously suspicious of everybody and everything in a paranoid way. Nineteen-eighteen was his finest hour and he judged everybody by how he related to 1918 and to his own October Revolution. It was amazing, but *everybody* – Brazilian bankers, Dutch poets, young men not yet alive at that time, related somehow to the 1918 revolution in Hungary. He was a split personality: the determined and ardent revolutionary and the old aristocrat at one and the same time. He was absolutely honest in his revolutionary enthusiasm; yet, the old aristocrat was always popping up to laugh in the face of the revolutionary.

At the beginning of the War the Károlyis and the Hatvanys lived in Oxford and saw one another a great deal. Baron Louis

My Political Career

Hatvany was a pillar of Károlyi's October Revolution, so he passed the test, yet the two were still addressing each other as 'Monsieur le Baron' and 'Monsieur le Comte' until one day Hatvany told Károlyi: 'You are penniless and so am I. What about saying *tu* to each other?'

Károlyi loved the cinema and so did Loli (Baroness) Hatvany, but Countess Károlyi and Baron Hatvany hated it. The two cinema-goers went to see almost every film shown in Oxford. Károlyi never accepted a penny contribution from Loli Hatvany towards the tickets but always booked seats in the front row because, so he said, only there could he stretch his long legs. One day they were watching an English saga about Queen Victoria. The Queen and her Consort were receiving guests on a ceremonious occasion, everybody in full evening dress, 'all decorations worn'. Károlyi suddenly sat up in his seat and whispered to Loli in an excited voice: 'Look. Look at that. Incredible!'

'Look at what?' asked Loli who did look but saw nothing.

'Albert. Look at Albert.'

'What about him?'

'Good God. He's a Protestant and he's wearing the Order of Maria Theresa.'

I am sure Count Károlyi was the one and only revolutionary who noticed that mishap.

Sometimes I met Jan Masaryk in his house, the future Foreign Minister of Czechoslovakia who ended his life so tragically after the war. Károlyi was the only politician who still advocated a Danubian confederation, so he kept in close contact with his Czech friends. Masaryk used to be regarded as a bit of a playboy before the war. He told us this story.

When he was Czechoslovak ambassador in New York he received an invitation to dinner from an ambitious socialite hostess. He accepted it and took one of his Czech friends along. The hostess was a millionairess, the dinner was superb but soon after the meal Masaryk felt that he had about enough and he got up to say goodbye to his hostess.

'But Mr Masaryk,' she said in dismay, 'surely, you won't go before playing something for us on the violin?'

Masaryk agreed. A Stradivarius on a silver platter was brought in by a liveried footman. Masaryk tuned the violin and started playing. He was a reasonably good pianist, he often played pleasant little tunes, Viennese operettas and Czech and Slovak folksongs at the Károlyis. The violin was a different proposition. He was musical enough, he could play it – just. He played two Slovak nursery rhymes on the *Ba-Ba Black Sheep* level. This was received with rapturous applause and overwhelming gratitude. He was forced to give an *encore* but after that he was allowed to leave.

When they were in the lift his friend said: 'Why on earth did she ask you to play the violin?'

'Heavens, you are slow-witted,' replied Jan Masaryk. 'They mixed *me* up with my father; they mixed *him* up with Paderewski and they mixed the piano up with the violin.'

Károlyi was one of the most hated men in Hungary. The aristocracy and the middle classes hated him because he was accused – wrongly – of having handed over power to Béla Kun's Communists in 1919. For us younger people he was a bogeyman; we were told at school that it was most unpatriotic not to hate Michael Károlyi so we hated him. His real crime, of course, was that he decided to divide up the big latifundia among the peasants and, in fact, started with his own lands. Such an act threatened the very foundation of the rule of the aristocracy and the landowners in a semi-feudal country. He felt very bitter about these false accusations and could not help feeling the hatred oozing out of his much beloved homeland. He hated the Hungarian aristocracy, especially his own family and, among them, especially his cousin, Gyula Károlyi, a successor of his as Prime Minister in the thirties and the immediate predecessor of the fascist Gyula Gömbös.

One day, while we were washing up, Károlyi spoke to me sternly:

'I want to tell you off. I've been listening to, and reading, your talks written for the BBC. They are perfectly all right but why on earth are these talks anonymous? Why don't you dare to give your name? What sort of cowardice is this?'

'But Mr President,' I replied, quite amazed, 'I have my family in Hungary.'

My Political Career

'So have I. But I give my name when I write something.'
'But there is a great difference, Mr President. *I* would not be happy if *my* family were hanged.'
The reply to this was a broad grin: 'A good point,' he said. The subject was never mentioned again.

Mihaly Richter was the most outstanding and interesting member of the Hungarian Club in London, the Communist outfit; a self-educated labourer with a delightfully sharp, quick and original brain. He was a devoted Communist, flexible and brilliant in debate. Zoltán Radó was the club's President, a happy little man who kept putting on weight, and Miklós Szücs was its Hon. Secretary, another well-fed comrade. The word 'Communist' was never uttered by them publicly but we all knew that they were receiving friendly 'guidance' from the Soviet Embassy, just as we were from our Foreign Office. They were agitating for the 'Second Front' and later for unity among the Hungarian groups.

Károlyi also wanted unity, provided he would be the acknowledged leader of the enlarged group. This seemed a reasonable wish; after all, there were not many former heads of state among us. But that was the very reason for which my own association opposed unification. We knew that Károlyi's leadership would push the movement to the left. Our group also feared that Károlyi – if he came to power after the war – would make over-generous territorial concessions to his friends, the Czechs.

I personally was not worried by these considerations. I never thought that Károlyi would come to power, neither did I think that any Hungarian politician who did come to power, would have a say about future frontiers after the war. But I found it disastrous that the comparatively few Hungarians in Britain should speak in three different voices. The BBC refused to put out our statements and proclamations. They said they would give publicity to one Hungarian voice but not to three. An Extraordinary General Meeting of our Association was called and I made a big speech in favour of unity. It was the first and last occasion in my life that I faced a deeply divided and mostly hostile crowd and managed in the course of speaking to turn hostility into enthusiastic support. The motion – after a long and bitter debate – was, in the end, unanimously carried; *nemo contradicente*, because the mood at the end was such that even members of the Executive Committee did not vote against me. This was the beginning and almost the end of my political career. Admittedly, it was brief; but I did enjoy that hour and a half while it lasted.

As a result of that meeting the three groups, while keeping their identities, formed a super-organisation, called the Hungarian Council in Great Britain, with Count Károlyi as its President. When various posts were discussed (I heard it later) my name was mentioned and some people said that I ought to be rewarded.

'Why should he be rewarded?' asked Countess Károlyi. 'He has done a service; he has played his part. He can't do much more. Now he can go and be forgotten.'

This was a second lesson I learnt during my brief political career.

But in spite of this I was appointed Press Officer of the Hungarian Council. I handled our communications to the papers and all our messages to Hungary, now accepted by the BBC.

After the great union, our organisation was about to arrange a great dinner in honour of Károlyi. Andrew Révai, our President, was a good and brilliantly clever man but a terrible snob. He rejected Károlyi as the left-wing oracle but revered him as the great aristocrat that he was. He was delighted that the Károlyis had accepted his invitation to dinner and was determined to make a fuss of his guests. He was also jealous of the others, he wanted to be seen as the only intimate of the Great Old Man. Someone asked me, before the dinner, whether preparing the seating arrangements was my responsibility. I replied that Révai had done that himself. Well then, what was the order? I told him: 'Károlyi will sit at the head of the table, with Révai on both sides of him.'

My work as the Council's Press Officer went on smoothly till nearly the end. With the help – and strict control – of my colleagues I wrote many messages to 'the Hungarian people' which were broadcast by the BBC. I had the strictest instructions never to submit one single line to the BBC without Károlyi's

My Political Career

personal permission to do so. I obeyed these instructions willingly and loyally until one April day in 1945, when the news came that the last German soldier had been expelled from Hungarian soil. Károlyi was not available, he was away on holiday. So I wrote a message – strictly on the lines of previous messages, approved by Károlyi – and this was duly broadcast. Károlyi, on his return, was all fire and fury. Urged by his wife, he would not listen to any explanation, I had been told not to submit anything to the BBC and I had broken my promise. As Hungary had been liberated, the Council decided to dissolve itself at its next meeting, so my friends – i.e. all the other members – suggested that the matter should be overlooked. Countess Károlyi, however, would not hear of it. I had committed a heinous crime and I had to be punished for it. So the agenda for the Council's last meeting was:
1. Dismissal of George Mikes as Press Officer.
2. Dissolution of the Council.

At the beginning of that session Károlyi – I thought under the strong influence of his wife – delivered a philippic against me. He said that while he fully approved of the text of my declaration, he could not tolerate the idea that a message had been broadcast to Hungary without his approval. He demanded my dismissal. It was in a very tense atmosphere that I was called upon to reply.

I said that the Council had issued statements and messages not only after the liberation of Budapest and the bigger cities, but also after the liberation of every nook and cranny, veritable dirt-holes. I thought it would be ludicrous – quite ludicrous – to remain silent when the whole country was liberated. Hungary – I went on – had an unfortunate history and it was liberated from foreign oppression, roughly speaking, every twenty-five years. Count Károlyi also had an unfortunate history and a hard life and went on holiday also about once in twenty-five years. What was I to do when these two rare events coincided? As I could not postpone the liberation of Hungary till after Károlyi's return, I had to rush in with our statement before his return.

My statement was received first with giggles, then with roars of laughter. Károlyi himself laughed the loudest. Countess Károlyi was the only one who was not amused but Károlyi brushed aside her attempt to insist on my dismissal. We proceeded to dissolve ourselves, so I, too, was dissolved but not dismissed.

The Hungarian Council in Great Britain was not a major episode in the history of Hungary, but it would be a hard task to write even a Ph.D. thesis on our activities. Mrs Ilona Dushinska kept our records, but at the last meeting she admitted that she had lost all the minutes.

'How could you lose the minutes?' Károlyi asked her.

'I lost them when I changed stockings on the top of a Number 13 bus.'

This explanation was deemed satisfactory and was universally accepted.

Perhaps world history did not lose much by not knowing the secrets of our Council. But I feel I lost a great deal by never finding out why Ilona Dushinska changed her stockings on top of a Number 13 bus.

In 1946 a Hungarian ministerial delegation arrived in London on its way to Washington. Its leaders were Ferenc Nagy, the Prime Minister of the coalition (Smallholders' Party), István Gyöngyössy, Foreign Minister (Smallholders' Party) and Mátyás Rákosi (Communist). We met them on many occasions and recorded interviews with them. Rákosi was all sweetness and understanding and was childishly pleased to show off his linguistic abilities – he spoke many languages, all (including Hungarian) badly. On one occasion he declared that he was one of the most ardent Anglophiles in Hungary but, alas, that record mysteriously disappeared when we wanted to play it back to him at a later stage of his career, when his Anglophilia was not quite so obvious to all observers. One day Rákosi called Béla Iványi and myself aside and asked us to return to Hungary.

'We need good democrats like you': those were his words.

Béla Iványi replied for both of us. He said that we tried to be good democrats but for the time being we would watch developments in Hungary and help the Hungarian cause – as much as it was in our power – from London.

I thought he was too guarded and too pessimistic. For about a fortnight I seriously considered returning. I was grateful to

My Political Career

Britain and hated the idea of leaving; but I thought I might be able to offer some help in the rebuilding of Hungary and that country, after all, was my country. Quite a lot of my friends had similar thoughts. Events, however, were happening rapidly and it was obvious that our dreams about a new, democratic and decent Hungary were being quickly buried. People here were changing their minds fast but they would not admit it. Not yet. They were talking of unavoidable delays; they still had matters to settle; yes, yes, they would go but only in the following month. I made a suggestion: 'Let's arrange a huge and splendid farewell dinner and after that we all stay here.'

That's what happened as far as I and most of my friends were concerned. I applied for, and received, British citizenship and never again, not for a moment, did I think of leaving this country.

A few of my friends, however, did go back. The luckiest among them was Mihály Richter, the idealistic Communist labourer, whose plane crashed at take-off in Surrey, killing him on the spot.

George Pálóczi-Horváth – an old friend and a colleague of mine at the BBC, an enthusiastic Communist when he left – spent four years in prison. My dear friend Paul Ignotus – who became Press Attaché at the Hungarian Legation after the war and went home for his father's funeral – spent seven years in prison. George Faludy, the greatest living Hungarian poet, was sent to the notorious concentration camp at Recsk. Count Károlyi received a hero's welcome on his return and was appointed Hungarian Minister to France. After the arrest of Rajk he – with breathtaking courage – returned to Budapest from Paris in order to resign his post. Afterwards he returned to France, becoming an exile for the second and last time. He died in France in 1955.

Zoltán Radó, the happy-go-lucky President of the Communist Club, was charged with industrial spying and sabotage and after the first of the Communist mock trials was hanged. Szücs, the Hon. Secretary of the Communist Club, seemed to be safe: his brother was the deputy of Gábor Péter, Hungary's own almighty Beria. Soon enough Szücs's brother (and eventually Péter himself) was accused of being a traitor and a foreign spy and the two brothers were arrested. Both were thrown into an acid bath, still alive. Their bodies disappeared without trace.

How to be Seventy

Bandi Havas, the ugly poet, Károlyi's loyal secretary, was happy to rejoin the Party, the 'family'. He was delighted to find himself among his brothers and sisters once again. After Rajk's arrest the country was stunned: a terrible chill descended on the land. Rajk was guilty of many crimes but – everybody knew that – not of those trumped up charges he was accused of. Havas was the only man who really believed that Rajk was guilty as charged and he went around Budapest, trying to convince others of Rajk's guilt. He could not bear yet another disappointment in the 'family'. He went around saying that Rajk was a criminal, a Titoist traitor. When he himself was arrested and beaten to death in the cellars of the Political Police, he died shouting: 'Long live Stalin! Long live the Soviet Union!'

How to be an Alien

One day during the war I went to Bush House to deliver a script to the French, when I met Ferenc Körmendi – a successful novelist of the pre-war days – in a corridor. He told me that a sudden vacancy had occurred in the Hungarian Section and that I should apply for the post. I said I would think it over. But before I could think, George Campbell appeared and Körmendi told him that I should be given a translation test and a voice test immediately. I took the test straight away. As soon as the tests were over, Campbell took me to the manager's office and about half an hour after my chance encounter with Körmendi, I was a member of the Hungarian Section. I stayed there as an employee for seven years and went on writing a weekly piece for another ten.

George Campbell, need I say, is a Scot. He is a brilliant man in more ways than one but his main claim to fame is his knowledge of fifty-seven languages. 'Claim to fame' – on second thoughts – is the wrong expression. First of all, he does not claim anything at all, he is the most modest and reticent of men; secondly, if he did claim anything it would not be fame on account of his many languages; indeed, he hates to be known as the champion of polyglots. But he cannot live it down. His knowledge of languages is phenomenal. He knows all the European languages, about seventeen Indian languages and a few such oddities (at least for Europeans) as Tagalog, the principal language of the Philippines. You could find him in the canteen – usually late at night – reading Japanese poetry or studying Georgian (Stalin's Georgia) proverbs. He was never doing it to show off, he covered up the book if someone approached. All the same, I became sceptical about his knowledge of all these tongues so I decided to investigate. On Hungarian I could check myself, and I found his knowledge superb. I checked on many other languages through my friends and was told by all, without exception, that his knowledge and understanding was amazing. Once he was persuaded to apply for a UN job (he did not take it in the end) and one of the questions on the form asked how many languages he spoke. He managed to list fifty-seven but remarked: 'I may have forgotten to mention one or two.'

He was a 'language supervisor' – his job was to check our translations into various foreign languages and then to check in the studio that we did not deviate from the approved text. He worked with a number of sections but ended up, after my departure from the BBC, as the boss of the Romanians. He learnt all these languages because he was interested in them, it became a compulsion and he simply could not resist it. He did not learn them because this knowledge was useful; in fact, it was not useful. The knowledge of a few languages is, needless to say, helpful. But knowing fifty-seven languages is like owning fifty-seven motorcars. We have been good friends from the first moment I went in to read my first talk in Hungarian – long before I joined the staff – and have remained on excellent terms ever since. But our relationship was not cloudless. Once I wrote a letter to the *Guardian* about his phenomenal accomplishments and after that he refused to speak to me for about two years because I praised him. After this piece here, he will never speak to me again.

Working for the BBC was regarded as an 'essential job' during the war but I felt I ought to do more. I had no idea what. If a foreigner volunteered for the army, he was taken as a member of the pioneer corps. He was not trusted with a gun. I would have been quite ready to fight for this country but to carry sacks for it failed to attract me. One day I received an invitation to visit the Ministry of Labour. I was asked to fill in a form. One of the questions was whether I would accept any job, even a dangerous one. I answered yes. Next question: was I prepared to go abroad? I said I was longing to. People scrutinised my replies and then led me into an inner sanctum where a gentleman informed me that he did not belong to the Ministry of Labour but to the War Office and they were recruiting volunteers to be dropped into Hungary by parachute or smuggled in from Yugoslavia. They were sending teams of five. Each team needed one Hungarian with a perfect knowledge of the language. That man would be trained as a parachute jumper as well as a radio operator and would get a commission after six weeks of training. If our team was caught by the Germans, well . . . I said yes, 'well' indeed, but one had to take risks during a war, other people were taking them too. I had never foreseen returning to Hungary that way but one of the beauties of life is that it does produce unexpected turns. A few days later I was called back to the 'Ministry of Labour' and asked by the same gentleman if my picture had ever appeared in newspapers. I said that it had appeared quite frequently – I often interviewed visiting celebrities and was photographed in their company – but all this had happened long before and I assured him that my face was certainly not a well-known one. No, he said, that ruled me out. About two months later I went to a party. There I met a young Hungarian, a second lieutenant, newly commissioned, who was about to leave for Yugoslavia. He said nothing, of course, and I asked no questions but I did not need to. Later I heard that he did get to Yugoslavia but no farther. The Russians, paranoid as always, protested against the infiltration of these British 'spy-teams' and the plan had to be abandoned.

My brother Tibor did much more than I; even more than Uncle Mundi who, as we know, practically won the war single-handed. Tibor got to America in 1939 and married his childhood sweetheart, Magdus Kemeny. He volunteered for the US Army and was enlisted into the 10th Mountain Division, a crack unit. The unit underwent very strenuous training, mostly rock-climbing and skiing in Colorado, which Tibor loved. Then the Division was sent to Italy where they fought their way up north, to the river Po. Tibor was in charge of a small reconnaissance unit. He lost many of his friends and comrades but he finished the war as a well-decorated (and luckily, unscathed) man.

He told me a story which is one of the most amazing coincidence stories I ever heard, including my mother-in-law's adventures at the butcher's.

It happened on one of the last days of the war. Tibor was sent on some mission with his men across the Po. It was a lovely spring day and the group was walking along the river bank when suddenly a shot rang out. They lay down in the grass and then one of them, Chuck Brian from Kansas City, noticed a German sniper in a tree. He aimed, fired and shot the German dead. The sniper fell out of the tree.

My brother ordered his group to proceed. He was pleased with Chuck Brian. He was a nice guy, a tough one like all of them had to be, but also a bit of a romantic. His wife wrote him two or three large pages every day and sent the lot – something around twenty-one pages – once a week in one envelope. Chuck lived for these letters and all the other guys teased him. Now he was rather worried because he had not heard from his wife for a week or two.

The group found out whatever it was supposed to find out and returned by the same route. The dead German was still lying on the same spot.

'You shot him, go and search him,' Tibor instructed Chuck Brian. Chuck did as he was told, turned out the man's pockets and took his wallet to establish his identity. There was a thick letter in one of the dead man's pockets. Chuck looked at it. It was in his wife's handwriting. Sender: Mrs Chuck Brian, Kansas City. It was addressed to him. It was his wife's delayed letter.

This sounds incredible and I hate to spoil the effect of the story with a logical explanation, but I must. A short while before that fatal encounter, the Germans had raided an American Army post office and the dead German (the *now* dead German, I should say) had taken part in the raid. Presumably the unusual thickness of Mrs Brian's letter seemed to promise a fat collection of dollars, and the man slipped it into his pocket. Before he had a chance of opening the letter, he was shot dead by the addressee.

An unusual way of delivery.

André Deutsch was, as I have already mentioned, released from internment after a very short spell. He has told me more than once that having been interned was the best piece of luck in his life. Most of the people who were kept in were anxious to send messages and Deutsch, when he was released, was inundated

How to be an Alien

with requests to deliver them, to run errands, to find out one thing or another and settle this and that. Feri Aldor asked him to visit Mr Minshall, the managing director of Simpkin Marshall, the big book-distributing firm. Minshall was a kind man and asked André what he was going to do next. He replied that he would have to get a job of some sort but his dream was to become a publisher. Mr Minshall made a few telephone calls on the spot and told André to visit Mr Roberts of Nicholson and Watson, a well-known publishing firm. André visited Mr Roberts and was engaged as a sort of man-of-all-work.

When interviewed by eager (but, if I may say so, not too bright) journalists abroad I am often asked: 'How did you become a humorous writer?' Or even: 'When did you decide to become blue-eyed?' I was born with blue eyes which turned greenish-grey during the vicissitudes of a humorist's life. Humour – as I am a 'beholder', like most of us – was in my blue eyes. But after all these protestations I am able to recount a particular incident which, perhaps, was decisive.

During the war I met a Yugoslav army captain who had escaped from a German prison camp and come to London. He had a thrilling story to tell – he was a brave and resourceful man – and he told it well. With André's help I got a contract from Mr Roberts and my book describing the Captain's adventures was published by Nicholson and Watson. The book was sold out in no time – like almost everything else in wartime. I got a number of good reviews which not only pleased me but also puzzled me. I described this in my book, *Shakespeare and Myself.**

I, quite rightly, regarded the book (*We Were There to Escape*) as the work of a reporter and not of a writer. I put down on paper what the Captain had told me in a number of long interviews. But I must have deviated from the rules of straight reporting without being aware of my deviationist tendencies. It was *The Times Literary Supplement* which brought home this fact to me. Its review began: 'There is a peculiar kind of Slav humour [why Slav I still don't know]. It came out delightfully in Čapek's work – and all through

---

* Allan Wingate, 1952.

this narrative it is more or less present. Even without it, the story would be one of the best that has come out of the war . . . It is something new in the way of escapes from P.o.W. camps and is full of thrills and exciting adventures. With humour added, it has the light touch that turns unpleasant and indeed horrifying experience into good reading. Even the appalling monotony of camp life . . . is presented in a comic light.'

This was a very important review for me. Of course, I was pleased with the praise, but this was the less significant part of it. I was somewhat shattered by the fact that the book had been called humorous. I was not aware of its being funny. I thought it was a thriller pure and simple, rather in the style of *War and Peace* and the *Odyssey*. If you can imagine Tolstoy receiving reviews after the appearance of *War and Peace* stating that his book was a pretty piece of fun, or if you can picture Homer, hearing that his epic poems were good examples of a peculiar kind of Slav humour, then you can imagine my feelings.

After some heart-searching I was driven to the conclusion that I might as well attempt to write something which would not cause me painful surprise to find described as humorous. One phrase especially reverberated in my memory: '. . . the light touch that turns unpleasant, indeed horrifying experience into good reading.' I sat down and told all about my unpleasant, indeed horrifying, experiences among the English. The result was a little book, called *How to be an Alien*.

André came to see me, as he often did – we used to play rummy in those days – and told me that he had decided to set up his own publishing firm. He would not leave his job at Nicholson and Watson's, indeed Mr Roberts was supporting him with avuncular benevolence. Did I have anything to offer him? I mentioned my manuscript and he took it away with him. (That's my recollection. André says I summoned him to the Isle of Wight and handed him the manuscript there.) Soon he informed me that he liked it but a) I had to add quite a bit to it because a book of 8,000 words could not be published (eventually I extended it to 12,000 words) and b) the book had to be illustrated. He would ask Nicolas Bentley. If Mr Bentley liked the book, he would go ahead. I was an admirer of Mr Bentley's, I knew his work for Hilaire Belloc's

How to be an Alien

verses and T. S. Eliot's book on practical cats and was delighted to hear that he had agreed. But then I realised that I had to call the whole thing off. I told André that I had suddenly remembered that I had signed an option clause in my contract with Nicholson and Watson and I had to offer the book to Roberts. André suggested that I should go to Mr Roberts and ask him to release me. So I went. The conversation went something like this:

'Well, what is this book of yours?'
'It's a humorous book.'
'A what?'
'A humorous book.'
Roberts: (taken aback, very suspiciously) 'What is it called?'
'*How to be an Alien.*'
'What?!?!'
'*How to be an Alien.*'
'Good God. You just take your little book to André.'

I took the book to André. It was followed by about thirty-five others, nearly all published by André. Among André's early books were Mailer's *The Naked and the Dead*, preceded by my little book. He never looked back. Roberts and Nicholson and Watson were out of business a year or two after that conversation. Later André told me that Roberts also turned down Orwell's *Animal Farm*. I introduced Orwell to André, he took him to Roberts but Roberts declined the book. I think that's what publishers call flair.

André, somewhat surprisingly, called his new publishing firm Allan Wingate. Who was Mr Allan Wingate? No one. He explained that he thought *Allan* to be a Christian name of considerable dignity. Then, he was a great admirer of Orde Wingate, the Chindit leader. That's how Allan Wingate got coined. He could not possibly call the firm *André Deutsch*, he said, no English publishing firm could be called that. But apparently it can.

In January 1945 my son, Martin, was born; in October 1946 *How to be an Alien* was published. I was delighted with both events. New editions were rushed out (of the book, not of the child) and

How to be Seventy

foreign publishers were buying rights left and right. A little money was coming in. But I was still thinking in the terms of my previous books. You publish something, it is sold out, you may or may not get a few good reviews and then the whole thing is forgotten. Not in my wildest dreams did I hope, or fear, that the little book would be remembered – indeed, would be in print – three and a half decades later. Minor immortality – I never even aspired for it. Still less did I think that after some thirty-six books and after thirty-six years I would be known – if at all – as the 'author of *How to be an Alien*'. Two days before writing this part of my autobiography, the *Observer* very kindly remembered my sixty-ninth birthday, referring to me as 'the Hungarian-born writer who taught us *How to be an Alien*'.

Somerset Maugham complained in one of his books that he had written many books and plays but he was only remembered as the author of *Of Human Bondage*. Maugham also remarked that Arnold Bennett was simply the author of *The Old Wives' Tale*. Without trying to infiltrate that august company, I cannot fail to notice that my fate has been similar or worse. Maugham has ceased to be the author of just that one book and Bennett has made progress too.

But why complain? It is better to be remembered for one book than for none. I do not think that *How to be an Alien* is my best book, but it was the luckiest. The timing of a book is as important, if not more so, than its quality. 'Alien' appeared at a moment when the English were in an introspective mood, preoccupied with themselves and with their status in the world. Their superb self-confidence had begun to be shaken but they still believed that they were the most magnificent people on earth. A little foreigner came along and made fun of them but that was all right, they had always been proud of being able to laugh at themselves. (Indeed, they boast so much of this great virtue that I have grown a little suspicious about it.) My book *flattered* them, although I never meant it to: it said they were very peculiar, they were more inscrutable than any Orientals – in short, that they were unique and inimitable.

No, I definitely do not complain. That little book has done as much for me as I have done for it.

How to be an Alien
* * *

At the end of the war I tried desperately to get news from or about my parents. I was prepared for the worst. After some anxious weeks I heard, to my great delight, that they had survived and were in good health. My mother and stepfather were hiding, with false papers, somewhere in the suburbs. They were posing as Transylvanian refugees – many of those appeared as the Russians approached. My parents' hosts were a vulgar and loquacious washerwoman with a drunkard of a husband. One day Arrow Cross thugs arrived in the building and went from flat to flat, hunting for Jews with false papers, posing as refugees from Transylvania. My parents' hosts had just had a bitter quarrel because the man had just eaten up the food his wife had prepared for the entire week. When the woman saw the Arrow Cross men, she went out to the corridor and began to shout: 'Come here. Take away my bloody husband, not those Jews. I shall be grateful if you rid me of this bastard . . .' and so on in this vein for quite a while. The Arrow Cross fled in panic, they wanted nothing to do with crazy Xantippe, and this probably saved my parents' lives. My sister also survived, hiding at a different place. My grandfather, Mishka Papa, was in a Yellow Star House, in the ghetto. All his life he shaved himself every morning and he insisted on shaving himself even in the most miserable circumstances. He was a somewhat clumsy man and kept cutting himself. He looked, as a rule, like a Nazi student after a particularly gruesome duel. In that Yellow Star House there were no mirrors but this did not put Mishka Papa off. *And he never cut himself.* So he kept to his new habits. When I went home on a visit in 1948, I saw him sitting in the middle of the bathroom on a stool, surrounded by mirrors but taking no notice of them. He shaved himself with great skill and never even scratched himself, ever again.

Our work at the BBC changed after the war. Instead of just reading the news and straight political commentaries we began – as the phrase had it – 'projecting Britain', i.e. we tried to explain to those ignorant and backward Central Europeans how our splendid democratic institutions worked (or didn't). I edited a weekly magazine programme, visited various institutions, intro-

How to be Seventy

ducing myself as a member of the BBC's Hungarian Section. The inevitable response was: 'Good God. The BBC has a Hungarian Section? Whatever for?'

Bush House, by the way, was a thrilling place to work. Mr Bush – an American gentleman – dedicated the building 'To the Friendship of English Speaking Peoples' but there was no other place in London – perhaps in the whole world – where English was spoken more abominably than there. Bush House managed to collect the cream of foreign journalists and actors, mostly from Germany and France. There was permanent excitement in the air, everybody cared for his work although he had no idea whether the whole country was listening to him or not a single soul. (The whole country *was* listening, as it turned out later. When Paul Tabori visited Hungary soon after the war and went into a shop to buy cigarettes, he was recognised by his voice.) In spite of our devotion to duty we all had time to chase the pretty English girls who, in turn, felt wanted and flattered in Bush. Everybody flirted with everybody else. Food, too was much better than in other BBC canteens because we bloody foreigners kept complaining against the muck they tried to serve us, and which was accepted without murmur in all the canteens with a majority of English.

Broadcasting House was a stiff and formal place. Everybody was Mr X or Miss Y – Christian names were unknown. When a girl in Broadcasting House was told that she was to go to work in Bush House, she felt as if she had been banished to Siberia. Three weeks later she would not return for love or money. Or perhaps only for money; in Bush House she got all the love she needed.

We Hungarians felt absolutely safe discussing everybody loudly in our strange and exotic language. Then suddenly a few Slovaks cropped up from somewhere.

'Be very careful,' Tarján, by now head of the Section, warned us, 'all these Slovaks speak good Hungarian.'

'Disgusting interference with our privacy,' we replied. 'How dare they? . . . Isn't there any language left those Slovaks don't understand?'

'Yes, there is,' said Tarján. 'English.'

How to be an Alien
* * *

The most illustrious Hungarian visitor I had to interview was Zoltán Kodály, a magnificent and almost terrifyingly austere man, with a tremendous natural dignity, yet completely unpompous. He was not an easy subject to interview. He was excessively meticulous, chewing over every word, objecting to his own wording when I put it down on paper for him to read – giving spontaneous answers was ruled out. The interview – a quarter of an hour on the air – took five hours to make. A great man, a significant artist but not exactly a humorist. Yet, during those five hours he told me a story I cannot forget.

In the early post-war days, when the Communists were taking over the country, the ordinary police, the cops on the beat, were armed with bayoneted rifles. You had the impression that if you crossed the road against the red lights they would shoot you; and if you talked back to them they would disembowel you.

Kodály – an absent-minded man – did cross one day against the lights and two policemen stopped him. (They always went around in twos or even more often in threes. When people asked: 'Why three of them?' the wits of Budapest replied: 'One of them can read, one of them can write and the third is there to keep an eye on those dangerous intellectuals.') Kodály was told off. He apologised but that was not good enough. One of the men took his notebook and told him that he would be booked. He started asking the usual questions: 'Your name.'

'Zoltán Kodály.'

None of them had ever heard the name.

'Profession?'

'Musician.'

Then a further dozen questions: age, address, father's name, mother's maiden name, grandfather's name, grandmother's maiden name. Then, at last: what is your monthly income? (This was a sensible question. A rich man should be fined more than a beggar.)

'I have no idea,' Kodály replied.

'Come on. You must know.'

'I can give you an approximate figure.'

'Out with it.'

How to be Seventy

Kodály thought, calculated and then mentioned the equivalent of £5,000 per month – an incredible fortune in those days, not just a 'monthly income'.

'What did you say?' asked the policeman. 'Just say it again.'
'I can't be sure. But it's roughly £5,000 per month.'
'Roughly?'
'Yes, roughly.'

The policeman looked at his colleague, then he looked at the poorly clad old man. He folded his note-book, put it back into his pocket and told Kodály in a sympathetic voice: 'Go home old man and take care next time how you cross the road.'

Two Kings

During the immediate post-war years I was kept busy with domestic affairs. My first marriage broke up and I married my second wife, Lea.

My attitude to marriage – as to almost everything else – was a cavalier one. I mentioned earlier that it was Isobel's idea that we should get married and I told her then: 'Very well, let's get married for five years. After that we'll see.' I had forgotten this not too chivalrous statement but Isobel reminded me of it when our marriage broke up after exactly five years.

My attitude to the major events of my life seems rather casual. I do not recollect the following incident but my friend Laci Hervey reminded me of it. (He informed me one day that he had changed his name from Héthelyi to Hervey.) Laci came to see us one day and noticed that Isobel, a matter-of-fact and no-nonsense woman, was ordering me about and that I was obeying her without a murmur. As this clashed with my general character as Laci knew it he asked me why I tolerated being ordered about. I am alleged to have given this answer: 'Look, this whole marriage business seems to be very important to her but it is utterly unimportant to me. Let her enjoy herself.'

Laci informed me in those days that he, too, wanted to get married. His intended bride was Joan, then serving in the WRNS, the women's auxiliary force attached to the Navy, and he asked for my views.

'Marry her,' I am reported to have said. 'Every marriage works for the first two years and no marriage works after that. So it doesn't really matter whom you marry. You might as well marry the girl you fancy.' He did.

But my cavalier attitude to marriage and divorce came to an end with a heavy thud. Isobel remarried in Lausanne and took

How to be Seventy

Martin with her to Switzerland. Losing – to a large extent – my little son was a terrible blow which I did not take light-heartedly at all. I had completely failed to foresee such an eventuality.

Lea, my second wife, was a colleague of mine at the BBC. She was a stunningly beautiful girl and I was very much in love with her. In 1949 we had a daughter, Judy, who became a journalist and is expecting her first baby as I write this. Martin came to see me once a year and I visited him once or twice a year in Lausanne.

My mother appeared in London in 1947. She was on her way to America to my brother's family and spent a few weeks with me *en route*. I wanted to go to America myself, to visit my brother and spend more time with my mother whilst she was there. It was Lea who suggested: 'Why don't you go to America and write a book about it?'

This simple and sensible question determined my activities for about two decades to come. I did go to America to write a book, *How to Scrape Skies*.

I must pause here for a few remarks. During the last thirty-five years I have written about as many books. I do not intend to mention all of them and take the reader from book to book. I enjoyed most of my journeys round the world. I have said what I had to say about various countries (and a few other subjects, involving no journeys) and see no point in repeating or summing up my impressions here. Books, of course, will unavoidably crop up here and there, after all this is an autobiography and writing books has been my life. Essentially, however, the rest of these pages will be given to name-dropping. I shall drop names in both senses of the word, writing about people I knew well or have something to say about, and dropping many other splendid names – even famous ones – into silence by not writing of them, because I have nothing to say. I could drag in such distinguished gentlemen as, say, Somerset Maugham or Ben Gurion – I met them both ... just. But although an admirer (with certain reservations) of both, I can add nothing interesting to people's knowledge of them, and shall not try to do so.

I left for New York during the 1947 fuel crisis when it was forbidden to use electric heating for four or five hours a day. Bread was rationed (it had not been rationed during the war) and

Two Kings

there was a general scarcity of food. Eggs were hardly available and although I am not really fond of eggs, scarcity made them desirable. My plane took off in the early evening hours one day at the beginning of February. We landed at Shannon, Ireland, as planes in those days could not fly London–New York non-stop. Our group was a jolly lot, nice people, all excited about the journey – a much greater adventure then than it is now when, if a five year old has not been to California yet, he feels deprived and unloved. We got quite friendly with one another on that plane, with the single exception of a haughty and aloof man who turned out to be a general. He obviously despised the *hoi polloi* and seemed to indicate with his behaviour that normally he flew across the Atlantic in a special military aircraft. He ignored us all and did not speak one single word to any fellow-passenger. Next dawn we landed in Newfoundland, at a small airport, Stephenville. I found there a huge Post Office which did not sell stamps. It was a military Post Office, I was told, and they had no stamps for my numerous postcards. What could I do? Just hand them in, they would send them for me. But they could not sell stamps, they were sorry. I accepted their apologies, handed in my postcards without paying a penny, and they all duly arrived. At Stephenville we were served a magnificent breakfast, with bacon and eggs. No one who did not spend the war years and immediate post-war years in Britain can imagine the wild fascination of those bacon and eggs. We all gobbled them down. While gobbling, I noticed two things. First, that I was sitting next to the haughty general, who ignored me as usual. Second, that on the trolley next to me there was another portion of bacon and eggs, unclaimed. The general was looking at the same plate at the same time; then he looked at me. I looked at him and raised my eyebrows, meaning: 'Are you interested?' He nodded slowly. I took the plate, cut the bacon in two and shared out the two eggs, shoving half of the dish onto his plate. The general shut his eyes for half a second, which I took to mean acknowledgement or, perhaps, even approval. That was all the human contact between him and the rest of us. After that flicker of his eyes (and eating his share, of course) he sank back into his Olympian silence and haughty disdain.

My brother's brother-in-law – his wife's, Magdus's, brother,

How to be Seventy

John Kemeny – was a kind of mathematical genius. He was a student at Princeton and had received so many prizes and scholarships that he had to refuse some of them for income-tax reasons. Before leaving for New York I came across a book called *Riddles in Mathematics*. I have always loved such books but now I meant to catch John out with a few good riddles. I found one I particularly liked. I did not have to solve it – I could not – but the solutions were given at the end of the book. I learned my favourite riddle by heart; it was very complicated but I made a great effort. Soon after my arrival I put the riddle to John. He thought for about five seconds and told me: 'I think you messed up the question. The right way of putting it would be *this*. And then the solution is *that* . . .' and he gave me the right solution.

John told me the fascinating story of his military career. When he was called up his professor, Robert Oppenheimer, gave him a letter to the powers that be, stating that John was an eminent mathematician and should be given a job in which he could use his talents. He hung onto that letter even when standing stark naked in front of the medical board. In the end he was given a choice: he could learn Japanese or become a radio operator. He decided that radio was a step nearer to mathematics than Japanese so chose radio. He did a tiny bit of square bashing, but before the word 'radio' was even mentioned again, he was given a week's leave. He was instructed by a high-ranking officer to proceed, after his leave, to Santa Monica, California, and take a bus to a secret military establishment at Los Alamos. But he was not to utter a word about any military establishment, nor even to say the words 'Los Alamos'. He should simply enquire which buses were going to Santa Fé and then take the special military bus in the opposite direction. When arrived at Los Alamos, he was to present himself to Colonel Soandso. John went home, spent a week with his family and took the train from New York to California, across the United States, as instructed. Somewhere in the Mid West military policemen – the snowdrops, so well known in Britain, too – were checking up on travelling soldiers and found John's story amusing but incredible. Did he really mean to say that after only a week or so in the army he was given a week's leave? And was he serious in saying that he, Private Kemeny, had

Two Kings

to report personally to a Colonel? John knew very little about army ways, but now that the matter was put to him, he did find it all a bit strange. But he had no choice: he had to insist on this extremely unlikely tale. He was detained. Next day he was released, not exactly with apologies, put on the train and told to carry on as instructed. He arrived in Santa Monica and, wandering around town, lost his way. He stopped a simple old woman and asked her where the bus station was.

'That depends, Son,' she said, 'on whether you want to go to Santa Fé or to the Secret Project.'

John, of course, was put to work on the atomic bomb. Twenty-four of the brightest young mathematicians in the United States were put to work on John Neumann's new computer and had to carry out all the necessary calculations. They worked in shifts of eight, day and night, every day of the week, all the year round. Twenty years later John told me that using a modern computer, any second-year maths student of average intelligence could perform *all* the calculations they performed in three years, working day and night, in about three hours.

John's knowledge of Hungarian came in handy, too. With Teller, Szilárd and Neumann in the team, they always said that it was only Robert Oppenheimer's presence among them which prevented their talking Hungarian all the time.

After the war, John went back to Princeton and from there he moved to Dartmouth where he first became head of the Maths Department and later President of the College. He was the first non-American-born president of an Ivy League College. Last year he presided over the Three Mile Island enquiry, appointed by President Carter.

In the early fifties he became Albert Einstein's assistant at Princeton. He gave my book on Israel – called *Milk and Honey* – to Einstein. One day I opened my post at our flat in St John's Wood and found a letter among the others, written in a small hand, in German.

'Look,' I told my wife, 'this chap is also called A. Einstein,' and pushed the letter aside without even bothering to read it properly.

About an hour later, I heard a shriek. My wife appeared with the letter in her hand.

How to be Seventy

'This is not from a chap "also" called A. Einstein. Look at the address.'

To be sure, the address was 112 Mercer Street, Princeton, New Jersey, USA. The letter reads in translation:

15th July, 1951

Dear Mr Mikes,

I have had so much pleasure out of your little book that I cannot resist sending you my special thanks. In all the miseries which plague mankind there is hardly anything better than such radiant humour as is given to you. Everyone must laugh with you, even those who are hit with your little arrows.

Best wishes,
A. Einstein

I answered him in English, apologising that my German was not good enough. I thanked him, of course, for his generous letter and sent him another little book of mine called *Wisdom for Others*. Einstein wrote me a second letter which reads in translation:

16th August, 1951

Dear Mr Mikes,

It was very kind of you to send me your little book, *Wisdom for Others*. Reading it I was, once again, much amused. I found the chapter dealing with Bores particularly well hitting the target, and original. One finds more or less perfect examples of them among one's best friends.

With friendly greetings and thanks,
Yours,
A. Einstein

In 1953 I went to the United States with my wife and daughter. I went to see Einstein with my brother. John Kemeny, who arranged the meeting, was also there.

Two Kings

Einstein, with his tousled snow-white hair, looked like his more extravagant portraits. In addition to being one of the greatest geniuses who ever lived, he was also a kind and friendly man who kept trying to joke with me. (This is a professional hazard for humorists.) I visited him in his house at Princeton. He was worried, indeed, distressed, by the fact that he could not visit New York. Even while he was walking from his car to the entrance of a hotel, he was recognised and mobbed. This preyed upon his mind.

'You don't have any difficulties in Princeton?' I asked him.

'None whatsoever. I walk to the Institute every morning and walk home in the afternoon. I love walking. This is the old German professor in me.'

'It could be the old English professor in you,' I told him.

'It could. People here recognise me, too. Some of them raise their hats. Others say, cheerfully: "Hi, Prof." All this is nice and warm, I appreciate their friendly greetings. They are civilised people, unlike those New Yorkers.'

'The trouble simply is, sir,' I told him, 'that you are the greatest physicist in the world.'

That wouldn't wash.

'All right. I am the greatest physicist. But Niels Bohr is then the second greatest physicist. Yet, if his name is mentioned, people ask: "How do you spell it?" Lucky man. He can move around as he pleases. Why do people, who haven't got the faintest idea about my work, make my life miserable?'

He felt pretty sore about this subject.

The other theme I wish to mention concerns Miss Dukas. She was Einstein's loyal and excellent secretary and assistant. She joined him in Germany and accompanied him into exile. Einstein said that he was not a rich man but would leave all his copyrights to Miss Dukas.

'Why are you smiling?'

I told him that I was not aware of having smiled. But he was aware of it and wanted to know what I was smiling about.

I told him.

'You may have changed humanity's view of itself, our picture of the universe and our concept of time. You have probably changed history, too. But you did all this with three equations. What can poor Miss Dukas do with the copyright of three equations?'

Now he smiled and said: 'Perhaps. But I could not leave her the copyright of *How to be an Alien*.'

What a world! – I thought. But I needn't have worried. Einstein's manuscripts and notes are worth a fortune.

I also told him that I had just finished a tour of Germany, collecting material for a little book called *Uber Alles*. I told Einstein that in 1952 I could not find a Nazi in Germany. Not one single man who would say: 'I see the errors of my ways now. I made a mistake. But yes, I was a Nazi.'

I told him that when I arrived in Bonn I could not get a room anywhere except in a hotel across the bridge. As that hotel was on the wrong side of the Rhine, it was empty, in fact, I was its only guest although Bonn was bursting at the seams. The proprietor became interested in me: he saw my English motorcar, he took messages for me from government departments or the university and, in the end, he asked me what I was doing. I told him. He enquired whether he could help me. I said he could: I wanted to meet a Nazi. A self-confessed Nazi, who admitted that he had been a member of the National Socialist Party and had joined it voluntarily. Oh yes, he would get a Nazi for me. Days passed, and I asked him: what about my Nazi? Yes, yes, he was getting one for me. One day, to be sure, he informed me that I should come back at 11 a.m., 'the Nazi' would be there. I returned as told and the Nazi was waiting for me in the garden. He told me that he had joined the Party voluntarily before it gained power but he discovered in 1933, at the end of the first year of Hitler's rule, that winter help was not distributed fairly – only Nazi party members were helped – and then he left the Party. He would have nothing to do with a Party which failed to distribute help to the poor in a fair and equitable manner.

'So the only Nazi,' I concluded, 'I managed to find after all this search, was a man who *left* the Party in 1933.'

'Because you went about it in the wrong way,' Einstein told me. 'You ought to have drawn up a few criteria and everyone who fell within your definition was a Nazi.'

Two Kings

'With great respect, sir,' I replied, 'that is the physicist's approach. I am only a simple journalist. I knew I could find people in Germany whom *I* would call Nazis. I was keen on meeting one who would call *himself* a Nazi.'

'That will come, too. But you have to wait a few years for that,' he said prophetically.

John Kemeny told me later that one day Einstein informed him that Bertrand Russell was coming to stay with him for a few days. John was excited, not only because it is a treat to be in the company of two such great men (although two great writers, when together, often discuss nothing but publishers and income tax) but also because Russell was the founder of mathematical logic, John's own subject. He prepared a number of questions in writing on various problems but when he put them to Russell, the great man shook his head and said: 'I have no idea. I have not kept it up. I just don't know what's going on in mathematical logic.' (Just as Columbus would know little about modern America.)

It was in connection with the publication of my book on the United States, *How to Scrape Skies*, that I got, once in my life, into personal contact with the royal family.

It turned out that the publication of my book in 1948 was scheduled for the day when the King and the Queen celebrated their silver wedding. Someone had the idea that I should send a copy to the royal couple. I hesitated a little but as everybody else thought it a wonderful idea, I agreed to it. I asked a friend, a court correspondent, how this should be done. He explained that one could not just send a book to the King, one had to ask permission first. If I got permission – he went on – I must not write anything in the book itself but I might write an accompanying note. I followed my friend's advice and soon enough I received a reply from the King's Private Secretary, telling me that the King (*sic* – not 'His Majesty') would be pleased to receive my book. It should be sent – the letter explained – to 'The King, Buckingham Palace,

How to be Seventy

S.W.1.' I loved that 'S.W.1' bit. Probably it was put in to avoid confusion; lest my book be sent to another King in another Buckingham Palace in Brixton or Woodford. Or in case the Post Office was not sure where to find Buckingham Palace.

The packing department of my publisher's spent a considerable time in finding a copy fit for a king but, in the end, the book with my accompanying letter was delivered to Buckingham Palace, S.W.1. by a messenger. As I had just become naturalised, I signed my letter: 'Your most loyal and most recent subject.' I got a letter from the Private Secretary, stating that the King had received my book and was looking forward to reading it. I thought that was the end of the matter; but it wasn't.

On the day of the Silver Wedding (and of publication) a paragraph appeared in the *Evening Standard*'s Londoner's Diary saying that I had offered a copy of my new book to the King who invited me to the Palace and had a long chat with me.

I was shocked. As a journalist I must have shocked other people on many occasions but this was the first time that 'the press' shocked me. Not only was the story distorted and blown up into something more significant than it really was, but it looked as if I myself had used the King's kindness for self-advertisement. I wrote a letter to the King's Private Secretary explaining that I was innocent, and that I regretted that untrue paragraph very much indeed.

I got a reply from the Private Secretary by return of post. The letter said that the King had instructed the P.S. to say that he, the King, had been much too busy on that day to read the *Evening Standard*. In any case, the King suggested that I should not worry because I was not the first, nor alas the last, person to suffer because of the indiscretions of the press. It was a most generous letter. I felt inclined to write back to tell the King that I knew a thing or two about the indiscretions of the press because I had committed one or two myself (indiscretions yes, untrue reporting never – not knowingly, at least) but I thought that no reply from me was called for and that the correspondence should come to an end. But I was wrong once again.

A few weeks later I received an invitation to one of the royal Silver Wedding garden parties. I duly appeared with my wife, and

Two Kings

wearing an elegant Moss Bros outfit complete with top hat. I felt a bit of a fool and swore that I would never again wear a morning coat, let alone a top hat, and I never did. Before leaving for the Palace, in my battered old Ford car which did not have even a starter and had to be cranked with a handle, my wife told me: 'I have never stolen anything in my life, but today I shall steal a silver spoon.'

But she did not. All the spoons – silver or otherwise – were engraved: *J. Lyons & Co.*

The Mogul

A few words on the Mogul, Alexander Korda. I did not know him intimately, but well enough to add a footnote or two to the Korda legend. I was a bit suspicious of him. Although his entourage included eminent and able Hungarians – Lajos Biró and Emeric Pressburger, just to mention two out of many – there were always a number of good-for-nothings, spongers and hangers-on around him and I had a horror of being ranked among them. Besides he preferred, on the whole, courtiers and flatterers to friends and he was prone to drop these favourites from one day to the next. I had to face my shortcomings and realise that I was not a good courtier. Nevertheless, in later years, every now and then he invited me for lunch.

Once we were talking of his preference for Hungarians and he reminded me of the famous notice he had once put up in his Hollywood office: 'It's not enough to be Hungarian.'

'But that wasn't really true,' I told him. 'It *was* enough to be Hungarian.'

After a moment's reflection, he agreed with me: 'Yes. I am afraid it was.'

Once I went to see him in his office and he asked me how my wife was. He was, of course, enquiring after Isobel who had been his secretary for years, but that was all in the past and now Lea had been my wife for quite a long time. If someone mentioned my wife, then – perhaps not unreasonably – I thought of my wife. So I told Korda how Lea was but it soon became obvious that we were talking of two different persons. He laughed and told me: 'I give you one piece of good advice for life. I have just broken my own golden rule but it remains a golden rule. *Never* ask anyone how his wife is. No one really minds if you don't. But if you do, more often than not, he will have a new wife. Or else they have

The Mogul

just had a terrible quarrel and he will tell you: "Don't mention that bloody whore to me." Next time you ask how's the bloody whore, but they have made it up in the meantime and he will never speak to you again. Just forget about people's wives.'

The last time I saw him, a few months before his death, he asked me to come to his office at Piccadilly at 12.30. I thought, naively, that we would go out for lunch together as we had done on a few previous occasions. But between the invitation and my appearance he had given up lunching because he wanted to slim. One good meal per day was the best thing for him, he decided. He was the most extravagantly and genuinely generous man I ever met; but he was also the most egocentric. If he had given up lunching, then humanity had given up lunching; if it was best for him to have one meal a day then no one else should have two. So lunch was not even mentioned. I thought of the subject several times between 12.30 and 2.30 but for some reason, unfathomable by now, I failed to tell him that I was still the slave of the obnoxious habit of lunching. We had a lovely chat. He was walking up and down in his office, talking in his lively, amusing and witty way. Suddenly he stopped and said: 'I've noticed that I keep changing my language all the time. I speak to you in English, then I switch to Hungarian, and then switch back to English. Can you explain why?'

'Easily. When you are telling the truth you speak English, when you are telling me a tall story you switch to Hungarian.'

He laughed aloud. When a few months later I read his obituary in *The Times* I read this remark quoted with the introductory words: 'He was fond of saying about himself . . .'

He was welcome to it. But he could have given me lunch in exchange.

Our Cricketing Career

'Our' means Vicky and me.

I met the cartoonist Vicky in the late forties in unusual circumstances: he interviewed me for a BBC radio programme. *I* was the journalist and *I* should have interviewed him. As far as I know, apart from that series he never made interviews. In any case, I was delighted to meet him. I had heard that he was Hungarian so I tried to speak to him in Hungarian but he knew only a few words of the language. His father, Mr Weisz, emigrated from Hungary to Berlin and became the president of the Hungarian Association, but his son never learnt the lingo. (If you do not speak it, it is a lingo; if you do speak it, it is raised to the rank of language.)

Vicky was tiny, rotund and bald, very amiable and delightful company. After our interview we went to have a cup of coffee at the nearby Quality Inn. He asked me whether, after finishing a book or even an article, I didn't always have the feeling that I would not be able to write another line again. I was surprised by this question. I did not know yet that he was touching upon the central problem – the main neurosis – of his life. So I told him that no, I did not have that feeling. Didn't I feel, seeing my work in print, that it was bloody awful, practically unreadable? I told him that when I finished a book, I was usually pleased with it. Then a few months later I received the proofs and they plunged me into despair. I always find my book, at that stage, silly, badly written, pointless and unreadable. The publisher ought to have warned me, he obviously means to destroy me as a writer. When the book is published, I can't face it and push it aside unread. A few months later I reread it and then I can form a more or less objective view of it: sometimes I still think that it has not come off, sometimes I think it is not too bad and occasionally I am even

Our Cricketing Career

pleased with it. But now I know, I added, that proofs always put me into a nervous and paranoid state, so I accept it as a phase and do not attach too great an importance to the matter. Vicky listened to me with tense interest. Having finished a cartoon, he told me, he had the feeling – in fact, the strong conviction – that he would never have another idea for a drawing. But he must know, having been a successful professional for many years, that he *did* have ideas and he had nothing to fear? Just as I knew in spite of my horror of proof-reading that whatever I might feel at that stage, the book might indeed be bad but it might also be quite good? No, he shook his head. Every morning he came here, to this Quality Inn. He waited outside the door, with all the daily papers under his arm, for the opening at seven o'clock. By 7.20 he usually had an idea for his daily cartoon. Did he not feel relieved then? I asked. He looked at me as though I had asked a most idiotic question. Relieved? No. How could he feel relieved when he knew that that was the last cartoon of his life?

I saw a great deal of Vicky in subsequent years. Our love-hate relationship with the English, our feeling like eternal foreigners in this country we both loved, probably formed a close and special bond between us. It was Vicky who first told the story which has become a well-known joke: in those crisis-ridden, pre-war days he saw a headline in the *Evening Standard*: ENGLAND IN DANGER. He rushed to buy a paper to find that England was in danger of being bowled out by the Australians. (Few people worried in those complacent days about the danger of England being bowled out by the Nazis.)

A few years after we met, Vicky got into trouble with the editor of the *News Chronicle*. His cartoons became too left-wing for the editor's liking and as they deviated from the general policy line of the paper, Vicky was in constant dispute with Mr Cruikshank. He decided not to publish a daily cartoon but to illustrate – once a week – an article to be written by me. Our first assignment was to go to the by now famous test-match, England v. Australia in 1953. Neither of us had ever seen a cricket match before and we regarded cricket as an English eccentricity, a closed book to foreigners, a dark secret hardly worth solving. We were taken out to the Oval by Brian Chapman, assistant editor of the *News*

How to be Seventy

Chronicle. Sitting in the press box Brian explained a few elementary things about batsmen and fielding and maiden overs and wicket-keepers, when I suddenly exclaimed, in a worried tone: 'Where is the other wicket keeper?'

I expected to see two wicket keepers as one sees two goal-keepers at football matches. Chapman turned to me and told me in an avuncular but pained voice: 'My dear George, I realise that you are bound to ask a few surprising questions. But look here ... that is John Arlott there ... this is Neville Cardus ... So please whenever you have a question whisper it, for goodness' sake, don't shout!'

The day was a great one for English cricket. We went on the fourth day and it became obvious, almost inevitable, barring disasters or bad weather on the next day – that the English would regain the Ashes. Brian Chapman, a cricket maniac, was indignant: he had been watching cricket all his life and we, Vicky and I, went out to see our first match and happened to hit on one of the most glorious days ever. As if it mattered to us in the least; as if we could tell good cricket from bad cricket. We published our piece next morning and as this day of euphoria was the one day when you could make fun of that sacred subject, our piece went down quite well. Vicky's drawings were magnificent.

But something quite unexpected happened. I got bitten by the cricket bug and became interested in the match. The fifth day was supposed (and indeed turned out) to be sheer formality but I returned to the Oval.

Vicky phoned me up to discuss our piece and was told by my wife that I was out. Vicky, smelling a rat, asked a question he would not normally ask: 'Where is he?'

'Well,' Lea replied, 'he's gone back to the Oval to watch cricket.'

Vicky did not quite take it in: 'But he didn't *have* to.'

'No, he went on his own accord.'

There was a few seconds of deadly silence at the other end of the line.

'Traitor!' Vicky shouted and banged the receiver down.

I could never live it down. He often remarked, most contemptu-ously, that I was the man who had gone to watch cricket for pleasure. If he had known how many times I repeated my dastardly crime he would not have spoken to me at all.

Soon after our cricket experience we were sent together to watch that famous football match between Hungary and England, somewhat flamboyantly to be called 'the match of the century'. The Hungarians were then on top of the football world: the English thought that was all rubbish and were – as they had never been beaten on English soil – determined to teach the upstarts a lesson. There was great excitement about the match for weeks beforehand but, at first, I could not get worked up about it. A few days before the match Arthur Koestler asked me which side I supported. I had never been in any doubt about it: 'I am a British subject now, I am supporting my own side.'

Koestler disagreed: 'Patriotism is one thing; football-patriotism quite another.'

On the day of the match Vicky and I were picked up by a huge black car and we went to pick up, in turn, Brian Chapman from a restaurant near Sloane Square. He got in, together with the football correspondent of the *Daily Herald*. Brian started teasing us: those famous Hungarians would be taught a lesson today which they would never forget. England would beat the hell out of them. *Daily Herald* agreed, most enthusiastically. I protested, and this argument began to bring out the Hungarian patriot in Vicky and me. Just wait and see, we said cautiously. Very well, said Brian, would we care to bet? Yes, we would. We bet quite a lot on it – Vicky and I against Chapman. But this was not enough for Brian. Would we like to put an extra quid on each goal? Yes, we would like to. But Chapman was still not satisfied. Would we care to name a Hungarian player, and he would name an English one? There should be extra bets on goals shot by these named players. As Puskás was the only name we had ever heard, we named Puskás; he named Sewell. (We ought to have named Hidegkuti, he put in three; Puskás only two.) By the time we reached Wembley Vicky and I were ardent Hungarian football-patriots.

The match started and the Hungarians (Hidegkuti) shot a goal in the first minute, even before the English (including Sewell) touched the ball. Vicky and I stood up and applauded. One does not applaud in the press box and most certainly not the enemy. But people in the box informed each other that it was 'only Vicky and Mikes' and that calmed them down. We didn't really count. The Hungarians won the game 6–3 (and the return match, later in Budapest 7–1). The ebullient Brian was conspicuously silent on the way back and *Daily Herald* declared that he was a Scot, consequently neutral. A few days after the match I received Brian's cheque, accompanied by a mock anonymous letter, telling me in red capital letters: 'Dirty Hungarian Pig Go Home.' I replied that alas I was as unwelcome at home as I seemed to be here, so I could not oblige. Vicky and I, however, invited him for lunch to the Hungarian Csárda in Dean Street, remarking in our letter of invitation that we hoped he would enjoy Hungarian food as much as he had enjoyed Hungarian football. He informed us later that he had tried both and there was no comparison between the two.

Vicky's relationship with the editor of the *News Chronicle* deteriorated and he left the paper. He consulted his friends, first among them Sir Gerald Barry, what to do next. He had two offers: he could join the *Daily Mirror* or the *Evening Standard*. Barry told him to choose the *Standard*: so did I; so did all his other friends. Upon which he joined the *Mirror*. He said he was a socialist and it was his duty to join a socialist paper.

Phil Zec, a *Mirror* director and a cartoonist himself, invited both of us for lunch to the Savage Club. We met in the bar and Zec asked Vicky what would he have.

'A brandy,' Vicky replied, as always.

Zec was taken aback: 'Brandy? *Before* lunch?'

'Brandy before lunch,' Vicky replied.

Zec shrugged his shoulders and remarked: 'Very well. I suppose you can always have a minestrone after your coffee.'

When we reached the coffee-minestrone stage, he asked us to continue our partnership in the *Mirror*. I declined with thanks. I am a great intellectual snob and working for the *Mirror* did not attract me. Besides, I was certain that I would not last there longer than a fortnight. I always fail whenever I try to be 'popular'.

Our Cricketing Career

'Why not?' asked Zec.

'First of all,' I replied, 'nobody reads the *Mirror*.'

Phil Zec blew up.

'You bloody, conceited, arrogant intellectuals! About twenty million people read the *Mirror* daily, and to you they are "nobody"!'

He added: 'But you are all after money. And we have the money. We can buy you if we want to.'

I resolved then and there that I would not be 'bought', whatever phenomenal fees might be offered. My noble resolution was quite pointless. He offered nothing; he never returned to the subject.

I met Vicky about two months later. He asked me: 'Do you remember what you said to Phil about nobody reading the *Mirror*?'

'I do.'

'Well, nobody *does* read the *Mirror*.'

He drew a daily piece for the *Mirror* (circulation about five million) and a weekly piece for the *New Statesman* (circulation 80,000). Everybody he met congratulated him on his *New Statesman* piece but he never met anyone outside Fleet Street who even mentioned his pieces in the *Mirror*. *Mirror* readers were not interested in him, he worked in a vacuum and he felt he was a failure there. (A feeling never too far from his soul.) *Mirror* readers knew that Page Three was occupied by a cartoon, dead loss of space for most of them; Vicky was thoroughly miserable. After a five year stint on the *Mirror* he joined the *Standard*, which gave him perfect freedom and the more he annoyed readers the happier the editor was. Vicky, too, was as happy as his neurotic fear that his latest cartoon was also his last permitted him to be.

The last time I saw him he made a terrifying effect on me. He asked me to come to lunch with him but explained that we must lunch somewhere in the City because he had to remain near the office. He named a restaurant. He came late – a very unusual thing for him – and was obviously under great stress. We ordered our lunch. Vicky was having his soup when someone came in, sat down at the next table, opened the *Standard* and we could read the headlines. Vicky put his spoon down.

How to be Seventy

'Excuse me,' he said, 'but I must go back to the office to do a fresh cartoon on that.'

I failed to see the point. I told him that there was a perfectly good Vicky cartoon in an earlier edition. I also told him that the new headline was really nothing, a commonplace event blown up. He would not listen. He was sorry but he had to go. I should finish my lunch, I must be his guest but he had to go straight away. And he left. I looked at the *Standard*'s later editions, and his original drawing had not been replaced.

Soon afterwards I heard that Vicky had remarried and was very happy with his charming new wife. In those days I often visited Eustace Chesser, the psychoanalyst. We planned a book together – a lighthearted one on psychoanalysis – and Chesser said that I must go through at least a brief analysis in order to know what we were talking about. I lay on his couch and he asked the first question: 'Did you have a happy childhood?'

'I am still having a happy childhood,' I replied.

Then, session after session, twice a week, I lay on that couch and Eustace spoke to me about *his* childhood, about *his* problems and dreams. I just lay there, listening to him. Four months later I told him I knew enough about his methods.

'Don't you think you need a little more treatment?' he asked.

'I don't. But if you feel that *you* need a little more treatment, I won't refuse.'

It was all very pleasant, we both enjoyed it. After one session I suddenly felt a strong urge to visit Vicky who lived almost opposite Chesser. It had never occurred to me to go and see him but this time the impulse was almost irresistible: I had heard how happy and content he was and I was keen on seeing a happy and content Vicky, having seen that miserable and distraught man in the City restaurant. I walked over to his house in Upper Wimpole Street, my finger was already on the bell when I changed my mind. I dislike it so much when people appear on my doorstep unannounced that I decided, after all, not to inflict myself on Vicky.

Just as well. Vicky had taken an overdose of sleeping tablets and was lying dead in his flat.

Daylight at Midnight

At the end of 1952 I wrote a long article on the Hungarian poet, Ady, for *The Times Literary Supplement*. Ady was a giant, a revolutionary both in the literary and in the political sense, and the seventy-fifth anniversary of his birth was being celebrated. (He died in 1919, at the age of forty-two.) Soon after the publication of that piece I left with my wife and daughter Judy for the United States. There I received a letter from the editor of *The Times Literary Supplement*, Alan Pryce-Jones, who, in turn had had a letter from Arthur Koestler, expressing his desire to meet the author of the article on Ady. But – Alan's letter told me – all articles in the TLS were strictly anonymous so he could not reveal my name to Koestler without my permission.

I wrote back to Alan, telling him (as I was several times to tell his successor, Arthur Crook) that anonymity was *their* rule, not mine. Contributors would be delighted to see their names above their articles, instead of being compelled to scurry round whispering in as many ears as possible that they had written this piece or that. (Often they republished their TLS essays in book-form, expressing their gratitude to the Editor of the TLS for permission to reprint, and then the secret was out in any case.) The rule of anonymity was finally ended by John Gross, Arthur Crook's successor – and I confess that although I agree with his sensible decision, I do rather miss the fun and mystery of the past.

On getting back from the United States I phoned Koestler. We talked English. Funnily enough, for Hungarians to talk Hungarian when in England implies a certain familiarity – it seems, perhaps, an intrusion on privacy. He asked me where he could meet me and I told him that I would come to his house.

'Why should you come to me when I want something from you?' he asked.

How to be Seventy

I replied that I would like to come along, all the same, and we made an appointment. Koestler has described in his autobiography his meetings with Sigmund Freud and Thomas Mann, and the way they proved rather disappointing because he was so tense and over-awed. I had more or less the same feelings of awe towards him. Much later I was to hear him give an excellent description of the let-down which can come when one meets an idol for the first time. I was at his house for dinner when a gushing young American woman – an unknown admirer with a letter of introduction – came in for a drink. On and on she went about how delighted she was to be there; how meeting him was the dream of her life and so on, when he broke in with these pithy words: 'Liking a writer and then meeting the writer is like liking goose-liver and then meeting the goose.'

But to return to our first meeting. He lived and still lives in a large house near Knightsbridge. He had an entry-phone, a great rarity in those days in London. I pushed the bell and was quite taken aback when a stentorian voice with a heavy accent asked me through a loudspeaker who I was. When I told him my name, he gave a buzz which opened the door and asked me to come up to the fourth floor, to his study. He came down at the same time to greet me. We met half way. He talked to me in Hungarian now, just a few polite sentences, small talk. His Hungarian was halting, he kept stopping and searching for words.

'You must forgive me,' he said, 'but I haven't spoken Hungarian for years.'

'Let's speak English if it is easier for you,' I suggested.

He replied with a broad grin: 'Mikes, you and I should sit here together, on a fourth floor in Knightsbridge and *we* should speak English? Impossible!'

It was that moment that I realised that this great writer was also a very likeable man.

The reason he wanted to see me was Attila József. Attila was the one poetic genius Hungary produced after Ady's death. He was a close friend of Arthur's and a friend – although not so close – of mine. When Koestler visited Hungary in 1933 he spent a great deal of his time with Attila. The poet was a Trotskyite, Koestler an orthodox Communist and they quarrelled a lot. Koestler tried to

Daylight at Midnight

convert Attila to orthodoxy but he failed.

Once I met Attila in a Budapest coffee-house and he told me that he was, as usual, broke. He would not accept a loan from me but he gave me three unpublished poems. 'You are friendly with those bourgeois editors,' he said, 'try to do something with them.' My own editor threw me out and told me that I ought to be investigating scandals, not hobnobbing with bloody Communists. The editor of *Pesti Napló* accepted one of the three poems, emphasising that he was doing so for my sake and not for the sake of that bloody Communist. The poem is recited today by every schoolboy. Attila himself became mentally ill, suffered from schizophrenia and committed suicide by throwing himself between the wheels of a fast-moving goods train, four years after Koestler's visit to Budapest.

We both agreed that Attila was an outstanding poetical genius. Arthur had translated some of his poems into English and wondered whether we should not do together a whole volume of translations. We agreed that we would give the idea a try. A rather hectic period followed. It would be an exaggeration to say that we failed to do any other work; but a slight exaggeration only. We rang each other up several times a day exclaiming: 'Listen to this!' The other had to listen. Although Arthur was convinced that no publisher would be so foolish as to be interested in the book, both mine – André Deutsch – and his – Hutchinsons – were ready to go ahead. But excited though we were by our work, we had a few lingering doubts and we needed reassurance.

Auden had just been appointed professor of poetry at Oxford and Arthur rang various university numbers there, to find out how to contact his old friend. None of them had ever heard the name of Auden. I don't know which colleges he tried, or who the people were who answered his calls, but I do know he had to spell the name a dozen times and even so no one knew who this gentleman called Auden might be. He gave it up on that occasion, but managed to get in touch with Auden a week or so later and handed over our translations, asking him whether they convinced him that the originals were true masterpieces. Auden briefly and courteously replied that he remained unconvinced, and that was the end of our plans. Some of Arthur's – to my mind very good – translations appeared in his autobiography, in which almost a whole chapter is dedicated to Attila.

Koestler and I have spent quite a lot of time together and a few small incidents made unforgettable impressions on me. In one of his books he remarked that most people suffer from an inferiority complex and if most people's complexes are little houses, his is a cathedral. Once we were sitting in his study, working on our translations at his desk, on which the telephone was placed. Two ladies, my wife and a Swedish literary agent, were sitting on the sofa by the wall. The Swedish lady spoke impeccable, accentless English and my wife has only a very slight accent. Usually, after finishing our work, we went down to his kitchen, raided the fridge and had a delicious, improvised meal, but this time Arthur suggested that we should go out. We picked a restaurant and then Arthur asked the Swedish lady to phone and reserve a table. The phone was right in front of him and me, so she must have thought the request a bit odd and did not respond. Five minutes later Arthur asked my wife to phone. She also failed to respond for the same reason. Another five minutes later he turned to me and asked *me* to phone. I was puzzled and said: 'I'll phone with pleasure. But why don't you just pick up the receiver and book a table yourself?'

'What sort of table are we going to get if I ring up with *my* accent?' he asked.

'You'll get the best table, of course,' I replied, 'and the proprietor will put out a notice in his window: "Arthur Koestler is dining here." '

He gave me a disapproving look and announced: 'We'll stay at home.'

At 3 o'clock in the morning, on the 24th October 1956, Arthur telephoned me. He told me that he was with a Hungarian journalist and I should get up and join them straight away. All right, I said, if they insisted – but would he tell me why? They had a few bricks on them, he explained, and they were going to throw them through the windows of the Hungarian Legation and thought I would like to join them. 'If you are going to throw bricks, I certainly want to throw a few, too,' said I, 'but what is the aim of the exercise?' He was slowly losing his temper with me but

Daylight at Midnight

replied politely. The bricks, he told me, would draw attention to the Hungarian Revolution, which had broken out about twelve hours earlier. I repeated that I would come along if they insisted on their plan, but as all the papers had published the news from Hungary on their front pages, with banner headlines, and as radio and television had been discussing almost nothing else, I failed to see the necessity of 'drawing attention' to the revolution. The Hungarian revolutionaries had already drawn all the attention there was. On the other hand, if we wanted to draw attention to ourselves . . . This was unfair, as Arthur not only does not want but positively abhors personal publicity.

'Damn you,' he said, 'and your calmness even on such a day. All right, we'll speak tomorrow.'

Next day we read in the papers that unknown people had thrown thirteen bricks through the windows of the Hungarian Legation.

On the afternoon of the 24th October we had a discussion. Koestler suggested that we should arrange a public meeting. We hired Denison Hall, near Victoria Station, and on Saturday evening – the night before our meeting – Arthur suggested that I ring up the local police station and ask them to send a constable in case Communists should try to disrupt our meeting. I did as I was told and detected a slight amusement in the voice of the police officer who answered the phone. Next day we could hardly reach Denison Hall. The neighbourhood of Victoria Station was cluttered up with cars, motor-bikes and people. Several thousand people were trying to get into the hall and about a hundred policemen were desperately trying to control the crowd. Jacob Epstein, J. B. Priestley and Koestler sat on the podium among others; Henry Green, Hugh Seton-Watson and I were the speakers. Press, television and radio were there and everybody wanted to hear Koestler. They shouted his name more and more vociferously, but he remained seated. At last he stood up and explained that in his latest book he had declared that he would not write or speak on political subjects and he could not possibly break his vow.

Next day I travelled to Hungary with a Panorama team.

It is sometimes said that Koestler is a difficult, stubborn,

How to be Seventy

opinionated and quarrelsome man. I suspect that occasionally he can be all that, but I personally have always found him kind, compassionate, courteous, good tempered and extremely funny, whenever he meant to be. He does carry the world's troubles on his shoulders and public affairs upset him more than private worries. Perhaps he quarrels with people who are better at quarrelling than I. Perhaps I am below his class, so that it is just no fun to quarrel with me; perhaps, even after so many years of friendship, I haven't lost my deep respect for him. Perhaps it is the influence of Cynthia, his angelic wife (and secretary, nurse, daughter, mother, cook, companion, lady of the house – everything a man can dream of). Whatever the reason, I have never heard an unpleasant word from him.

When Koestler was seventy (in 1975), I was President of the PEN Club's Writers in Exile Branch. Our group invited Solzhenitsyn to come to London. He accepted our invitation on condition that we did not make it public. He explained that he meant to spend a few days in London incognito. The request puzzled me, coming from a man who wore one of the best known faces in the world and had a beard into the bargain, making recognition even easier. I asked him if he would shave his beard off. No, he would not, he said.

He did spend a whole week here incognito. His publishers supplied him with a car and a chauffeur but he hardly ever used the car and took buses and the underground everywhere, or just walked. I asked him whether he had been mobbed?

'Mobbed?' he said. 'No one even recognised me. They don't know that I'm here so they do not expect to meet me.'

'But surely people look at you and looking at you they *must* recognise your face.'

'Occasionally I detect the light of recognition in people's eyes but they dismiss the thought. I can read what's going on in their minds: this chap looks like Solzhenitsyn but he is not in London so he cannot be Solzhenitsyn. Even if he were in London he would not be on the top of a bus or travelling by the tube. So this chap cannot be him. It's logical.'

Before Solzhenitsyn arrived, I meant to arrange an anniversary PEN Club dinner-party in Koestler's honour. I wanted Solzhenitsyn

Daylight at Midnight

to propose the toast. Koestler seemed to be tempted but he hesitated. In the end he gave in: 'All right. In this case my vanity is stronger than my horror of such occasions.'

I asked Solzhenitsyn to come along and deliver the main speech of the evening. I repeated Koestler's remark to him. He smiled: 'I have a high regard for Arthur Koestler but even in this case my horror of such occasions is greater than my vanity.'

Koestler started his writing career as a Hungarian poet. There was a boys' paper in Hungary, called *Én Ujságom* (sort of 'Boys' Own') which we all read avidly. We loved and revered its editor, Lajos Pósa. Koestler was nine years old when the First World War broke out. Soon afterwards the Hungarian army occupied Belgrade, the capital of Serbia – the country regarded as responsible for the assassination of Francis Ferdinand. This was a moment of national glory and it inspired Koestler to write a poem which he is able to recite even today. The poem is bloody awful even for a nine-year-old. He sent it in to *Én Ujságom*. Lajos Pósa sent it back with the remark that while Arthur's patriotic zeal was laudable, it was, alas, only too obvious that he had no talent whatsoever for writing.

Arthur Koestler is still not published in Hungary. Lajos Pósa's verdict seems to be still regarded there as valid.

Revolution

In the mid-fifties I started working regularly for Panorama, the BBC television magazine. On one occasion I got into one of those national rumpuses television was apt to generate in those days. It broke out on a Tuesday, the morning after transmission, raged for two days and was forgotten before the next Panorama was transmitted. I visited two of our sea-side resorts and drew a parallel between the honest vulgarity of Southend and the shabby gentility of Bournemouth, favouring Southend all the way. The somewhat unexpected result was that Bournemouth was delighted and Southend deeply offended. A Southend official declared that Southend was a high class resort, it was only the day-trippers who spoilt and vulgarised it. This, in turn, incensed the day trippers and the chairman of the Day Trippers Union (or some such body) declared that if they were regarded as vulgar, they would not go to Southend any more. (Perhaps to Bournemouth, instead.) Southend protested to the Director General of the BBC and newspapers kept ringing me up but I, of course, was not allowed to comment, the quarrel being between Southend and the BBC. The Director General Sir Ian Jacob (a retired general, who used to be my boss at Bush House) sent a message to me through his secretary, telling me that I should not worry. I was not worrying, but it was a generous gesture. (Jacob was a remarkable man. When he became Director General he went around Bush House and about eight hundred people were introduced to him on one day, I among them. About a fortnight later I met him in the Savoy, at a lunch of the Foreign Press Association. I saw him at the bar but decided not to greet him as I hate to seem to be flattering bosses. But he came up to me and said: 'I think, Mikes, you must be one of my hosts here.' To remember me, remember my name, and to know that I was

Revolution

likely to be a member of the FPA is proof of a quite remarkable memory of the kind given only to royalty, generals and barbers.)

When the Hungarian Revolution broke out Panorama sent me to Hungary to film it. Charles Wheeler was the producer, Tubby Englander the cameraman. Before leaving I was interviewed on Panorama by a new boy on the programme called Malcolm Muggeridge, and I remember Malcolm telling me then that I would be the first person he had ever interviewed on television. I reminded him of this twenty-three years later, when I was chairman at a talk he was giving to the English PEN. He corrected me and said that I was, in fact, the second person he interviewed, the first being Billy Graham, the evangelist. I did not argue. Perhaps he was right. Even if he was not, who am I to stand between Saint Mugg and Saint Billy?

In Vienna we, the whole BBC team, went to the Hungarian Legation in order to obtain a visa, but no one came to the door when we rang. There was not even a porter for us to talk to. As the unfortunate Hungarian envoy could not possibly know whether he still *was* the Hungarian envoy, I could not blame him for this cautious attitude.

Next morning we drove to the Hungarian border. The notorious AVO – political police – guarded the frontiers too and the man in charge flatly refused to let us in. I mentioned the extraordinary circumstances but he told me he knew nothing about extraordinary circumstances. I told him that we had tried to get a visa but there was no one at the Hungarian Legation in Vienna. He replied that this was not his problem. Without a visa we could not cross the frontier and that was that. At that moment a lorry-load of revolutionaries arrived, on their way to Austria to collect medical supplies. In Budapest revolutionaries hanged AVO men but here the relationship seemed to be quite cordial. The leader of the freedom fighters and the AVO man were on Christian-name terms but the AVO man was obviously frightened of the revolutionaries.

The leader enquired who we were. I introduced myself and told him that I had come from London to report on the events inside Hungary.

How to be Seventy

'But Jóska (Joe),' said the leader, 'surely you will not stop Mr Mikes from the BBC?'

'Of course not,' replied the AVO man in enthusiastic agreement.

'He is most welcome,' said the revolutionary.

'He most certainly is,' echoed the AVO man.

'Thank you very much,' said I. 'Thanks to both of you. There is, however, a small problem.'

'What is it?' asked the freedom fighter.

'I am not alone. There are my colleagues outside – from BBC television.'

'BBC television?' asked the revolutionary, genuinely astonished. 'Does the BBC also have a television service? Whatever for?'

I was delighted. Having been asked so often in London 'Good God, does the BBC also have a Hungarian Service? Whatever for?' I felt that the clock had turned full circle. It was my total vindication. For these people the BBC was the Hungarian Service alone – to which they had been listening during the war and the days of Communist tyranny, sometimes risking their lives for so doing – and the rest was superficial luxury.

I should not like to give the impression that my recollections of the Hungarian Revolution consist of anecdotes only. Far from it. It was a great and inspiring event, one of the greatest of post-war history and I, rather a cold fish in most circumstances, was deeply moved by it. I published a book about it, *The Hungarian Revolution* (André Deutsch, 1957), and anyone interested in these events can have a look at the book in a library. I came face to face with the people who had shaken off a powerful foreign and domestic tyranny without any outside help – and I was proud of my former compatriots.

Here, however, I wish to recall only two further events.

After the initial difficulties, we crossed the frontier daily without any trouble at all. The AVO man just saluted and waved us on. We had to return to Vienna every evening because there was a general strike in Hungary, the post did not function and we had to send our material to London every day. The last time we recrossed the frontier from Hungary into Austria was on Saturday, 3rd November. Shortly afterwards the frontiers were closed, and at dawn on Sunday the Russians opened fire and

Revolution

their tanks started rolling back into Hungary. It was owing to no foresight or premonition on our part that we left practically in the last minute. We had to leave on Saturday because Panorama was being transmitted on Monday. If Tuesday had been Panorama day, we would have been caught.

I returned to Austria on several occasions, mostly to interview refugees. A few people, quite wrongly, call me a good man. I am a misleading phenomenon and look a better man than I really am. But I have performed two really good deeds in my life. One was to my second cat, Ginger – he was chucked out in mid-winter by my neighbour, his previous owner, and he would have frozen to death and starved if I had not taken him in. The other was to a pair of human beings, a married couple.

In 1955 I went to Wells, in Austria, and wrote two articles for the *Observer* about refugee camps there. The little series was called 'Forgotten People'. Refugee camps are rarely cheerful places but the Wells camps were particularly dismal and heart-breaking, full of human wrecks and rejects. Most of the inhabitants were Yugoslavs but there were quite a few Romanians, Hungarians and Bulgarians among them. They were nearly all sick and elderly. The young and healthy ones, particularly those with useful skills, were picked out and sent to the United States, Canada, Australia and other desirable countries. Only Sweden took a number of sick or blind people; for the others 'helping refugees' meant helping themselves to a few well-trained and much needed specialists. Many of the people I met at Wells had been there for years and few had any hope of getting out. A few were still optimists, collecting documents busily and visiting consulates, only to be told that more and more documents were needed, or to be turned away with a few kind words. Or unkind words.

One day after the Revolution I travelled to the Hungarian frontier and stopped at the bridge at Andau. It was not much of a bridge any more. It was broken down and people waded through the mud to reach Austrian soil. There had been an invasion of people, a veritable flood, but by the time I got there, the flood had dwindled to a trickle. But people kept arriving. I stood there, watching them wading through the mud, exhausted, almost collapsing, yet happy. Suddenly someone standing on the bank beside me greeted me by name. It was an old man and he asked me if I remembered him. No, sorry, I did not. He was Mr Horváth. The name did not mean a thing to me – it is a very common name in Hungary. He reminded me that we had met in Wells. Then I remembered all right. 'Forgotten People', I thought; I had forgotten them just as everybody else did. How was his wife? I asked him. She was there – and he pointed to a frail little woman, standing a few steps away. He dragged out a huge pile of documents from his pocket.

'I've got almost everything now,' he told me proudly. 'Just one more to come. Perhaps two. They won't be too difficult to obtain. Then we are off to Cleveland, at last.'

Two more documents, I thought. How often had I heard that. Then two more. And two more. No one ever had enough documents if he was old and sick.

'A very different proposition for those,' he said, looking at the newcomers without bitterness. 'They just come over and are asked: Where do you wish to go? They say: The United States. Or New Zealand. And a week later they are there.'

I told him: 'May I give you some advice, Mr Horváth?'

'What is it?'

'Go back to Hungary.'

He stared at me, obviously thinking that I had gone mad.

'Go back?' he asked with horror.

'Yes. Not too far back. Just cross the frontier here, it is quite easy and not dangerous. Go behind the first bush. And there tear up all your papers. Burning would be better but tearing up will do.'

He still thought I had taken sudden leave of my senses.

'I spent five years collecting these papers.'

'Never mind. Just tear them up. All of them. Don't keep any souvenirs. Not even the most precious ones. When you've got rid of them, come through that bridge – or whatever is left of it . . . through the mud. With your wife. As new refugees. And when they ask you where you wish to go, say Cleveland, Ohio.'

He understood. He looked at his wife – who had come nearer and was listening in. She nodded. A fortnight later I received a

Revolution

postcard from them, from Cleveland, Ohio, USA. And eleven years later I received another postcard from Mrs Horváth, telling me that her husband had just died. He obviously thought that my suggestion – cheating the authorities – had contributed to his last years of happiness in America. I am proud of that misdeed.

I travelled once again to Vienna with Charles Wheeler and Richard Dimbleby. I was to interview Hungarian refugees on Panorama. The refugees wore black masks, so as not to be recognised – a dramatic innovation, invented, I think, by Wheeler.

Richard Dimbleby was standing in front of the Rathaus –Town Hall – from where he was supposed to introduce the programme. We were inside the Rathaus, feeling a little lonely without Richard, who was a real anchor, a tonic, a rock, a good man to have nearby. Then there was a mechanical breakdown of some sort and Richard did not come on. Richard could cope with almost all conceivable emergencies, but even he could not overcome mechanical breakdowns. The rest of the participants were much less experienced, in most cases utter novices. Charles Wheeler was just about to tear out his stupendous crown of hair. This would be the worst Panorama disaster of all times. But everybody realised what had happened and all those beginners, novices and foreigners introduced themselves with the words they had heard at rehearsals, led themselves out and handed over to the next person like old hands, while poor Richard was desperate and impotent outside the Rathaus, unseen by any television viewer. He remarked later that his journey had not been really necessary.

But I was glad that he was there. I shall never forget Richard Dimbleby in Vienna. We arrived on Saturday for Monday's Panorama (Richard and I were travelling together, the others travelled one day earlier). I told the television crew that I knew a splendid Hungarian restaurant and we should go there to have dinner on Saturday.

'You and your wretched Hungarian restaurants,' said Richard. '*Must* we?'

'We must.'

'But I am on a very strict diet,' he insisted.

We went to that excellent Hungarian restaurant and had a delicious dinner. Richard had a splendid appetite. After a first course, a soup and a main dish – all huge portions – I suggested that the others should have a Sacher cake (I eat no sweets, as a rule, and do not like cakes). Richard always stayed in the Sacher Hotel but had never tasted a Sacher Torte. The sweet trolley was rolled to our table. To *look* at a Sacher Torte is 500 calories; to eat one is 5000.

'All right,' Richard gave in, 'I'll try one.'

After the cake I suggested coffee.

Richard said, somewhat hesitantly: 'I wouldn't mind another Sacher Torte.'

He had another 5000 calories. Coffee came at last and I pushed the sugar-bowl towards Richard. He lifted his hand, shook his head firmly and pushed it away again. He put two saccharins into his coffee. Then put a huge spoonful of whipped cream on top of it. A diet, after all, is a diet.

The Decline of Invective

Here comes another character sketch – and in a modest way, another footnote to the Hungarian Revolution, or rather to the effect it made on people.

My wife and I were invited to a Sunday morning party by Rooney Pelletier, Controller of the BBC's Light Programme. Among the guests was Gilbert Harding. We rarely watched television apart from the news and a few news programmes, consequently we often failed to hear even the names of some of the most famous people in the land. It was quite impossible, however, never to have seen Gilbert Harding; he had one of the best-known faces in Britain. When he was introduced, my wife looked at him, scrutinized him carefully and remarked: 'I think I've seen your face somewhere.'

I expected one of his famous rude outbursts but no outburst followed. Instead, Gilbert knelt down and kissed my wife's hand in the best Central European manner. He was delighted that someone did *not* recognise him, did not gape at him and did not even know who he was.

He was lively, quick-witted, amusing but the archetypal 'television personality': not a writer, not a performer, just a personality. I always felt that his greatest asset was his rudeness. Rudeness and command of invective have regrettably declined in Britain. English may be the richest language in the world but it is pitifully poor when it comes to swearing. A Hungarian sergeant major is able to swear at a recruit for three minutes on end without repetition, using the most colourful language and incisive imagery as he tells his victim what to do with his mother and how to do it. And that Hungarian sergeant major is a beginner compared with a Russian sergeant who, in turn, fades into insignificance compared with his Arab counterpart. A

How to be Seventy

country which more than a century later is still proud of Queen Victoria's rude remark 'We are not amused' is not even in the second eleven when it comes to swearing. The British admire rudeness and regard it as evidence of virility because they are taught from early childhood to suppress all their healthy impulses towards it.

Gilbert Harding reaped the benefit of the English longing for a rude hero. Gilbert was the ideal: a genuinely rude man with appalling manners, a master of invective.

During our second meeting he did not kneel down and kiss *my* hand. On the contrary. BBC radio planned a new series. Gilbert Harding and Basil Boothroyd, two very English Englishmen, were to form a panel and interview foreigners – visitors and residents – about their views on England and the English. I was to be the first in the series. Basil Boothroyd described what followed in one of his books.

We met at 9 o'clock in the morning – not the best time to be witty and relaxed. I had the impression that Gilbert had had a few quick ones before arrival. He picked up a glass of water, took a sip, and spat it out angrily on the carpet, shouting: 'This must be the water in which Reith kept his false teeth overnight.'

Not a bad remark but not an auspicious beginning. Fresh – at least slightly fresher – water was brought for him and he was anxious to start and get the whole thing over. But there was some slight hitch caused by the assistant studio manager, a nervous young girl. Gilbert thundered something very personal about her, making a reference to her showing off her tits under her pullover. The girl jumped up and rushed out of the cubicle. Harding's rudeness to this defenceless girl put my back up. I am not a naturally rude man but one can always try, and I did not do badly. During the recording I was very critical of the English and a lot of things in England, and Harding took this personally and became ruder and ruder to me. I reciprocated vigorously and quite enjoyed the duel. I said something about the 'British' and he blew up. There were English, Scots, Welsh and Irish but there were no British. I retorted that being British was an ideal. The others in the studio were only English; I was the one person there who was British. We were so rude, offensive and sometimes

The Decline of Invective

vulgar to each other that they had to abandon not only this first programme, but the whole series.

After the programme Harding wanted to go to the Duty Room. I had no idea why, but we went to the Duty Room, and it turned out that that was the place where drinks could be served.

'Oh, so that's your great devotion to duty,' I said. 'I should have guessed.'

We were given large gins and tonic. I lifted my glass and said: 'Gilbert, I have been very rude to you.'

He, expecting an apology, said mildly: 'Yes, you were.'

'And I meant every word of it. You, of course, were just as rude to me. And if you think that I am going to have drinks and a friendly chat with you, you are bloody well mistaken.'

I banged my glass down and stalked out of the room.

The producer phoned in the afternoon, expressed his full approval and told me that the little assistant studio manager attacked by Harding had suffered a hysterical sobbing attack and had needed to be given an injection by a doctor to calm her down.

When I came back from Hungary, after the Revolution, I took part in a number of television and radio programmes. One day a producer of the Light Programme invited me to come along and take part in a feature. He told me that he wanted four minutes from me on a certain aspect of the problem. The channel would be open, I could come along at any time to record my piece. He added that Gilbert Harding was the anchor man. I hesitated for a moment, but decided that I would not give up professional engagements because of stupid personal quarrels and accepted the invitation to take part.

When I went along I was pleased to find that Harding was not there. I recorded my piece and was about to leave when Rooney Pelletier, the Controller, and Lawrence Gilliam, Head of Features, emerged and told me that Gilbert was sorry for not being here to greet me but he had left a recorded message for me. They played it. He said that he knew how I must feel about events in Hungary and he expressed his sympathy. This was the gist of it, but it was the warmest, kindest, most generous and moving message I ever heard. I was deeply moved. I recorded my thanks and appreciation for his kind words.

How to be Seventy

I often met him after that. We both frequented the Hungarian Csárda, a restaurant in Soho. Whenever we met, he was courtesy and kindness itself. Our erstwhile quarrel was never mentioned. Harding could certainly be a churlish and cantankerous bastard but his kindness and generosity could be equally overwhelming. He was a sad and lonely figure. A master of witty invective and wounding rudeness; an even greater master of the disarming, perfect apology.

Abstract Paintings

For quite a few years – between 1947 and 1970 – I travelled a great deal. I visited the four other Continents and wrote books about most of my journeys. One long journey was to the Far East. The PEN Club arranged a Congress in Tokyo and that enabled me to get there at a reasonable price. I have given a full account of that journey, but there are two broad events I should like to recall.

The actual journey itself was a much longer and more arduous affair in 1957 than it is now. About fifty English writers – Angus Wilson, Stephen Spender and Philip Hope-Wallace among them – boarded the chartered place in London and another ninety or so French writers joined us in Paris. There was little communication between the English and the French, they hardly spoke to one another beyond the absolute necessities and unavoidable courtesies. We flew for three days and two nights (plus a night spent in a Bangkok hotel). I was astonished and amused to see that when each Frenchman woke up in the morning, as soon as he opened his sleepy eyes, he went round and shook hands with every other Frenchmen. All ninety of them shook eighty-nine hands every morning.

During the journey in South East Asia, from Hong Kong through the Philippines to Malaya, I could not avoid being celebrated as a brave and indomitable Hungarian freedom fighter. Paul Ignotus and George Pálóczi-Horváth, two members of our group, were real participants in the revolution, had written articles putting their futures at risk (having been in prison previously), and they had faced grave dangers during the fighting. Paul and Kate Tabori and I – who were travelling together – were often in their company, so we, too, were treated like heroes. It was no use protesting. If you were a Hungarian you were a hero and that was that.

How to be Seventy

Later a small number of Hungarians blotted their copybooks and that changed everything. After doling out all that admiration the world was only too happy to turn against them and start treating every Hungarian as a nuisance and a troublemaker.

Another long journey, once again with the PEN Club, took me to Latin America in 1960. My starting point was Rio de Janeiro where the Congress was held. On the day after our arrival we were invited to a party by the British Council representative. It was a nice party in a beautiful house and we looked forward to the arrival of our most famous colleague, Graham Greene, who had come from Paris under his own steam (I mean not in our chartered plane). We were having our first drink when someone told me that Graham Greene had arrived at the party and was looking for me. I dismissed this as absolute nonsense. I had never met him and I felt pretty sure that he was unaware of my very existence. But when the fifth person informed me that Graham Greene was there and was looking for me I was driven to the conclusion that Graham Greene must be there, and must be looking for me. Suddenly I caught sight of him and I walked up to him and introduced myself.

'Oh yes,' he said, 'I have a letter for you.' He handed it to me. It was written by Marie Schebeko, my French agent. The letter explained that Marie had something urgent to communicate and as she knew that postal services were rather slow and pretty unreliable in South America, she took the opportunity, etc. She went on to say whatever she meant to say and concluded: 'This letter will be given to you by my dear friend, Graham Greene. He is a shy man. But behind the forbidding exterior there is a heart of gold. It's worth while taking the trouble to reach it.'

I read the letter on the spot and having finished it, said to Graham Greene: 'Mr Greene, Marie says that behind your forbidding exterior there is a heart of gold. She also tells me to make an effort to reach it. Time is short here. Do you think we can take a short cut to your heart of gold?'

He replied: 'If you have nothing better to do, wait for me at the end of the party.'

We left together and during the following week I spent a lot of time in the company of a brilliant and amusing man. I discovered

Abstract Paintings

neither shyness nor a golden heart in him. He could be quite devastating on occasions.

One day the whole PEN Congress was invited by some artists' association for lunch and after lunch we were supposed to visit an exhibition. The lunch was outside in the garden, the exhibition inside the house. We were sitting at small tables, Graham Greene not far from me, and we agreed that we would leave together. He stood up at the end of the lunch, looked into my direction, I joined him and we were ready to leave. At the gate a very domineering lady pounced on him.

'But Mr Greene,' she said, 'you can't possibly leave without seeing the exhibition.'

He was annoyed and I told him, not without a *soupçon* of *Schadenfreude*: 'Certainly not, Mr Greene. You *must* see the exhibition. I'll go home now and see you later.'

The school-marm turned to me and said curtly: 'But you can't leave either, Mr Mikes, without seeing the exhibition.'

'Definitely not,' said Graham a little vindictively, and we were led back to see a lot of abstract pictures. They were pretty awful but we made no comment. After going round the room, the lady asked Graham: 'How do you like the pictures, Mr Greene?'

'Not at all,' he replied in a quiet voice.

There was deadly silence for a few seconds. The lady just did not know how to cope with this. Then she found the obvious way out: 'You don't like abstract pictures?'

'I love them,' Graham replied politely.

I had never heard anyone deflated so totally, more courteously and with fewer words.

One day Graham Greene, Alec Waugh and I were invited to lunch with the British Ambassador in Rio. The ambassador was Sir Geoffrey Wallinger, and as he had been Minister to Hungary between 1949 and 1951, which era included the trial of Rajk and Cardinal Mindszenty (particularly horrible times) I was much interested to meet him. We, the three guests, arrived together and were greeted by Lady Wallinger, who was very apologetic and told us that the Ambassador seemed to have been detained. We all said that we understood that perfectly well. Lady Wallinger kept looking at her watch and was obviously a little nervous. She apologised again and Alec told her that the Ambassador must be a busy man and we fully understood. At last he arrived and his own apologies, we thought, were a shade more profuse than the situation warranted. We all felt that thereby hung a tale but we could not ask any questions. But after an excellent lunch accompanied by equally excellent wine and brandy Sir Geoffrey became more relaxed and told us the story.

'I had to see the Brazilian Foreign Minister this morning. Kubitchek, the former President who invented Brasilia, the new capital, and had it built, decreed that no foreign envoy must be received by the Foreign Minister in Rio, only in the new capital. But, as you know, everyone loves Rio and detests Brasilia. This morning I had to take an early plane to Brasilia. At the airport I saw the Brazilian Foreign Minister, who was obviously flying there in order to meet me. We politely and considerately ignored each other. On arrival I lingered on a bit to give him a chance of reaching his ministry before me. Then I was driven there, saw him, we settled our business, while I kept a nervous eye on my watch, as I did not want to miss my plane back to Rio. I took my leave in a bit of a hurry and managed to reach the plane. I was the last but one passenger to board. The last was the Brazilian Foreign Minister.'

This has all changed by now. I returned to Brazil in 1976 and by then all diplomatic missions had been exiled to Brasilia. The new capital is a strange and artificial place. I had the feeling that most of its inhabitants – diplomatic personnel and also all the other people – were whistling in the dark, singing, shouting, banging the table and howling how happy they were to be there, how much nicer it was to live in the middle of a desert in a small and pleasant town, than in Rio with its fumes and traffic jams. But Rio is one of the most beautiful and exciting cities in the world; and Brasilia is not small any more, neither is it free from fumes and traffic jams.

From Rio a number of us – including Graham Greene and Alec Waugh – went over to Montevideo and from there to Buenos Aires. I was keen on seeing an *asado* – the roasting of a whole ox on a giant spit. Alec Waugh got an invitation to an *asado* and very kindly suggested to his hosts that they should invite me, too. Next

Abstract Paintings

morning we drove quite early to the smaller Buenos Aires airport, in the middle of the town. The *estancia* was sending a small plane to fetch us. The plane was a four-seater and there were four passengers: Alec Waugh and myself, a young man from the British Council and the pilot.

Alec looked at the plane and declared: 'I don't like the look of it. I don't trust this plane.' I told Alec that if the pilot could get here from the *estancia* he would be able to get back. So we got in. I sat next to the pilot, Alex with the British Council chap in the back. I love flights in small aircraft. In them you really *fly*. We flew over gardens and saw what people were having for breakfast. Cows looked up at us and we could see their sad, brown eyes. We crossed a small stream. The pilot tossed a map to me and asked casually: 'Was that the river or the canal?'

This did not augur well for the future. 'The river,' I replied without looking at the map. A few minutes later the single engine of the plane stalled for a few seconds, then picked up again.

'The engine has cut out,' said Alec.

'Nonsense,' said I.

'It did not,' said the British Council.

A few minutes later it cut out again and this time it failed to pick up. We glided down and crash-landed in the middle of nowhere in the Argentine pampas. We landed on huge, hard slabs of earth which shook the hell out of us, but nothing worse happened.

'You are lucky,' said the pilot. 'Last time I landed in a tree.'

'How often do you do this?' I asked.

'A strange idea to make a habit of it,' murmured Alec.

The pilot ignored these remarks with haughty dignity.

We walked three hours, then reached an *estancia*. The owner was having his lunch. He listened to our story, left his lunch and in spite of our protestations he insisted on driving us to Mar del Plata without delay. From there we got a plane back to Buenos Aires – minus the pilot who stayed behind with his plane, delighted that it was on the ground and not in a tree, like last time.

We arrived just in time for Alec Waugh's lecture in the British Council. Alec began with the conventional words: 'I am glad to be here tonight . . .'

How to be Seventy

I could not resist remarking loudly: 'You bet . . .'

People looked at me and as I had given a talk there on the previous evening, recognised me. The glances all implied: 'What a rude and superfluous interjection!'

'My friend is quite right,' Alec nodded and explained that he was indeed pleased to be there instead of lying dead somewhere in the pampas.

Just a few words to add. I did get to an *estancia* later, although I never saw an *asado*. The owner led me round his estate at seven in the morning. I saw a very old and feeble gaucho having a huge steak for breakfast. His hands were shaky but he was obviously enjoying his enormous steak. I asked him, through the owner, my interpreter, whether he ever had coffee for breakfast.

'I can't afford coffee,' the old man replied.

'Steaks are dirt cheap, coffee is very expensive,' the proprietor explained. Then the old man spoke again: 'And coffee gives me indigestion.'

Snobs

One day in 1964 I was rung up by Michael Russell, a literary agent, who told me that he and his partner had approached the Duke of Bedford and suggested that he should write a *Book of Snobs* – a guide to being snobbish in the approved manner. The Duke was willing but he needed some help and they had thought of me. Would I be ready to do the book with him? I said that in principle I should be delighted but I had never met the Duke – indeed, when I came to think of it, I had never met any Duke – so I had no idea how we would get on. We might take an instant dislike of each other and that would make collaboration difficult. Michael Russell agreed that we ought to meet and arranged a lunch at the Ritz.

Like most people, I had read a great deal about the Duke and I was pleasantly surprised when I met him. He looked like an assistant bank manager of a suburban branch – a small branch at that – and he was courteous and modest, but not without the inborn self-assurance of the aristocrat. Peter Owen, the publisher of the book, and Michael Russell were also there.

When he was ordering his lunch the Duke told the waiter: 'I would like roast pork, but only if you give me a lot of crackling.'

Then he turned to me and said: 'I understand you want to put me on probation.'

'The probation period is over,' I replied. 'You have passed with flying colours.'

He was surprised: 'But we haven't talked at all.'

'No. But you want a lot of crackling. A man who loves crackling is a man after my own . . . a man of taste and insight.'

'All right,' he nodded. 'We shall get on.'

(Years later I was amazed and amused to see what a different impression this little scene had made on someone else present.

How to be Seventy

Peter Owen did not get on with the Duke at all. Their dislike was mutual and on one occasion they had a flaming row. I met Peter at a party about ten years after the publication of the book and Bedford was mentioned. He asked me: 'Do you remember that awful fuss he made about crackling?')

Bedford and I had to spend a lot of time together, partly in his house in Regent's Park occasionally in my Club but most often at Woburn Abbey, where I spent several days on occasions. I have a very strong anti-authority streak in me; royalty and aristocracy put my back up. I cannot tolerate a boss and do not want to be anybody's boss – there were periods in my life when I could hardly do without a full-time secretary but I would rather spend twice as much money on typists than have an 'employee'. I am, I suppose, as snobbish as the next man – to be in the company of a great writer or to be the friend of a great scientist (like for example that delightful and lovable man, the late Denis Gábor, the Nobel Prize winning physicist) fills me with pride – but kings, princes, dukes and multi-millionaires kindle a latent hostility in me. So it was to my utter amazement that I grew genuinely fond of the thirteenth Duke of Bedford.

I asked him – as soon as we started working together – what he thought about dukes. Did he not think that it was a ridiculous anachronism in the second half of the twentieth century to venerate a man and allow him to keep a vast fortune because a distant ancestor, many generations ago, did something laudable? In many cases (not in the case of his family) the noble deed of the ancestor amounted to being a royal whore.

'I quite agree with you,' he replied. 'It's ridiculous. There is no excuse or proper explanation for it. I fail to see why modern society tolerates dukes. But it suits me. I won't complain when society decides it has had enough of us, but you certainly won't see me in the forefront of the fight for abolishing dukedoms.'

I always found his sane, cynical and self-derogatory views refreshing.

'What's the most interesting thing in Woburn?' I asked him once.

'I am.'

He explained: 'There are the most marvellous paintings to be found there, from Rembrandts downwards. Carpets, antique furniture, ancient porcelain, marvellous jewellery, all the miracles of artistic creation. But when I am there – and I am there most of the time – people are more interested in me than in all those wonders. Look at me. I am a very dull, utterly uninteresting man, I have nothing to offer. I shall never understand this interest in me. But if people are determined to touch the hem of my garment, they may do so. For a small fee.'

Whenever I stayed with him in Woburn, we always had lunch – not surprisingly, perhaps – in the dining room. It had the famous twenty-two Canalettos and was opened to the public from 1 o'clock, so we had to have an early lunch (cooked by his excellent French chef), hurry up with it and have our coffee in the library, which was private. One day, when we had to pack up and move on as usual, I asked him: 'Must we always flee? You charge a shilling for the Canalettos. Can't you charge two shillings and include yourself in the spectacle? You say you are the greatest attraction. I am sure people would be pleased to pay a shilling to see you having lunch.'

His grandfather Herbrand the eleventh Duke of Bedford was a repulsive character, the last of those autocratic, opinionated and stupid local tyrants who were more at home in the thirteenth century than in the twentieth. But he was a fascinating relic all the same. Herbrand hated Ian's, the present Duke's, father and they both hated Ian. This is more or less traditional in the Bedford family.

'In the last twenty-seven years of his life,' Bedford told me, 'my grandfather and my father met only once – because they were not on speaking terms. They met in order to discuss how they could deprive me of the title, but that wasn't possible.'

When Herbrand, the eleventh Duke, came up to London he travelled in a horse-drawn coach. In Hendon he always changed coaches. When he was persuaded to give up horses and buy motorcars, he bought two Rolls Royces and changed Rollses at Hendon. It took some time to convince him that one Rolls was up to the whole journey. He still owned the whole of Covent Garden. The place is full of names connected with the Bedford family: Bedford, Tavistock, Howland, Woburn etc, places, streets,

How to be Seventy

squares and mews. Herbrand was persuaded by some financial wizard to sell the lot. He sold out for two million pounds. To have your money in bricks and mortar – the financial wizard told him – was plain silly. He advised him to put the two million into Russian, Czarist bonds – not, in 1912, an astute investment.

The best story of male chauvinist piggery emanated from Herbrand, the eleventh Duke.

Woburn Abbey was in a terribly dilapidated state and he decided that it had to be redecorated. He called in the most fashionable interior decorator of the day, a woman, and told her to look around and make suggestions. Among other things she suggested the creation of a Corridor of Duchesses.

'A what?'

'A Corridor of Duchesses . . .'

'What's that?'

'Well, Your Grace, there is a Corridor of Dukes, with the portraits of all the eleven Dukes of Bedford in a row – plus the Earls of Bedford who preceded them. I suggest that you have a Corridor of Duchesses, with the portraits of all the Duchesses.'

He was much taken aback.

'But my dear, the Duchesses don't belong to the family.'

The present Duke's father and grandfather had £300,000 of annual income between them, at a time when £300,000 was still money. They allowed Ian £96 per annum. He was so broke that he was always happy to accept invitations for dinner. 'They invited me because I was the future Duke of Bedford; I went because I was hungry. I put on my dinner jacket and went to those ducal soup-kitchens.' His grandmother, the Flying Duchess, was another unforgettable character. She flew out over the sea and disappeared with her machine, never to be found. Probably she committed suicide partly because she had become stone deaf (she took up flying in the first place because the pressure up there was less and her ears hurt less) and partly because her husband refused to endow a hospital where she wanted to work and spend most of her time. Many people believe that Ian's father also committed suicide but Ian himself is convinced that his death was a genuine shooting accident.

When his father died and he was summoned to return from South Africa, where he was farming, he was faced with £3m of estate duties. Everyone told him that the case was hopeless: he had to close down Woburn (no one would buy it, of course) with all the junk in it and forget about it. How could he possibly raise £3m? Those Czarist bonds – which the Communists forgot to revaluate – would certainly not pay the estate duties. But the new Duke would not listen to reason. He rolled up his sleeves, opened the windows, swept out the three hundred rooms, dusted the junk (Rembrandts, Canalettos etc) and opened Woburn to the public.

'I am extremely unpopular with the aristocracy and with other owners of so-called stately homes,' he told me. 'Not because I became a businessman but because I became a good businessman. To open your house to the public is all right. To let the mob in and look down upon them is quite acceptable. But to *like* them, treat them as your customers on whose money you live, that's unforgivable. To be a showman is bad enough; but to be a successful showman is downright disgusting.'

After the book we kept in touch, in fact, we wrote another book together. One day he telephoned me and invited me to lunch at Woburn. After lunch, he explained, a chap would come from French television to discuss a plan. The Duchess, before she married him, had worked for French television, hence the contact. I went to Woburn, we had lunch under the Canalettos, then moved, as always, into the vast library. The French TV man arrived on time. He was overwhelmed by the occasion. He, too, wanted to kiss the hem of the Duke's garment, but he restrained himself. The Duke behaved like a normal and simple human being; his visitor like a French nobleman of the sixteenth century, visiting one of the Earls of Bedford. The Frenchman told us that the French TV planned to turn our *Book of Snobs* into two one-hour shows and they wanted to film in Woburn. The Duke nodded. They wanted me to write the script and I nodded, too. They wanted the Duke to be the narrator and, generally, play the principal role in it. Would he do it?

'How much do you pay?' Ian asked.

How to be Seventy

'Well,' said the TV man deeply embarrassed, 'that will be discussed by someone else.' His tone implied: discuss this sordid question of money with some inferior being.

'Will you do it?' he turned to the Duke again.

'How much do you pay?' Ian asked again.

The French producer started sweating. How to deal with such incomprehension? But he did not dare show annoyance, so he explained again, very patiently: 'Another man will discuss finances. I am a producer and an artist. I should like to discuss the matter in principle. Do you agree in principle?'

'If you pay enough, I agree; if you don't pay enough I don't agree. And I have no other principles.'

I loved him for that. Of course, there are many things a writer does for the love of it, for little or no money, but turning our *Book of Snobs* into a television show was not among them. That sort of thing one does only for the money involved. But only a non-professional equipped with aristocratic arrogance would have the courage to say so.

Last time I saw him (to date) was in Woburn. I went down to have lunch once again and he drove me round his new zoo. We admired the lions, cheetahs, elephants, zebras and hundreds of monkeys, we drove amid them and they all – apart from the monkeys – kept a respectful distance from the car. The monkeys jumped on the bonnet, tried to remove the windscreen wiper, fought one another, searched for sandwiches and were very funny and sweet. The zoo was a roaring success. The Duke of Bedford's establishment was in friendly competition with the establishment of the Marquess of Bath.

'Henry Bath,' said Bedford, 'has stolen many of my good ideas; but I have stolen his *best* idea.'

He was referring to the zoo. Money was pouring in. Yet he looked less relaxed than before.

'The success of this zoo has wiped out my overdraft. It's terrible.'

'What's terrible about it?'

'Not to have an overdraft. It used to be a constant challenge, threat and excitement to me. Fencing with the bank manager, struggling with that overdraft. It's all gone now.'

Snobs

His voice was full of nostalgia. He was quite sentimental about the romantic – and bygone – beauties of the overdraft. He looked into the distance.

He could not bear it. He handed over the management of Woburn to his son, Tavistock, and went to live abroad. In France he has no zoo and can, perhaps, still run an overdraft.

A Gentleman at Last

Perhaps, after all, I have fulfilled my mother's hopes for me and although I have spent a life in journalism and as a writer, I have also become a gentleman. The evidence, admittedly, is circumstantial: I am a member of several gentlemen's clubs.

When I left the BBC in 1951, I felt that I ought to have a base in town. My friend David Langdon – who illustrated a number of my books – suggested that I join his club, the Savage, at Carlton House Terrace. I made many enquiries about club life among my friends. I asked Tony Gibbs, the publisher, which club he belonged to. He mentioned a distinguished little club, founded originally by King Edward VII when Prince of Wales, but he told me that he was leaving it.

'Too many people got to know me,' he explained. 'They talk to me.'

Innocent as I was, this did not make sense to me. I asked Tony if he had not joined the club in order to talk to people.

'Most certainly not,' he replied angrily. 'I am leaving my club and joining the RAC. It has a million members – and I shall take the utmost care not to get acquainted with a single one of them. I'll go there, have lunch, put my feet up and have a nap in front of the fire.'

'But you could do that more cheaply at home,' I argued. 'You can have lunch at home, you have a fire and you can take a nap undisturbed.'

He looked at me as if I had suggested that he should murder the porter of the club or steal silver spoons from his best friend's house. He told me curtly: 'An English gentleman does not sleep at home. An English gentleman sleeps in his club.'

Once or twice the Duke of Bedford invited me to *his* club. He took me for dinner to Pratt's, and his son, Lord Tavistock, was

A Gentleman at Last

there on one occasion. Tavistock had been put up for the club and was waiting to get in. I asked the Duke if he was using the club a great deal. He told me that he went there once or twice a year.

'Is it worthwhile? Why don't you leave it?' I asked him.

'One can't leave a club when other people are waiting seven years to get in.'

His relationship with his son was in the true Bedford tradition although it was considerably better than his own relationship with *his* father, and his father's relationship with *his* father. But I had a vague feeling – perhaps unjust – that the Duke refused to leave the club for fear that his son – who was on the waiting list – might get his place.

My own debut at the Savage was disastrous. My name was put up and I was elected a candidate member. The idea was that you became a candidate member for a month – put on probation, so to say – and after that period unless the others found you totally repellent you became a full member.

On the first day when I visited the club as a candidate member, an old and popular music hall actor – one of the Lanes – came up to me and asked me if I wanted to buy a sweepstake ticket. I am not a betting man and did not have the faintest idea what a sweepstake was. Nevertheless, I inferred from his demeanour that this was something I was expected to do, so I bought a ticket and forgot all about it.

Now it was all right – indeed compulsory – for a candidate member to buy a sweepstake ticket, but it was very much against the accepted rules – indeed against morality and decency – that he should win first prize with a single ticket – with, in fact, the first ticket he had ever bought in his life. (Winning sweepstakes and tombolas is now quite a habit of mine. Once I bought three tombola tickets at a Foreign Press Association dinner for three ladies around my table, and they won first, second and third prizes. The only snag was that my first wife got third prize, which was a book written by me.)

Winning first prize at the Savage was bad enough but there was worse to come. It was the ancient custom of the club that when the winner entered the bar for the first time after his win he stood drinks all round. I knew nothing of this custom; and even if I had known it would not have made any difference; because I did not know that I had won. I slipped into the bar, hid myself modestly in the corner as befits a mere candidate, and ordered a gin and lime – the fashionable drink of a bygone age.

Miraculously, in spite of my repulsive behaviour I was accepted as a full member and received a letter asking me to pay in a certain sum: the entrance fee plus the first year's subscription. Before I could do so, I received a cheque from the club by post, for almost exactly the sum I was supposed to pay. I went into the club's office and explained that *I* was supposed to pay this sum to the club, not the club to me. They told me that as I had failed to claim my winnings – although my name had been posted for weeks on the notice board – they had sent me the cheque.

I liked the Savage except for what I felt was its forced bonhomie. There was a buoyant, effervescent, chest-beating atmosphere, proclaiming: we are the happy band of Savages, the finest and most delightful band of chaps in the land, full of funny stories and waggish jokes. Occasionally I found this a trifle tiresome, but I met enough charming and likeable men there to be very happy in the club. In the early sixties, however, they were forced to give up their beautiful house in Carlton House Terrace and moved into the premises of the National Liberal Club. That place looked to me like the operating theatre of a vast American (Mid-Western) hospital and we happy and vociferous Savages were completely lost there. One day I complained about this to Malcolm Hilberry, the judge, who put me up for the Garrick. Arthur Crook, editor of *The Times Literary Supplement*, seconded me and I – probably thanks to my formidable sponsors – was elected a member in 1963.

My first visit to the Garrick was not much more auspicious than my first to the Savage had been. When I arrived on the first occasion as a member I went to have a drink at the bar. Coming down to the coffee room, I met Satters – Commander Satterthwaite, a retired naval officer, the Secretary of the Club – who greeted me: 'Oh, you are a new member . . . Let me take you into the coffee room.'

He took me to the far end, to a small table with six places, five of which were occupied. I had no idea, of course, that this was the

A Gentleman at Last

publishers' table, and putting me there was like throwing not merely a Christian, but a particularly innocent Christian baby, to the lions. When I arrived Daniel Macmillan was holding forth to Ian Parsons, Alan White and two others, fuming about those bloody foreign publishers who had invaded gentlemanly British publishing. As soon as I opened my mouth and he heard my Central European brogue, he realised that this was not the best way of receiving a brand new member, so he cut himself short: 'All I mean to say is that I wouldn't trust Deutsch any farther than I could throw Weidenfeld.'

It is hard not to plunge into a eulogy of the Garrick Club but I shall restrain myself. More or less. Tony Gibbs would be thoroughly miserable there as this is the club where people talk to one another. There is a long table running the length of the coffee room and members coming in on their own have their meals there. You must sit down next to someone at the table, without leaving a gap, and you must talk to him. If you are in a bad mood and just say: 'Lousy day, isn't it?' you have fulfilled your obligation, but in most cases something livelier develops. As likely as not, you will find someone interesting and fascinating next to you and that's why nearly all members of the Garrick know all other members, from Her Majesty's Lord Justices of Appeal and the Editor of *The Times*, through Kingsley Amis and Robin Day down to myself. Yes, the Garrick enjoys a notoriety of friendliness which many people in Clubland find hard to swallow. Anthony Sampson tells a story about this in his *Anatomy of Britain*. Once upon a time, when the Garrick was closed, we used Brooks. One Brooks member remarked wrily: 'I always know when the Garrick is closed. There is laughter in the bar.'

These reciprocal arrangements with that august club ceased abruptly some years ago. When I asked why, a friend told me: 'We've been chucked out. A Garrick member asked for a fish-knife.' (For the benefit of those few people who did not read our *Book of Snobs* I ought to add that in some circles fish-knives are regarded as the most despicable symbols of middle-class pretensiousness.)

I must confess that I am the most unsuitable person to be a member of any club. I have a most rotten memory for faces. As

How to be Seventy

some people are colour-blind, I am face-blind. I may have seen a person fifty times and still have no idea who the hell he is. I remember names very well, but this does not help. It is very rare, all the same, that I get into trouble on this account. First, after a few sentences I usually recognise people's voices – I am not very musical but, happily and miraculously, I do remember voices. Then, people usually give me a clue. Someone may ask: 'Have you seen Eleanor and Matthew again?' and the penny will drop. Finally, constant, life-long trouble in this field, equips you with a certain amount of cunning. For instance, when I have to introduce people in my club – old friends who would not even suspect that I do not know their names – I just say: 'Of course, you two know each other.'

They may look at me a little puzzled, but I look inscrutable. They proceed to introduce themselves – and I listen eagerly.

Now and then, however, I do get into deep trouble. Once I failed to recognise my son, Martin, at Zurich Airport. It was all his fault, he was supposed to be in Geneva. But still. The worst troubles crop up in the club.

One evening I entered the coffee room and, according to the regulations, I sat down next to a diner whom I recognised without a moment's hesitation as Lord Gardiner, the Lord Chancellor. I knew his features well, I had heard him on several occasions and, in fact, a few days before I had heard him on the radio, so his beautiful voice and diction made recognition easier. We had a fascinating conversation – but at the sweet-stage he made a remark in which he used a legal term wrongly. As it seemed to be extremely unlikely that the Lord Chancellor would used a legal term wrongly, I was driven to the logical conclusion: the man next to me was not Lord Gardiner, after all. But who? I *did* know his features; I *did* know his voice.

I did not give myself away. When I went to pay my bill, I asked the cashier if she happened to know who the gentleman sitting next to me was. She happened to know. She said: 'It was Lord Olivier.'

I was shattered. His was one of the best known faces, and voices, in the land. But I was consoled a week or two later. Once again, I strolled into the coffee room for an early dinner. There

A Gentleman at Last

were only two people at the long table: Alec Guinness (and although he had a beard because he was appearing in a Russian play, I recognised him immediately and, I might as well state here, the man *was* Alec Guinness) and a doctor whom I also knew and recognised rightly. They were engaged in vivacious, amusing and friendly chat. Great chums, obviously. A quarter of an hour later Guinness stood up, he had to go to the theatre. As soon as he was out of earshot, the Doctor turned to me: 'I say, I know this chap is in show-business, but do you happen to know his name?'

This, of course, did not diminish my previous blunder in any way. Yet, it was nice to know that I was not the only idiot in the club.

Mania

No portrait of myself and no picture of my life would be complete without confessing to the one and only mania of an otherwise cool and sober man. It's tennis.

In my young days I used to enjoy rowing on the Danube, like almost everybody else; tried fencing – with sabre – at Italo Santelli's famous establishment in Budapest, with extremely modest success; even tried boxing. In fact I got to the point of loving boxing. Jenö Rózsa, a former European boxing champion, was a patient of my stepfather's, which started Tibor and me on it. After the very invigorating gymnastics and shadow-boxing, I always had a friendly bout with a young man called György Murin. We never hurt each other too much but his family was anxious about it, saying that boxing was a wild sport, fit for bullies but not for reasonably educated men. One day Murin told me that his fiancée and his mother would be coming along to watch us, so would I please be particularly considerate to him, and so would he be to me, in order to convince the two ladies that boxing was a nice and harmless sport, fit for gentlemen. On that occasion he hit me on the jaw and I spat out two of my teeth. At the end of the next round I hit him in a most unfortunate manner – somewhere around his solar plexus – whereupon he lifted in the air, flew to the far corner of the room and lay there lifeless, like a sack of coal. On the same evening my brother Tibor – a pathetically thin and sickly looking youth at the time – had an exhibition bout with Rózsa's brother, another champion. Young Rózsa was chatting with someone while boxing with my brother, fending off his feeble attempts at attacking him and caressing Tibor's face instead of really hitting him. Suddenly my brother managed to hit him in the solar plexus and the huge, powerfully built champion collapsed and passed out. Curiously, all this seemed to convince the Murin ladies that boxing *was* gentle fun, fit for gentlemen, and Murin continued to come to box with me. All our subsequent bouts went off without any incidents.

But tennis was my real sport, the one which truly fascinated me, both as a player and as a spectator. I played a lot in Budapest. My brother Tibor, much more athletic by now, observed my passion with curiosity and decided to try his hand, just to see what the fascination of the game was. He had a great deal of natural talent for tennis – as he had for many other sports – and six months after taking it up he beat all the teaching professionals in the club. A little later he was spotted by some talent-scouts, enrolled in one of the great tennis clubs of Hungary, trained by the best people and soon he reached the semi-final stages of junior championships both in singles and doubles. But he was essentially bored with tennis. One day his coach made him practise the half volley for five hours on end. He got fed up, declared that tennis should be pleasure and not a chore and said that in the future he would play for his own enjoyment only, and had finished with competitive tennis. And he stuck to it. During the war, as I have described, he served in the American Army and was otherwise engaged, but even afterwards he never went back to it, while I plodded on with my pedestrian and mediocre game all my life.

In 1961 I joined Hurlingham Club. Hurlingham is a beautiful place and it is something of a miracle to have such a club in the middle of London – well, not quite in the middle but not too far out.

Since I joined I have been playing about four times a week, all the year round, always in the open. When my second marriage broke up (I am not divorced and I am on friendly terms with Lea, my wife, but we do not live together) I moved to Fulham, very near Hurlingham. On Tuesdays and Thursdays we organise our own games and for twelve years or so I have been playing with Stewart Ramsay, a retired Colonel. A few years later John Briance, a retired diplomat, joined us and various friends make up the four. It is believed we are terribly lucky with the weather and miss very few games. This 'terrible luck' must be explained. Once I heard an American radio-announcer declare: 'Today's weather is unacceptable.' We are more tolerant. We accept all sorts of weather. And this is the secret of our 'terrible luck'. If people are ready to play in rain, sleet, fog and gale they will miss fewer games than those who are deterred by a slight drizzle.

Friends keep telling me that 'tennis is good for you'. It probably is, and perhaps it helps to keep me in some sort of shape. But I do not play because it is good for me. If tennis were bad for me, something like smoking, I would still play with equal zeal.

Non-players – should I call them normal people? – find it difficult to understand this tennis mania. I heard of its most splendid manifestations from Ernest Wittman, a Hurlingham friend. He was born in Hungary and his mother tongue is Hungarian but he lived in Poland for a long time and played Davis Cup tennis for the Poles in the thirties. In his heyday he was a magnificent player and one day before the war, when he arrived in Stockholm, King Gustav – another maniacal tennis player – heard about his arrival (he made it his business to be informed about such events) and invited him to come and play tennis in his palace, outside Stockholm. Ernest went, played with the King and returned to Stockholm. He was pleased to play with the King but got slightly irritated. The one and only subject the King discussed with him was tennis. No other subject was even mentioned.

One day, to Ernest's delight, King Gustav told him that he would be driving to town after their game and would be pleased to give him a lift. This was his opportunity to prove to the King that he was an intelligent and knowledgeable man, not just an empty-headed knocker-about of tennis balls. It so happened that Count Koudenhove Calergi was also in town, holding meetings for the propagation of his notion that the countries of Europe should unite. He was listened to with courtesy but not taken too seriously – people doubted whether Hitler was ready to join. Nevertheless, Ernest saw this as a splendid theme for a serious and wide-ranging political conversation with King Gustav.

As soon as the two men had settled in the back of the King's car, Wittman said to the King: 'I see, Sir, Count Koudenhove Calergi is in town.'

Mania

The King nodded, thought for a few seconds and replied: 'Koudenhove Calergi . . . Koudenhove Calergi . . . Oh yes . . . If he had a better backhand he might be quite a good tennis player.'

Another memorable tennis-moment happened two years ago. After a summer game on a lovely day – when the dressing room was chock full – I was discussing something with John Briance. We had both just taken our showers and were stark naked. He suddenly heard a somewhat unusual sound – unusual in men's dressing rooms – and turned round, to display a full, frontal nude to a charming young lady. She was utterly unperturbed and asked him in a chatty and natural voice: 'Is this the ladies' dressing room?'

John, a very quick-witted man, was, for once, lost for words and he simply replied: 'Next door.'

'Thank you,' the beautiful visitor nodded, turned and left with perfect composure.

John was speechless for a few seconds, then told me: 'I've served as a British diplomat in a dozen countries, but I've never been so insulted in my life.'

The Last Anecdote

I suppose that readers who have stayed with me up to now are entitled to be told what sort of person I essentially am, so perhaps at this stage I ought to sum up – not my 'philosophy of life' because I do not possess anything so grand – but my views on various basic principles. I have, however, decided against it. I myself would not be at all keen on being plunged into ideas and first principles at this stage – or, indeed, at any stage – of an autobiography, and I suspect that most people would agree with me; and anyway, those readers who are still with me must surely have gathered, whether I like it or not, what sort of person I am.

I would, nevertheless, like to go further into one subject because it has been so important in my life ever since I left the country I was born in. It is my relationship to Hungary and to Great Britain. Although in 1970 I was thrown out of Hungary as a dangerous imperialist spy (an event which I described in my book *Any Souvenirs?*) I do still have a relationship with it. Quite soon after my expulsion I received semi-official, or at least officially inspired, messages telling me that I ought not to make too much of the incident (after all, what is a little spying between friends?) and that if I were to apply for a Hungarian visa it would be granted. I replied that it was nice to know this and that when I next wanted to visit Hungary I would apply. I did so in 1979, and they did grant me a visa. They also rolled out – well, not a red, but a pale pink carpet for me, received me with perfect courtesy, and enabled me to enjoy my stay at home – as I still call Hungary, although I do not think of it as 'home'.

My feelings about Hungary have always been very ambivalent, but some things about it I definitely love: the countryside round Siklós, for example – those gentle hills and green mountains of Transdanubia. As a child it never occurred to me that the village's

The Last Anecdote

surroundings could strike anyone as beautiful, but when I saw them again in 1970 I realised that they were (the little town itself was always rather ugly and still is, with the single and important exception of the ancient castle in which King Zsigmond was imprisoned at the beginning of the fifteenth century). I also love dearly, almost passionately, my mother tongue, a strange and sometimes cumbersome language, an instrument from which its great poets have produced ethereal and seraphic music. When I wish to turn to poetry – and I often do – it is to Hungarian poetry that I turn. Nothing, absolutely nothing in my whole life, has given me more superb pleasure than the poems of Babits, Gyula Juhász, Heltai, Ady, Attila József, Faludy and a few others. I also have many friends in Hungary who are near my heart, and I am always much interested in what is going on there.

I am not even against the Hungarians for their regime. They did not choose communism. True, official Hungary behaved abominably before and during the Second World War, and was Hitler's last loyal ally; but had the Hungarians been devoted to the Western Allies their fate would have been exactly the same: the fate of Czechoslovakia and Poland proves as much. Kádár is a reliable communist from Moscow's point of view; but from my point of view (however much he may object to it) he is also a patriot, heir to the princes of Transylvania who tried to navigate between Turk and Habsburg. Kádár's declarations of love (never too profuse) for Brezhnev are probably sincere – after all, his rule depends on Moscow's confidence in him – but he does try to keep Hungary as Hungarian as he can; he tries to preserve the nation's unique character. Hungarians often say: 'We have survived the Tartars, the Turks, the Austrians, the Germans. We shall survive the Russians too.' I should be surprised if that thought had never crossed the mind of Kádár as well. He has made Hungary into by far the most agreeable hut in the great Russian concentration camp, no more of a police state than the nature of the regime compels it to be. Even the most reactionary former Horthyite army officers go to church every Sunday morning to pray for Kádár's life. Which is no mean achievement.

It is only as a distant observer that I find all this interesting; I am not at all involved: that is what I try to persuade myself. But of course I *am* involved. How could I not be when I was born and brought up a Hungarian? Yet I have to admit that I will not die a Hungarian. In Hungary I shall die as that man who emigrated and became an English writer; it is only in England that I am and shall remain Mikes the Hungarian.

So what about my feelings for Britain? The English took me in at a critical period and probably saved my life: if I had not been here I would have been sent to a concentration camp or would have had to serve in a Labour Battalion: I might have come out of it alive, or I might not. But gratitude is no basis for a solid relationship, and my love for this country is not based on it. I like it here, and I always have liked it here . . . although in an earlier book I was not so positive about it. I said that during my early time in this country 'I admired the English enormously but did not like them very much; today I admire them much less but love them much more'. Perhaps the first part of that statement ought to have been put a little differently, but the second part of it remains exactly true.

Could I ever leave England? Friends often urge me to spend at least half of my time abroad – to buy a little house in France or Italy. I always refuse to do so. One change of country is enough for a lifetime. 'But don't you want to live abroad?' they ask me. I tell them: 'But I *do* live abroad.' And I mean it. I feel perfectly at home here, this is my country, I belong to this place – yet I continue to feel that I am living among strange and peculiar people and that my real kith and kin are those even stranger and more peculiar people on the banks of the Danube. It ought to be an unsettling situation, but it is perfectly all right with me. In any case, what can I do about it?

Would I stick to England in all circumstances? No, I would not. It would not occur to me to run away if it were threatened by a nuclear holocaust because I have lived long enough and although I would not mind going on a little longer, if London went up in flames I would like to claim the honour of going up with it. But if Britain turned fascist – either black or red fascist – that would be an utterly different matter. Then I would like to try to get away, and brood for the rest of my life. Fortunately, in spite of race riots, inner-city battles, football hooliganism and all the

The Last Anecdote

rest, I do not take such a threat at all seriously.

The important question for me is this: is there a conflict between my allegiance to Britain and my love for Hungary? There is not; but it is possible that such a conflict might arise. Allegiances are strange things. It is possible to be loyal to our family, our town or village, our football club, our political party, our country, and none of these loyalties conflict. But allegiance to two different countries *can* conflict. Ideas change, of course. The supreme loyalty of an ancient Greek was to his city state; medieval man's loyalty was to his faith; modern man invented nationalism but can often feel that the primary loyalty belongs to an idea – communism, for example. There is nothing sacred about a state, it is an association formed for our convenience, to be our servant, not our master. But we are illogical beings, and I, being a child of my times, accept the idea of allegiance to a country – or rather, to two countries.

We all know that we do not choose our principles in the way we used to imagine. We do not sit down, reflect, weigh up arguments and accept the conclusion which is most logical. We have inborn, *a priori* prejudices which drive us in one direction or another, and we seek logical arguments to confirm them, whereupon we like to call them principles. This is what I have done.

I am a devout European. I want the whole of Europe to unite into one democratic state. For a long time I believed that I wanted this for solid and logical reasons: Britain, as a little off-shore island, could not survive alone; being insular was absurd; our economic future is bound up with that of the rest of Europe, etc etc. I still think all this is true, but now I know that my original conviction – like all convictions – was based on purely personal considerations. If Europe becomes one, if national frontiers disappear, then no conflict can possibly arise between my allegiances and I will be able to love both my countries with a clear conscience, just as one may love, say, Nottingham and Birmingham, or Northumberland and Essex.

I have not told in this book the story of that tennis ball that hit my right eye in 1975 and nearly blinded me in both eyes. I told it in my book *Tsi-Tsa* (and also in a long article in the *Sunday Times*, 24th July, 1977). Anyway, I did not lose my eyesight, and I hope my eyes – though none too good – will last as long as I do.

And I have said almost nothing about my cat Tsi-Tsa, because I have already written her biography. She is still with me, in good health, happy and content. Her biography was dedicated to three cats of my acquaintance, among them Ginger, 'a Saint among cats'. I called Ginger a saint because he has a kinder, gentler and more unselfish disposition than most saints I know about. Tsi-Tsa had a bad accident that left her a cripple, despised, tormented and persecuted by the other cats of the neighbourhood. Ginger was the only exception: although Tsi-Tsa had never been particularly nice to him, he was sweet and protective to her; and in the days when he himself was a hungry stray, he used to share the little food he managed to get with a tiny kitten, even more miserable and forlorn than himself. When, eventually, he was thrown out by his owner – who had never really cared for him – I had to take him in. I could not allow an old friend to starve and perish in the cold, but I also wanted to express my gratitude for his kindness to Tsi-Tsa. Tsi-Tsa herself, however, confronted Ginger with jealousy and hostility. In his early days with me he had to be fed outside in the patio, to avoid clashes with Tsi-Tsa. Having finished with his breakfast or dinner, he would come in to see what had been left on Tsi-Tsa's plate. As he approached the plate Tsi-Tsa would start groaning and moving towards him menacingly. Ginger retreated. Then he advanced again. The same scene would be repeated several times, until Tsi-Tsa got bored and moved away, whereupon Ginger would advance and quietly eat up what was left on the plate. He invariably got what he wanted by patience and perseverance – *non vi sed saepe cadendo* as we used to say a few years ago, when Latin was still a living language. But today all this has changed and the two cats are best friends. They groom each other, sleep on the same armchair (or on the same man) and usually embrace each other while asleep. They are both devoted to me too, and I – I know that this is silly – am even more devoted to them. Having joked for about forty years about the ridiculous cat-worship of the English, now I can include myself in the joke.

The Last Anecdote

* * *

Let me continue with the list of lightly-treated subjects. I have said little about my literary and broadcasting activities. I have written for almost all the daily papers and a great deal for various weeklies, have contributed regularly to *That Was the Week That Was*, have written many features and talks for radio and used to appear regularly on television until 1970. I disliked television, its breathless, always excited atmosphere, its constant panic and high tension. I disappeared from the scene – and from London – for a while but hoped that when I re-emerged they would still occasionally invite me to express my views on events of the day – and on events in Hungary – as they used to do. But they can exist without me quite comfortably. A pity. It is quite useful for a writer to show his face occasionally on the box and it is a joy, mixed with embarrassment, when you are recognised next morning in the butcher's queue.

I have not said much of Martin and Judy, my two children. Martin, who lives in Lausanne, has married recently for the second time and has made, I am sure, an excellent choice at last. Judy has just had her first baby in London. She told me that her child would be a girl and would be called Sarah. And what if it is a boy? I wondered, only to be assured that it was quite impossible, the baby would be a girl. I tried to impress on Judy that there really are two possibilities. I had heard of a notice somewhere in Germany, in a park, beginning: 'It is strictly forbidden for people belonging to different sexes, for example male and female . . .', and I quoted this to Judy, but she promised me that in her case there was only one example. In April 1981 she had a boy. Because of the impossibility of this event Judy and her husband had no name for him. The little boy was one day old when I went to visit him. I asked if he seemed to be an intelligent child and Judy thought he was fairly intelligent. I told her I knew that he was very small and it would be foolish to expect him to be able to speak fluently but could he, at least, say 'Mummy'?

'No, he can't,' said Judy. 'In fact, our relationship is pretty formal. We are not yet on Christian name terms.'

How to be Seventy

They are now. The little boy's name is Alex. Alexander George, to be precise.

I did not write much about my children because I think most people feel about other people's children as Churchill felt about Mrs Kennedy's. She had a great many children and grandchildren and thought that as they were so numerous and different, at least one of them was bound to interest the person she was talking to. During the war, when her husband was ambassador to Britain, she sat next to Churchill at a dinner. Churchill spent most of his time talking to his other neighbour. At last he turned to Mrs Kennedy who remarked, chattily: 'I think, Mr Churchill, I haven't told you anything about my grandchildren yet.'

To which Churchill replied: 'For which, Madam, I am infinitely grateful.'

All my books, with very few exceptions (always in exceptional circumstances) were published by André Deutsch. I met him about fifty years ago (as I have described) when he went to school with my brother Tibor in Hungary. But I am sure it is easier to survive half a century of friendship than thirty-five years of publishing connections. Yet we have survived remarkably well. Of course, we have quarrelled now and then; at some periods frequently, sometimes bitterly. Occasionally, I am sure, he wanted to get rid of me and sometimes I swore that I would never look at him again. I spread malicious stories about him and I am sure – indeed, I hope – that he reciprocated in kind. I never left, of course. Partly this was because of his brilliant chief editor, Diana Athill, who had to read, poor thing, all my books from beginning to end, several times. When she herself published a book, called *Instead of a Letter*, I settled down to read it with a sigh. It's only fair, I thought, that I should read her one and only book, when she has read all mine. I am glad I did. It is one of the most moving and beautiful books I have ever come across – it was mentioned among the best books of the year. But, as I said, my staying with Deutsch has been only partly due to Diana. Mostly it has been because of André himself. To be published by someone for thirty-five years is like a marriage. It has its trials, quarrels,

The Last Anecdote

exasperations and crises like all marriages but on the whole it has been a good one. Certainly, my most successful marriage; and André's only one.

About my other marriages, and about other ladies who played important parts in my life, I have also chosen to be reticent. I was just over twenty when I was wanted in Czechoslovakia for 'the forcible abduction of a married woman' – the forcible abduction consisting of meeting the lady's train when she arrived in Budapest, although I must admit that I gave her a warm welcome. That's how I started and I cannot claim to have become much more mature and responsible with advancing years. I felt, however, that I could be frank and outspoken about myself but not about others. My private affairs are also *their* private affairs. So I prefer not to go into details. But I can make one rather unusual claim. I am on the best possible terms with my two wives and I have pleasant contacts with all the important ladies of my life, including that forcibly abducted girl from Czechoslovakia who now lives in this country.

I have a large number of male friends, some of my friendships originating in Hungary.

Emeric Pressburger spent a few years in Austria but then he decided that 'I have been a fool to leave the best country in the world' – and now he leaves his charming Suffolk cottage only when he absolutely must. (He recently bought a new car in which he has managed to do 400 miles in five months.) He – and his partner, Michael Powell – are enjoying a renaissance; their old films have been shown at special festivals in London, New York and Paris, they received the highest honour from the British Film Academy, and their *Red Shoes* is being turned into a musical on the grand scale. My friendship with Emeric means a great deal to me, but I must admit that selfish considerations play a part in it. He may be among the best film-makers of the world; he certainly is its best cook.

I have written a good deal about Arthur Koestler. Here I must add a few words about Laci Hervey. In 1966 I was collecting material for a book in Jamaica and was invited to dinner by Arthur Brown, the Finance Minister. He mentioned some of Jamaica's economic difficulties and I said that I had a friend who could solve all their problems. Of course he paid no attention to this. Later in the evening – without any definite purpose – I started telling him stories about Laci, including the following one.

For years Laci had been employed in a factory as a Public Relations Officer. He hated his boss and his boss hated him, although he appreciated Laci's brain and brilliance. When Laci left the job, they parted as intimate enemies. Years later I was sitting in Laci's study when the phone rang. It was his former boss's wife.

'I am sorry to tell you,' she said, 'that my husband has died.'
'I am sorry to hear it,' replied Laci.
'The funeral will be on Wednesday. Will you come to it?'
'No. I believe you.'

In the end, Arthur Brown decided that he ought to see that fellow. Laci happened to be in New York so we put through a call and asked him to come down to Jamaica. He was seen by the Prime Minister who, after a short chat, decided that he needed Laci.

'This will be a great change for you, Dr Hervey,' he said. 'Jamaica after Hungary.'

'Not at all,' Laci replied, 'one is as corrupt as the other.'

This finally convinced the Prime Minister that Laci was his man – certainly not a sycophant – and that's how his Jamaican career started. Today he holds a high rank in the Jamaican Civil Service, having survived all changes of government. He started negotiations with the Hungarian government, first about bauxite (of which both Jamaica and Hungary have a fair deposit) and then about many other matters on which the two countries can cooperate. When they first sat down to negotiate, Laci and two black Jamaicans opposite three stern-looking Hungarians, the latter obviously felt a little dubious about Laci as a Jamaican spokesman. The ice melted, however, as soon as he said: 'And none of your wicked Hungarian tricks, gentlemen. I know them all.'

Since then relations between Jamaica and Hungary have been cordial.

The Last Anecdote

When in a hundred years' time historians try to explain the close friendship between two such unlikely countries, they will think of many portentous and impressive reasons, but few of them will spot Laci Hervey's jokes.

The death of Paul Ignotus – dear, vague, witty, brilliant and absentminded Paul – was a great blow to me. I am at an age when friends depart – well, that's the natural order of things. It is only Paul whom I acutely miss every day.

I have many dear friends in the Garrick and the club is an important spice in my life.

Money and I have never attracted each other. I have run away from possessions all my life because I have seen so often that a man belongs to his possessions instead of his possessions belonging to him. I have just read that Somerset Maugham contemplated moving from the Riviera to Switzerland in order to save money on taxes. He did not in fact make the move, but the very idea that a multimillionaire of nearly ninety could *think* of moving house to save money – why? for whom? – is abhorrent to me. So is the idea of living a tax-exile's wretched and miserable life on a tropical island or in some other boring place, instead of enjoying one's wealth. Maugham spent the last years of his life in dread that his paintings might be stolen. Another couple I know, also on the Riviera, can never go out together: one of them must always stay at home to mind the Picassos and Monets. What a life! What belongs to whom? Do the pictures belong to them or do they belong to the pictures?

I do not think that animals are superior to men *in everything*. Their greatest glory, however, is that they do not deal in money. I have never seen a parsimonious panda or a wastrel of a rattlesnake. Never met a monetarist horse or a Keynesian ostrich. No squirrel or kangaroo ever wants to buy something cheap and sell it at a profit.

Once, for a short time, I had a large house in London. As soon as my wife and I had signed the contract in a solicitor's office, she turned to me and said: 'We should never have bought this house.'

I wished she had said it thirty seconds earlier. We did our best to get rid of it, but did not succeed until a short slump in the price of houses occurred – a period of about six months. During that time I managed to sell my house – at a loss, of course. If I had kept it I would be a rich man today.

But I do not *want* to be a rich man. I have never visualised myself living in a huge house with a park and a lake, owning a big car and being driven around by a chauffeur. It was Elsa Maxwell, the American society hostess, who made the remark: 'Been poor. Been rich. Rich better.' I am not sure. I have always felt a slight contempt for those rich people who become rich by their own efforts, in other words who spend their lives chasing money. Those who inherit money may be better; they cannot help it. I have some rich friends but they had to prove themselves before they were accepted.

I used to be proud of my attitude to money. I thought it reflected a noble and non-materialistic approach to life. Today I know that it is sheer conceit. Of course, I need money myself: I must be able to feed myself, pay my rent and my bills, run my car. Neither would I mind having a few thousand more per annum to *spend*. But basically I feel that most rich people need money because without money they would be nobodies. I am what I am – not much, I agree, but a fortune would add nothing to my value. And it would make me feel pretty uncomfortable.

Some years ago I explained this theory of mine to a beautiful and clever girlfriend, Eva. I told her: 'In my old age I want to be poor.'

She replied: 'My dear George, this is one of your few ambitions which you have already achieved.'

Looking back at my life it seems that it has been a long string of anecdotes. Naturally, when I received blows they were blows, and not jokes; but somehow I have forgotten the blows and remember only the pleasant events and the anecdotes. The anecdotes are very important. Jokes reeled off without rhyme and reason can be awfully boring, but apt and well-told stories are the spice of life and the treasures of a life-time.

The Last Anecdote

I was in Greece with Eva, dining with my friends, Antonis and Eleni Samarakis, he a writer, she a lawyer. Antonis started telling a story and Eleni exclaimed: 'Oh Antonis, I've heard that one two hundred times!'

Then I started a story, and Eva sighed: 'God, that one again . . .'

And so it went on. Finally, when Eleni protested yet again, Antonis turned to her and said gently: 'My dear Eleni, if a man's wife is bored by a man's stories there is one thing the man can do: change his wife. He can't possibly change his stories.'

Quite. But it is because of all these stories (I must say it again) that I am not a more significant writer than I am. Happily, being significant has never really been my ambition – nor being a proper humorist. Every humorist worth his salt is neurotic, depressed and afflicted with a gastric ulcer. What sort of a humorist is a man who accepts the world as it is (not without a sigh, but accepts it), adjusts to it and likes it here?

Great writers are nasty, as Evelyn Waugh seems to have been. I am what people call 'nice'. Or that's what I used to think. In the mid-sixties I spent some time in Australia and stayed in the hospitable house of my childhood friend, Martin Vida. A few years later he came to London and told me that he had brought kind regards from half of the people I had met – the half who had liked me. 'What do you mean?' I asked. '*Everybody* liked me.' He appeared to be greatly surprised by this remark, and told me that on the contrary, the blood freezes in many people's veins when my name is mentioned. 'Don't you know how you treat people when you are bored by them?' he asked. 'Don't you realise that you look through people as if they didn't exist? Don't you know how bloody awful you can be?' I thought this was a splendid joke and reported it to various friends – male and female – who knew me well. They all agreed with Martin.

So obviously I can be – and often am – bloody awful. That notion cheers me up. Perhaps there is still hope for me.

All my life I have tried to be a little unhappier, but I didn't succeed. It has been my good luck to do all my life what I wanted to do and make a reasonably comfortable living on it. Who wants more? Many people do. I don't.

If I had the choice . . . I mean the choice between having a deep Slav soul like Kafka's, being read a hundred years from now like Kafka, being as miserable as Kafka . . . But why continue? We never have a choice. People sometimes say: 'I'd rather be blind than deaf', or vice versa. Perhaps in the course of history some cruel and sadistic tyrant did offer this very choice to some of his victims, but such situations are few and far between nowadays. We may be unfortunate enough to go blind (I myself was near enough to it); or to go deaf. But we have no vote in the matter.

A friend of mine once declared somewhat grandiloquently: 'I'd rather be a dead lion than a live mouse.'

To which a German writer replied: 'You have no choice. You already are a dead mouse.'

And I, too, had no opportunity to make the choice between being a profound thinker and living a perhaps superficial but contented life. I had to resign myself to being a happy man whether I liked it or not. And I believe I can claim that although I have always been aware of its weight, I have borne the cross of happiness courageously enough.

Unlike Malcolm Muggeridge, I do not look forward to death with eager anticipation. He hopes to get to heaven but he may, of course, get the shock of his death by getting nowhere at all. I do not expect to survive in any form or fashion and have no desire to do so. What a horrible place this world would be if all the people ever born were still around. What a burden it would be on the Ministries of Pensions all over the world.

Being born involves the certainty of death. Only those countless millions, the unborn ones, are really safe. They will not die, but neither can they have any fun. I think it is one of the beauties of life that it is not eternal. It would be a frightful bore to go on and on and on, even in reasonable health. Besides, I am used to being dead. Death is simple non-existence and we are all used to non-existing. I did not exist in 500 BC or in 50,000 BC or in 1793. Why should not existing in 2117 or 3117 be any different?

The Last Anecdote

Death is simply the end of the story. If one is lucky, a good end to a pleasant story. For me, if I am lucky, it will be simply the last anecdote.

INDEX OF NAMES

Ady, Endre, 189, 231
Áldor, Feri, 132-, 143, 161
Alex, grandson, 236
Alpár, Imre, 134
Amis, Kingsley, 223
Anna, Auntie, 9, 20, 37
Arlott, John, 184
Asquith, Earl of Oxford, 3
Athill, Diana, 236
Auden, Wystan, 191

Babits, Mihály, 231
Bajor, Gizi, 113
Barr, Mr, 3
Barry, Sir Gerald, 186
Bauer, Bandi, 46
Bauer, Elze, 46
Básti, Lala, 110-, 122-, 126, 127-
Bedford, Duke of, 213-
Bedford, 11th Duke, 215-
Bedford, 12th Duke, 215
Bedford, 11th Duchess, 216
Bedford, Duchess, 217
Belloc, Hilaire, 162
Ben Gurion, David, 170
Bennett, Arnold, 164
Bentley, Nicolas, 162
Beöthy, László, 88-
Bertha, Aunt, 11, 13
Bernát, Pal, Dr, 83
Biró, Laoš, 180
Bonar Law, 3
Boothroyd, Basil, 204
Bottomley, Horatio, 3
Bözsi, 58-
Brian, Chuck, 160

Breuer brothers, 42
Brezhnev, Leonid, 231
Briance, John, 227-
Brown, Arthur, 237
Buch, Mr, 155

Campbell, George, 157-
Cardus, Nevile, 184
Coward, Noel, 110-, 115, 123, 127, 129
Chamberlain, Nevile, 126
Chapman, Brian, 183-
Chesser, Eustace, 188
Churchill, Winston, 3, 121, 132, 135, 236
Csóri, 24-
Crook, Arthur, 189, 222
Cruikshank, Ed. *News Chronicle*, 183

Dán, Etelka, 113, 145
Day, Sir Robin, 223
Deutsch, André, 122-, 143, 160-, 191, 223, 236-
Dimbleby, Richard, 201-
Dollfuss, Chancellor, 120
Dóra, 13
Dostoevsky, Fedor, 5
Driberg, Tom, 139
Dukas, Helen, 175
Dushinska, Ilona, 154
Dybwad, Ejnar, 6, 137-

Egyed, Zoltán, 67-, 71-, 73-, 85, 91, 92
Einstein, Albert, 173-

Einzig Dezsö, 21
Einzig, Ilonka, 31
Eliot, T. S., 163
Elizabeth, Queen, 177
Englander, Tubby, 197
Epstein, Jacob, 193
Eva, 240, 241
Eve (Biró), 116-, 126, 130

Faber, Mr, 3
Faludy, George, 142, 155, 231
Farkas, István, 57
Fenya, 65
Foley, Thomas, 132-
Fraenkel, Dr, 12
Francis Ferdinand, 195
Francis Joseph, 1, 11, 26, 49, 79
Freud, Sigmund, 190
Friedrich, István, 68

Gabor, Denis, 214
Gál (Gale), Mundi, 120-, 159
Gardiner, Lord, 224
George V, 3
George VI, 177-
Gibbs, Anthony, 220, 223
Gilliam, Lawrence, 205
Ginger, 199, 234
Gizi, 36
Gòmbös, Gyula, 86, 94, 150
Graham, Billy, 197
Granville, Barker, 111
Green, Henry, 193
Greene, Graham, 4, 207-
Gross, John, 189
Guinness, Alec, 225
Gustav, King of Sweden, 228
Gyöngyössy, István, 154

Haldane, Lord, 3
Halmos, Dezsö, Dr, 39, 45-, 48-, 53, 57, 59-, 65, 125, 165

Harding, Gilbert, 203-
Havas, Bandi, 147-, 156
Hatvany, Lajos, Baron, 148
Hatvany, Loli, Baroness, 149
Hédy (Halmos, later Mrs Denes), 20, 46-, 57-, 59, 165
Hervey, Laci, 92-, 96-, 101-, 115, 119, 130, 143, 169, 237-
Héthelyi: see Hervey
Heisler, Feri, 40
Herczeg, Ferenc, 89
Hevesi, Sándor, 111
Hidegkuti, 185
Hilberry, Sir Malcolm, 222
Hitler, Adolf, 9, 26, 30, 94, 97, 126, 231
Homer, 162
Hope-Wallace, Philip, 207
Horthy, Adml, 26, 79, 147
Horváth, Mr & Mrs, 200

Ibolyka (*née* Gál), 45
Ignotus, Paul, 145, 155, 207, 230
Imre, Uncle, 14
Incze, Sándor, 91, 117
Iványi, Bela, 119, 143, 144, 154

Jacob, Sir Ian, 196
József, Attila, 190-, 231
Julia, 114
June, 105-, 125-

Kafka, Franz, 5, 242
Kaiser, The, 1
Kádár, János, 231
Karinthy, Frederic, 47
Károlyi, Countess, 140-
Károlyi, Gyula, Count, 150
Károlyi, Mihály, Count, 145, 147-, 155
Kaufmann, Tibor, 22-
Kató, 66-

Kennedy, Mrs Joseph, 236
Kemeny, John, 172-
Kemeny, Magdus (Mrs T.
　Mikes), 159
Khuen-Héderváry, 2
Kiss, Dezsö, 68
Kodály, Zoltan, 167
Koestler, Arthur, 5, 134, 147,
　185, 189-, 237
Koestler, Cynthia, 194
Korda, Alex, 111, 119, 186-
Koudenhove-Calergi, Count,
　228-
Körmendi, Ferenc, 157
Kossuth, Lajos, 67
Krausz, Simon, 89-
Kubitschek, Pr of Brazil, 210
Kun, Béla, 150
Kuratani, Na'omi, 8

Lambda, Peter, 146
Langdon, David, 220
Lázár, Miklós, 66-, 72, 76, 85,
　89-
Leonard —, 126
Lloyd George, David, 3
Lohmeyer, Brigitte, 64
Lukács, Gyula, 91
Lukács, Robert, 96

Macmillan, Daniel, 223
Mann, Golo, 7
Mann, Thomas, 190
Márkus, Miksa, Dr, 34
Mary, Queen, 3
Masaryk, Jan, 149-
Maugham, Somerset, 164, 170,
　239
Mayer (MGM), 75
Maxwell, Elsa, 240
Metternich, 1
Micike (Márkus), 31, 37
Mikes, Alfred, Dr (Author's
　father), 9, 10, 11, 14, 15-, 17,
　26, 32, 36-
Mikes, Alice, 12, 13
Mikes, Erzsi, 12
Mikes, Judy (Mrs Evans), 170,
　174, 189, 235
Mikes, Isobel, 30, 141, 167, 180,
　221
Mikes, Lea, 169-, 173, 174,
　178-, 180, 184, 189, 192, 203,
　227, 239
Mikes, Marcel, 11, 12, 15
Mikes, Margit (later Mrs D.
　Halmos, Author's mother), 9,
　20, 32-, 36-, 46-, 59, 165, 170
Mikes, Martin, 64, 163, 170,
　224, 235
Mikes, Tibor, 32-, 35, 38, 45-,
　53, 122, 125, 159-, 226-, 236
Mindszenty, Cardinal, 239
Minshall, Mr, 161
Mishka, Papa, 9, 19, 47, 165
Molnár, Ferenc, 82
Moreau, Mathieu, 3
Muggeridge, Malcolm, 197, 242
Murin, György, 226-

Nagy, Ferenc, 154
Neumann, John, 173

Olivier, Lord, 224
Omama, 10, 11, 13, 15-, 21, 34-,
　41-
Oppenheimer, Robert, 172, 173
Orwell, George, 5, 163
Owen, Peter, 213-

Pálóczi-Horváth, George, 155,
　207
Parsons, Ian, 223
Paula, Auntie, 35-
Pauncz, 58
Pepi, Uncle, 11

Péter, Gábor, 155
Petöfi, Sándor, 11, 113
Pista (Papus, Dr Márkus), 24, 31
Pósa, Lajos, 195
Powell, Michael, 237
Pressburger, Emeric, 118-, 180, 237
Priestley, J. B., 193
Pryce-Jones, Alan, 189
Princess Royal, 3
Puskás, 185

Rajk, László, 155-, 209
Radó, Zoltán, 151, 155
Rákosi, Jenö, 89
Rákosi, Mátyás, 6, 65, 94, 145, 154
Ramsey, Stewart, 227
Révai, Andrew, 144, 152
Richter, Mihály, 151, 155
Roberts, Mr, 161-
Róza Mama, 9, 45
Rózsa, Jenö, 226-
Rudolf, Archduke, 11
Russell, Bertrand, 177
Russell, Michael, 213

Sampson, Anthony, 223
Samarakis, Antonis and Eleni, 241
Sandhurst, Lord, 3
Satterswaite, Cmdr, 222
Santelli, Italo, 226
Schebeko, Marie, 208
Schuschnigg, Chancellor, 94
Selznick, David O., 112, 115, 124, 127, 129
Seiber, Mathias, 145
Sewell, 185
Seton-Watson, Hugh, 193
Shaw, G. B., 111
Solzehnitsyn, Alexander, 5, 194

Soós, Károly, Gen, 32
Sophocles, 5
Spencer, Lord, 3
Spender, Stephen, 297
Spengler, Oswald, 5
Strasser, Jani, 145
Sugár, Miklós, 30
Sun-Yat-Sen, 3
Szamuelly, Tibor, 26
Szilágyi, Dezsö, 66-
Szilárd, Prof, 173
Szóhner, Sándor, 17
Szomory, Dezsö, 97-
Szücs, Miklós, 151, 155
Szunyogh, András, Capt, 103-

Tabori, Kate, 207
Tabori, Paul, 36-, 166, 207
Tarjan, George, 113-, 115, 116-, 122-, 130, 138, 145, 166
Tavistock, Lord, 220-
Teller, Edward, 173
Titkos, Ilona, 71-, 90
Tisza, Kálmán, 26-
Tisza, István, 26
Tolstoy, Leo, 162
Tsinna, 22
Tsi-Tsa, 234

Vértes, István, 20, 70, 84
Vian, Capt, 132-
Vicky, 182-
Vida, Márton, 22, 241

Wallinger, Sir Geoffrey, 209-
Wallinger, Lady, 209
Waugh, Alec, 209-
Waugh, Evelyn, 241
Weidenfeld, Lord, 139, 223
Weisz, Laci, 40
Wells, H. G., 141
Wheeler, Charles, 197, 201
White, Allan, 223

Wilson, Angus, 207
Wingate, Orde, 163
Wittman, Ernest, 228

Zec, Phil, 186-
Zsiga, Lord, 14
Zsigmond, King, 231
Zsilinszky, Antal, 144